Churchill

CHURCHILL

The Unexpected Hero

PAUL ADDISON

OXFORD
UNIVERSITY PRESS

OXFORD

UNIVERSITY PRESS

Great Clarendon Street, Oxford ox2 6dp

Oxford University Press is a department of the University of Oxford.
It furthers the University's objective of excellence in research, scholarship,
and education by publishing worldwide in

Oxford New York

Auckland Cape Town Dar es Salaam Hong Kong Karachi Kuala Lumpur
Madrid Melbourne Mexico City Nairobi New Delhi Shanghai Taipei Toronto

With offices in

Argentina Austria Brazil Chile Czech Republic France Greece
Guatemala Hungary Italy Japan South Korea Poland Portugal
Singapore Switzerland Thailand Turkey Ukraine Vietnam

Oxford is a registered trade mark of Oxford University Press
in the UK and in certain other countries

Published in the United States
by Oxford University Press Inc., New York

ISBN 0–19–927934–9

Printed in the U S A

For Rosy

Acknowledgements

This book originated with an invitation from the late Colin Matthew to write the article on Churchill for the new *Oxford Dictionary of National Biography*. I owe a debt of gratitude to him, and also to his successor Brian Harrison, and the staff of the *DNB*, for all their encouragement and support. Having completed the article, which ran to about 30,000 words, it occurred to me that it could be expanded into a short book in which I would be able to give more space to the analysis of Churchill's character and career. I am grateful to Ruth Parr at OUP for supporting the initial proposal, to Bonnie Blackburn for impeccable copy-editing, and to Kay Rogers and Anne Gelling for seeing the book efficiently through the press. My agent Bruce Hunter has been an unfailing source of wisdom and encouragement.

I am grateful to the University of Edinburgh for granting me the study leave in which to complete this book. Dr Jeremy Crang and Dr David Stafford, my colleagues at the Centre for Second World War Studies, have been the most supportive of colleagues and friends. My thanks are also due to many others for their generous assistance or advice, and especially Professor Geoffrey Best, Dr Angus Calder, Professor Antoine Capet, Mr Sebastian Cox, Dr Frances Dow, Mr Owen Dudley Edwards, Sir Martin Gilbert, Professor Rhodri Jeffreys-Jones, Dr Richard Mackenney, Professor James McMillan, Dr Nicholas Phillipson,

ACKNOWLEDGEMENTS

Professor John Ramsden, Dr Victor Rothwell, Professor George Shepperson, and Mr Ian S. Wood. As ever my greatest debt is to Rosy, James, and Michael.

Paul Addison
October 2004

Contents

Abbreviations   xi

Prologue   1

1. The Youngest Man in Europe, 1874–1901   7

2. The Renegade, 1901–1911   29

3. The Lilliput Napoleon, 1911–1915   57

4. The Winstonburg Line, 1915–1924   82

5. Respectability Won and Lost, 1924–1939   112

6. The Making of a Hero, 1939–1945   153

7. Climbing Olympus, 1945–1965   216

8. Churchill Past and Present   246

Notes   255

Bibliography   275

Index   287

Abbreviations

TNA   The National Archives

PRO   Public Record Office

RSC, *WSC*   Randolph S. Churchill, *Winston S. Churchill*,
                i: *Youth 1874–1900* (1966); ii: *Young States-
                man (1901–1914)* (1967)

WSC Companion i, pt. 2: *1896–1900*, ed. Randolph S.
                Churchill (1967); ii, pt. 1: *1901–1907*, ed.
                Randolph S. Churchill (1969); iv, pt. 2:
                Documents, July 1919–March 1921, ed.
                Martin Gilbert (1977); iv, pt. 3: *Documents,
                April 1921–November 1922*, ed. Martin
                Gilbert (1977); v, pt. 1: *The Exchequer Years,
                1922–1929*, ed. Martin Gilbert (1979); v,
                pt. 2: *The Wilderness Years, 1929–1935*, ed.
                Martin Gilbert (1981); v, pt. 3: *The Coming
                of War, 1936–1939*, ed. Martin Gilbert
                (1982)

Prologue

Winston Churchill won two great victories in the Second World War. The first was a victory over Nazi Germany. The second was a victory over the many sceptics who, for decades, had derided his judgement, denied his claims to greatness, and excluded him from 10 Downing Street on the grounds that he was sure to be a danger to King and Country. The roar of approval which greeted him on VE Day, as he addressed the crowds from the balcony of the Ministry of Health in Whitehall, was a moment of triumph in a battle over his reputation that had been going on ever since the turn of the century. The epic struggle between Churchill and his critics is the underlying theme of this short life.

Churchill's victory was never complete. Even at the height of his power and glory there were some who resisted the enchanter's spell. The day before he became Prime Minister in 1940 the Permanent Secretary to the Foreign Office, Sir Alexander Cadogan, wrote in his diary: 'I don't think they'll get a better P.M. than Neville [Chamberlain].' Nearly five years later he was writing: 'I *long* for poor old Neville Chamberlain again. He *did* know how to conduct business.'[1] The general acclaim for Churchill as a war leader concealed the views of critics for whom he was at best a hero with feet of clay, and agnostics for whom he was never a hero at all. Nor was the permanence of Churchill's triumph guaranteed. In 1918 Lloyd George was the great war

1

hero, but afterwards his reputation went into a decline from which it has never entirely recovered. The heroes of one generation can be unmade by the next, and it remained to be seen whether Churchill would win the battle of the history books.

When I began historical research, Churchill was still alive. My subject was the transition from the Chamberlain to the Churchill governments, but I knew little of Churchill beyond his fame as a war leader. A few months later, on the afternoon of Saturday, 30 January 1965, I stood in the hushed and reverent crowd as his funeral train, the coffin draped in the Union Jack, passed slowly through Oxford station. I was awestruck: the ground seemed to tremble beneath our feet. The following Saturday afternoon I was waiting for a train at the station when I noticed a frail and elderly man sitting alone on a bench with a little battered suitcase. It was Churchill's wartime deputy, Clement Attlee, who had been one of the pall-bearers of his coffin. No one on the crowded platform was taking any notice of him. When his train came in he found it difficult to climb aboard and a porter came forward to give him a helping hand. I said to the porter: 'That was Mr Attlee, wasn't it?' 'I think it was', he replied.

Attlee was the giant-killer who had defeated Churchill in the 1945 general election. His Labour government had constructed a new post-war settlement at home and abroad while Churchill languished in opposition. He had even nationalized the railway which carried Churchill on his final journey. Attlee was a thoroughly comprehensible type of Englishman who applied the service ethic of the public schools and the officer class to the Labour party and the socialist cause. There was very little mystery about him and no hint of charisma. Churchill was evidently something else. His exuberant image, complete with V-sign, giant cigar, and outlandish costumes, was as familiar around the world as Charlie Chaplin's tramp. But who was this exotic visitor from another world and what exactly were his claims to greatness?

Churchill was the only British politician of the twentieth century to become an enduring national hero. In a sense this was no accident. From youth onwards he was possessed by the ambition to be a great military hero, like his ancestor the first duke of Marlborough, and a great democratic hero, like his idealized father, Lord Randolph Churchill. In his more exalted moods he imagined that he was a man of destiny, intended by Providence to play a heroic role on the stage of history. As he remarked to Asquith's daughter Violet, at their first meeting in 1906, '"We are all worms. But I do believe that I am a glow-worm."' That night she burst into her father's room with the news that for the first time in her life she had encountered genius. '"Well", Asquith replied, "Winston would certainly agree with you there—but I am not sure you will find many others of the same mind."'[2] His dry comment set the scene for decades of conflict between Churchill's heroic self-image, communicated to the world through a stupendous barrage of publicity in which oratory, journalism, and history were all pressed into service, and the hard-bitten observations of politicians, civil servants, and military men, conversing in their clubs after another difficult day with Winston.

Between 1900, when he was first elected to the House of Commons, and 1940, when he succeeded Neville Chamberlain as Prime Minister, Churchill's career was one of snakes and ladders. The longest of the snakes was Gallipoli, the ill-starred campaign that all but destroyed his career in 1915. In the eyes of many observers at the time it was a disaster that epitomized his weaknesses and flaws. All but the most hostile conceded that he possessed great abilities, remarkable eloquence, a streak of genius, and some of the more amiable qualities of a mischievous schoolboy. But it was almost universally agreed that he was a shameless egotist, an opportunist without principles or convictions, an unreliable colleague, an erratic policy-maker who lacked judgement, and a reckless amateur strategist with a dangerous passion for war and bloodshed. Trade unionists and Labour politicians added that he was a class warrior of obsolete and reactionary views. 'The true tragedy of Mr Churchill', wrote one critic in 1931, 'is that whilst he has in reality nothing to *offer* the genuine Labour man or Liberal, he fails to command the confidence of the genuine Conservative. For the ghosts of the Gallipoli dead will always rise up to damn him anew in times of national emergency . . .'[3]

1940, Britain's 'finest hour', was the longest of the ladders which restored Churchill's fortunes. The transformation was all the more astonishing because it was so unexpected. A politician who had at one time or another offended every party and faction became the embodiment of national unity, an uncrowned king whose charisma threatened to eclipse the monarchy. A man who had been written off as too dangerous and irresponsible for the premiership, and most dangerous of all in wartime, was acclaimed as the greatest war leader and statesman since Chatham. No less surprising was the fact that his heroic status outlived the glory days of 1940 and survived the string of disasters which followed in 1941 and 1942. In 1943 the historian A. L. Rowse dedicated his book *The Spirit of English History* to 'Winston S. Churchill: Historian, Statesman, Saviour of his Country'.[4] It was not a controversial judgement.

Churchill's fame even survived the electoral defeat he suffered in 1945. Over the next ten years Churchill, as leader of the Conservative party, played a robust part in the rough-and-tumble of party politics. On controversial issues of the day he dealt his opponents blows which they returned with interest. But as the great war leader of 1940 to 1945 he continued to occupy a unique and almost unchallenged position in the British hall of fame. The philosopher Isaiah Berlin described him in 1949 as 'the saviour of his country, a mythical hero who belongs to legend as much as to reality, the largest human being of our time'.[5] However restrained, criticisms of Churchill's war leadership were sure to be met with howls of wrath, and the outpouring of grief at his death transcended class and party. Towards the end of his life Attlee called him 'the greatest citizen of the world of our time' and the historian A. J. P. Taylor, in a footnote to his *English History*, once more proclaimed him 'the saviour of his country'.[6]

Churchill's fortunes, like those of other politicians, depended as much on the person he was thought to be, and the things he was thought to have done, as upon the realities. Furthermore he was such an extraordinary character that everything about him was heightened and magnified. Wherever he appeared he cast fantastic shadows, a distorting effect that laid him open to myth-making of both a negative and a positive kind. Indeed there grew up in Churchill's lifetime two contrasting and incompatible mythologies. The personality depicted by the negative myths of 1900 to 1940 was remarkably different from the great man as he was generally perceived to be in the forties and fifties.

We can be sure, however, that Churchill did not suddenly turn into a different person at the age of 65. There survives from 1909 a recording of a snatch of one of his speeches on Lloyd George's budget. The voice and the mannerisms are unmistakeable: it is the Churchill of the Second World War. As with his oratory, so with his character and beliefs. Young Winston, the Winston of middle age, and the Winston of old age were all of a piece.

Churchill himself changed little, but perceptions of him were transformed when late in life he overthrew a long-established critique of his strengths and weaknesses in favour of his own vision of himself as a man of destiny. This book is the story of a politician who was underrated before the Second World War and overrated for a long time afterwards, but eludes all attempts to belittle or discredit him and lives on as a hero of past and present.

ONE

The Youngest Man in Europe, 1874–1901

Winston Leonard Spencer Churchill was born at Blenheim Palace, Oxfordshire, the home of the dukes of Marlborough, on 30 November 1874. His mother, Jennie Churchill, was the daughter of a New York financier, Leonard Jerome, and his wife Clara. Jerome, an unscrupulous wheeler-dealer who twice won and lost a fortune on the stock market, cut a dashing figure as a patron of the New York turf, transatlantic yachtsman, and prominent supporter of the North in the American Civil War. While he remained for most of the time in New York, Clara settled in Paris with her three daughters and the burning ambition, thwarted by the collapse of the second Empire in 1870, of marrying them into the French nobility. According to Jerome family lore Clara's great-grandmother Meribah had been an Iroquois Indian.[1] This may be a romantic myth but it was passed on to Winston by his mother as a matter of fact. In his eighty-fifth year Churchill told an American physician that he was descended from a Seneca Indian squaw[2]—the Senecas being one of the six nations of the Iroquois confederation.

Winston's father, Lord Randolph Churchill, was a younger son of the seventh duke of Marlborough, a substantial Tory statesman who had held office under Disraeli. Like his wife Frances, the eldest daughter of the third Marquess of Londonderry, the duke was devoutly religious, and spent most of his political career championing the Church of England against rival denominations. Both the dukedom and the Palace of Blenheim had been gifts bestowed by Queen Anne on the commander-in-chief of her armies, John Churchill, in recognition of his victory over Louis XIV at the battle of Blenheim (13 August 1704). The Palace, designed by Vanbrugh to rival the magnificence of Versailles, and set in a park laid out by 'Capability' Brown, was as much a national monument as a home. After the duke's death his widow, Sarah, added a triumphal arch, and a victory pillar a hundred and thirty feet high, on top of which still stands a twenty-five-foot high statue of John Churchill, clad as a Roman warrior. Though the Palace was never Winston Churchill's home he spent many of his school holidays there in the shadow of his great ancestor, and often revisited it in later life.

The Marlboroughs belonged to a network of landed families that had governed the country since the 'Glorious Revolution' of 1689. By the late nineteenth century their political power was on the wane as the income from landed estates fell and the political centre of gravity shifted from the countryside to the towns. In spite of this aristocratic dynasties like the Cavendishes, the Cecils, and the Churchills fought an impressive rearguard action to maintain their political ascendancy in a more democratic age. The last two Prime Ministers of the nineteenth century were the Liberal Earl of Rosebery and the Conservative Marquess of Salisbury, the latter succeeded in 1902 by his nephew, Arthur Balfour. The Churchills, meanwhile, had produced Randolph and his son Winston.

The seventh duke and his wife had six daughters and two surviving sons. The older son George, Marquess of Blandford, later the eighth duke, has been described as 'one of the most disreputable men ever to have debased the higher ranks of the British peerage'. He scandalized contemporaries with his adulterous affairs, sold off the Blenheim art collection, and died in his laboratory at Blenheim 'with a terrible expression on his face'.[3] His younger brother Randolph was less of a rebel and more of a dutiful son but gave no sign at first of political ambition. His passions were drinking and hunting until he was introduced, at the annual Cowes regatta in August 1873, to Jennie Jerome. The two fell instantly and passionately in love and got engaged three days later.

The match was strongly opposed at first by the duke, who feared that Jerome was 'a vulgar kind of man' and 'a *bad* character' and 'of the class of speculators'. The connection, he warned Randolph, would be one that 'no man in his senses could think respectable'.[4] His brother, Blandford, was alarmed for a very different reason. He thought that Randolph was marrying for love, a state of madness and delusion from which he would recover to find himself trapped in an unhappy marriage. Randolph and Jennie, however, were unshakeably committed. After tortuous financial negotiations the duke relented and the couple were married—in the absence of the duke and duchess—at the British embassy in Paris on 15 April 1874. Winston's date of birth has given rise to speculation that he was conceived before the wedding, but the only certainty is that he was born prematurely. Preparations were made for the birth to take place at his parents' home in London, but during a visit to Blenheim Jennie went into labour, the local doctor was summoned from Woodstock, and the baby delivered at 1.30 a.m. on 30 November.

In 1876 Blandford was the centre of a society scandal when the Prince of Wales's friend Lord Aylesford proposed to divorce his wife for adultery with Blandford, and Lord Randolph threatened to expose the Prince's own adultery with her. The growing vendetta between Randolph and the Prince led Disraeli to arrange for the appointment of the duke as Viceroy of Ireland (1877–80). In effect the Churchills had been ostracized from Society and sent into exile. The experience seems to have galvanized Randolph. Hitherto a somnolent MP for the family borough of Woodstock, he developed rapidly into a major politician. In the years between 1880 and 1885, when the Conservatives were in opposition, he outmanoevred the leaders of his own party with audacious attacks on the Gladstone government. During the Home Rule crisis of 1885–6 his masterly if Machiavellian tactics were crucial in turning the tables on the Liberals and ushering in a period of Tory rule. By July 1886 he was Chancellor of the Exchequer, with every expectation of the premiership in the fullness of time.

Winston Churchill's earliest memories were of Ireland. His nanny, Mrs Elizabeth Everest, took him for walks in Phoenix Park and warned him against a group of evil men known as Fenians. Shortly after the birth of his brother Jack, in February 1880, the family returned to London, where Winston began to build up an impressive collection of toy soldiers in the nursery. At 8 he was sent to a boarding school at Ascot where the headmaster took a pleasure in flogging the boys till their bottoms ran with blood. Winston performed well in some subjects but his reports often referred to his unruly behaviour. According to one account, he was birched for stealing sugar from the pantry and retaliated by kicking the headmaster's straw hat to pieces.[5] When he fell ill his parents transferred him to a school at Brighton, where he was much happier but came bottom of the class for conduct.

Neither of Churchill's parents lacked affection for Winston, but they saw little of him and he felt profoundly neglected. Lord Randolph's feverish life was devoted mainly to politics: Winston could recall only two or three long and intimate conversations with him. Lady Randolph, meanwhile, revelled in high society. 'She shone for me like the Evening Star', Churchill wrote. 'I loved her dearly—but at a distance.'[6] Unlike his brother Jack, Winston developed a powerful ego. His letters home from boarding school were full of demands for attention, and protests against his parents' failure to meet his wishes. He was fortunate to discover in Mrs Everest a surrogate parent who gave him the love and admiration he craved. He responded with remarkably open displays of affection for his 'Woom' or 'Woomany'. Inviting her to Harrow, he showed her around the school and walked arm-in-arm with her up the High Street while other boys jeered at him. During her final illness in July 1895 Churchill, by this time a Sandhurst cadet, rushed to her bedside, afterwards arranging the funeral and the erection of a headstone on her grave. In his novel *Savrola* (1900) he brought her to life again as the hero's faithful housekeeper, Bettine.

Churchill entered Harrow in April 1888. Convinced that his son was not clever enough for university, Lord Randolph was impressed by the enthusiasm with which he manoeuvred his army of toy soldiers and arranged for him to enter the Army Class, which prepared boys for Sandhurst. Legend has it that Winston was academically a bit of a dunce, but he demonstrated great ability in English, History, and Chemistry, subjects that captured his imagination. The Harrow archives contain a 1,500-word essay imagining the course of a future war between Britain and Russia, written when he was 14, which deeply impressed his English master, Robert Somervell.[7] Mathematics, however, baffled him, and in spite of personal tuition from the headmaster, J. C. Welldon, he detested Latin.

Like Richmal Crompton's fictional hero William, whom in many ways he resembled, the schoolboy Winston was a courageous individualist who flouted the rules and got into scrapes. He lacked self-discipline and his teachers often complained of slovenly or unruly behaviour, but censure or punishment served only to provoke him into a long and indignant defence of his actions. Inevitably, perhaps, team sports held little appeal for him, but in spite of frequent bouts of ill health he was a strong swimmer, excelled at rifle-shooting, and won the public schools fencing championship in 1892. None of this could appease his father's wrath when he twice failed the entrance exams for Sandhurst, passing in at the third attempt with marks too low to qualify him for the infantry. Lord Randolph's response was a remarkably cruel letter in which he threatened to break off all contact with his son and warned: 'if you cannot prevent yourself from leading the idle useless unprofitable life you have had during your schooldays & later months you will become a mere social wastrel, one of the hundreds of the public school failures . . .'[8]

Sandhurst was a liberation for Churchill. Military topics such as tactics or fortifications were far more appealing than maths, and horsemanship his favourite recreation. In high spirits, and working hard, he eventually passed out with honours, eighth out of 150. During his final term he also plunged for the first time into public controversy. When the eminent moral reformer Mrs Ormiston Chant organized a campaign to exclude prostitutes from the bar of the Empire Theatre in Leicester Square, Churchill incited some of his fellow cadets to riot and pull down the screens which had been put up to separate prostitutes from theatre-goers. 'Ladies of the Empire', Churchill declared in an impromptu speech, 'I stand for Liberty!'[9]

Churchill's adolescence was overshadowed by the physical and mental decline of Lord Randolph. Having risen to be Chancellor of Exchequer in Lord Salisbury's government of 1886, he overplayed his hand, resigned, and never held office again. In spite of Lord Randolph's rebukes, Churchill had grown up to adore and revere his father. At the time of his father's resignation he had been a schoolboy of 12. Taken to a pantomime at Brighton where a sketch of Lord Randolph was hissed by the audience, he burst into tears and turned furiously on a man behind him: 'Stop that row you snub nosed Radical!'[10] As a gentleman cadet Churchill had began to win his father's respect, but Lord Randolph's health was declining rapidly and his final appearances in the House of Commons were excruciating occasions on which he struggled in vain to articulate the right words. As his friend Lord Rosebery wrote: 'There was no curtain, no retirement, he died by inches in public.'[11] Just as the relationship between Winston and his father was about to ripen it was blighted. Lord Randolph died at the age of 45 on 24 January 1886. His neurologist, Dr Buzzard, diagnosed his illness as syphilis, though it has recently been argued that his symptoms were compatible with those of a tumour on the brain.[12]

Although he was unaware of Buzzard's diagnosis, Churchill believed that Lord Randolph's death, like that of his brother the eighth duke of Marlborough, 'was yet further proof that the Churchills died young'.[13] Driven by the need to appease his father's ghost and vindicate his reputation, he was desperate to make his mark before it was too late. But he was also free at last of Lord Randolph's restraining hand and ready to embark on adventures of his own. After passing out from Sandhurst he obtained his commission as a cavalry officer in the Queen's Own Hussars. Here he acquired a passion for polo, a game he was to enjoy playing for the next three decades.

Much as Churchill enjoyed soldiering he regarded it as a means to an end: the making of a reputation that would propel him into the House of Commons. In October 1895 he travelled with his friend Reggie Barnes to Cuba to report on the rebellion against Spanish rule for the *Daily Graphic*. Visiting New York en route he was entertained by the Irish-American politician Bourke Cockran, an old flame of Lady Randolph's, whose eloquence and oratory made a lasting impression on him. Churchill's twenty-first birthday (30 November 1895) found him in the company of Spanish forces suppressing a rebellion in Cuba. Here he saw shots fired in anger for the first time, and acquired two lifelong habits: Havana cigars and siestas.

In October 1896 Churchill sailed with his regiment to India and set foot for the first time in the British Empire. Comfortably quartered in the British military compound at Bangalore, he displayed little interest in the subcontinent around him, but followed the political news from home with the eagerness and frustration of an exile. With his thoughts fixed firmly on a parliamentary career, he was worried by the fact that unlike so many other ambitious young men he lacked a university education. Enlisting the aid of Lady Randolph, he pursued a remarkable programme of self-education. During the long afternoons while the regiment rested, he devoured the works of Plato, Adam Smith, Gibbon, Macaulay, Hallam, Lecky, Darwin, and Winwood Reade, supplemented by volumes of the *Annual Register*, in which he annotated the summaries of old parliamentary debates with imaginary contributions of his own. Churchill's reading affected both his prose style, which he modelled on Gibbon and Macaulay, and his view of the world. He was going through a phase in which orthodoxies of all kinds, including the Toryism in which he had been raised, were suspect. 'I am a Liberal in all but name', he wrote to his mother in 1897. 'My views excite the pious horror of the Mess. Were it not for Home Rule—to which I will never consent—I would enter Parliament as a Liberal. As it is—Tory Democracy will have to be the standard under which I shall range myself.'[14]

Winwood Reade's *Martyrdom of Man*, a classic of Victorian atheism, completed Churchill's loss of faith in orthodox Christianity and left him with a sombre vision of a godless universe in which humanity was destined, nevertheless, to progress through the conflict between the more advanced and the more backward races. The young Churchill was a free thinker inclined to dismiss religion as a form of superstition harmful to reason and progress. 'How dreadful are the curses which Mohammedanism lays on its votaries!', he wrote in 1900. 'Improvident habits, slovenly systems of agriculture, sluggish methods of commerce, and insecurity of property exist wherever the followers of the Prophet rule or live . . . Individual Moslems may show splendid qualities. Thousands become the brave and loyal soldiers of the Queen; and know how to die; but the influence of the religion paralyses the social development of those who follow it. No stronger retrograde force exists in the world.'[15] His reflections on Roman Catholicism were scarcely more flattering: 'Catholicism—all religions if you like, but particularly Catholicism—is a delicious narcotic. It may soothe our pains and chase our worries, but it checks our growth and saps our strength.'[16] Churchill nevertheless retained a residue of quasi-religious faith in the workings of Providence and the fulfilment of his own personal destiny.

Always ready to lend destiny a hand, Churchill embarked on a daring and spectacular scheme of self-advertisement. 'A few months in South Africa', he told Lady Randolph, 'would earn me the S.A. medal and in all probability the Company's star. Thence hot-foot to Egypt—to return with two more decorations in a year or two—and beat my sword into an iron despatch box.'[17] Between 1897 and 1900, with the aid of assiduous lobbying by his mother, he managed to fight in three of Queen Victoria's wars while doubling as a war correspondent and turning all three of his experiences into books.

When the attacks of Afghan tribesmen on the north-west frontier of India led to the formation of a punitive expeditionary force, under the command of Sir Bindon Blood, Churchill obtained an attachment to the force and a contract as a war correspondent with the *Daily Telegraph*. He took part in several skirmishes in which he came under fire and witnessed acts of barbarism by both sides. The experience helped to confirm his belief in the racial superiority of the British. 'Nothing is so remarkable', he wrote, 'as the ascendancy which the British officer maintains over the native soldier. The dark sowars follow the young English soldier who commands them with a strange devotion . . . To save his life they will sacrifice their own.'[18] On his return to Bangalore he expanded his reports into his first book, *The Story of the Malakand Field Force* (1898), which combined an incisive narrative of the fighting with vivid accounts of the landscape and its inhabitants. By this time he was also writing a novel, *Savrola* (1900), a melodramatic tale of a liberal revolution in an autocratic Mediterranean state: the hero, Savrola, was a compound of himself and Lord Randolph. His work on the book was interrupted, in the summer of 1898, by the final stages of the campaign for the reconquest of the Egyptian Sudan.

Churchill's career as a subaltern was played out against the background of an Empire that was expanding rapidly under the stimulus of competition from other European powers. The scramble for territory was accompanied at home by the rise of imperialism, a many-sided movement that celebrated both the ties of kith and kin that bound Great Britain to the white settler colonies of Canada and Australasia, and the exotic spectacle of British rule over 'primitive' or 'barbarous' peoples in Africa and Asia. Like any other young man of his time and social class, Churchill absorbed the spirit of imperialism with the air he breathed, but for him the rhetoric and the sentiment bore the indelible imprint of personal experience.

Since the opening of the Suez Canal in 1869, Egypt had acquired a new strategic significance for the British as a territory which straddled the imperial route to India. Technically Egypt was a largely self-governing state under a Khedive who owed allegiance to the Sultan of Turkey. But the British increasingly interfered in its affairs, and sent in troops to quell a nationalist revolt in 1882. At first the occupation was intended to be temporary, but the British were soon drawn into the reform of the government of Egypt under a great proconsul, Sir Evelyn Baring, who was virtually the civilian ruler of the country from 1883 to 1907. On the military side a British general, Sir Herbert Kitchener, was appointed Sirdar or Commander-in-Chief of the Egyptian Army in 1890. Egypt was therefore firmly under British control, but the Egyptian province of the Sudan to the south, nearly a million square miles of desert watered by the River Nile, and inhabited by a diversity of Arab and African tribes, was not.

In 1881 a sucessful revolt against Egyptian rule was led by a slave-trader who styled himself the Madhi, or Messiah. The British response, tragically bungled, led to the defeat and death of General Gordon at Khartoum in January 1885, and the evacuation of the Sudan. The Mahdi himself died, in the fullness of triumph, later the same year and was succeeded by the Khalifa, whose rule proved to be even more corrupt and oppressive than that of the Egyptians.

In 1896 Kitchener was put in charge of an expeditionary force which began to make its way slowly up the Nile with the aim of reconquering the Sudan. By the spring of 1898 he was poised for the final assault on Khartoum, and Churchill hastened to join the expeditionary force, which consisted mainly of Egyptian troops with some British units attached. This time it was the *Morning Post* which commissioned him to report the war. Overcoming Kitchener's objections, Churchill obtained a temporary posting with the 21st Lancers, and arrived in the Sudan just in time to take part in the last great cavalry charge in British history, at the battle of Omdurman (2 September 1898). After the battle, on Kitchener's instructions, the Mahdi's tomb was destroyed and his corpse flung into the Nile. Kitchener proposed at first to send the skull to the Royal College of Physicians, but following a protest from Queen Victoria it was secretly buried at Wadi Haifa.[19]

Churchill once more expanded his war correspondence into a book—*The River War* (1899), a two-volume work in which the story of the campaign was prefaced by a remarkably sympathetic history of the Mahdi's revolt against Egyptian rule. 'Those whose practice it is to regard their own nation as possessing a monopoly of virtue and common sense', Churchill wrote, 'are wont to ascribe every military enterprise of savage people to fanaticism.

They calmly ignore obvious and legitimate motives . . . upon the whole there exists no better case for rebellion than presented itself to the Soudanese'.[20] Churchill also censured Kitchener for his part in the desecration of the Mahdi's tomb and the slaughter of the wounded Dervish soldiers. For all that, he never doubted the 'civilising mission' of the British in Asia and Africa, or the 'barbarism' of the dervishes.

Churchill returned once more to India for the sole purpose of taking part in the Inter-Regimental Polo Tournament, an annual event which took place in Meerut. The officers of the 4th Hussars subscribed for the cost of a special train which carried the team's thirty polo ponies, accompanied by 500 tons of luggage, 1,400 miles from Bangalore to Meerut. Churchill was one of the winning team which beat the Dragoon Guards in the final on 24 February 1899—the only occasion in the history of the Tournament, which ran from 1877 to 1939, when the 4th Hussars were the victors.[21]

In the spring of 1899 Churchill resigned his commission and returned home. In an aggressively Tory speech in Birmingham on 1 June he attacked the Hague Peace Conference then in session, and the spirit of liberal internationalism. 'We are not meant to find peace in this world', he declared; 'the spirit of life cannot exist without effort. Destroy the rivalries of man and of nations and you will have destroyed all that makes for betterment and progress on earth.' War itself was an engine of progress, since the better nation usually won. Hence it was for the good of the world that the Greeks had triumphed over the Persians, Rome over Carthage, and Germany over France in 1870. 'I do not want to preach a gospel of war', Churchill continued. 'I only contend that all the virile virtues spring from competition—and from fierce competition.'[22] Churchill was putting into his own words Winwood Reade's vision of history as a Darwinian struggle in which the fittest races and civilizations were destined to prevail.

Writing many years later, in the aftermath of the Great War, Churchill recalled the boyish excitement with which he and his fellow Sandhurst cadets contemplated the prospect of taking part in battle. 'It did seem such a pity', he wrote, 'that it all had to be make-believe, and that the age of wars between civilised peoples had come to an end for ever. If it had only been 100 years earlier what splendid times we should have had! Fancy being nineteen with more than twenty years of war against Napoleon in front of one!'[23] As a war correspondent he wrote with more ambivalence of the nature of war, reflecting at times upon the grim realities. Observing the funeral of British officers and men killed on the north-west frontier he wrote: 'Looking at these shapeless forms, confined in a regulation blanket, the pride of race, the pomp of Empire, the glory of war appeared the faint and unsubstantial fabrics of a dream . . .'[24] During the war in South Africa the sight of dead Boers prompted him to write: 'Ah, horrible war, amazing medley of the glorious and the squalid, the pitiful and the sublime, if modern men of light and leading saw your face closer, simple folk would see it hardly ever.'[25] Churchill was also repelled by displays of vengeance and cruelty, especially when committed by his own side. In 1912 he gave his friend W. S. Blunt a graphic description of the treatment of the wounded Dervishes after the battle of Omdurman by the men of the 21st Lancers. He had seen them

spearing the wounded and leaning with their whole weight on their lances after the charge to get the points through the thick clothes the Dervishes wore as they lay on the ground. As the points went in the Dervishes would kick up their feet and hands. One trooper had boasted of his kind-heartedness because he had only put four inches of steel into his man. 'He ought to be thankful', he had said, 'to find himself in the hands of a good-natured chap like me.'[26]

Churchill understood the tragedy that war inflicted on the dead and their families, and he understood the barbarity into which it could so easily descend. At the same time he was enthralled and intoxicated by war and his mental faculties stimulated by the analysis of weaponry, strategy, and tactics. Wars, in Churchill's view, were the ultimate means by which nations competed, and empires rose and fell, and if a war had to be fought, it must be fought to a decisive conclusion.

While he was on leave from India during the summer of 1897 Churchill had made contact with Conservative party managers and delivered his first speech, at Claverton Manor outside Bath (26 June 1897). Two years later, when the sudden death of the Conservative MP for Oldham created a vacancy in one of the constituency's two seats, Churchill was adopted as the Conservative candidate at the forthcoming by-election. Before it could take place the other Conservative MP for Oldham decided to retire, and the local party adopted a trade unionist, James Mawdsley, the general secretary of the Amalgamated Society of Operative Cotton Spinners, to run in harness with Churchill. In a predominantly working-class constituency, the alliance of Mawdsley with Churchill was intended to convey the message that the Conservatives had the welfare of the working classes at heart. Here Churchill had a card to play: his father's identification with 'Tory Democracy'. It was a resonant phrase, suggestive of a long-term strategy, but defined by Lord Randolph in so many different ways, for so many different tactical purposes, as to empty it of all meaning beyond the need for daring and unashamed opportunism. At Oldham his son interpreted it in ringing terms as a carefully hedged commitment to social reform: 'I am a Tory Democrat', he announced;

I regard the improvement of the condition of the British people as the main end of modern government. I shall therefore promote to the best of my ability all legislation which, without impairing that tremendous energy of production on which the wealth of the nation and the good of the people may depend, may yet raise the standard of comfort and happiness in English homes.[27]

The contest, however, was dominated by religious issues and here Churchill ran into trouble with his party. In the course of the campaign he abandoned the party line on the government's Clerical Tithes Bill, a contentious measure unpopular with religious nonconformists in the constituency. 'I thought he was a young man of promise', Balfour remarked, 'but it appears he is a young man of promises.'[28] If Churchill's electoral tactics had succeeded, Balfour might have taken a more charitable view, but both seats were lost to the Liberals.

Destiny soon came to the rescue with a summons to South Africa, where the competition between the British and the Boers for supremacy at the Cape led to the outbreak of war in October 1899. Imbued as he was with the fervent imperialism of the late Victorian era, Churchill had no doubts about the justice or necessity of a war that also held glittering prospects for him personally. Anticipating the event, he had already negotiated a contract with the *Morning Post* which made him the highest paid war correspondent of the day, with a salary of £250 per month and all expenses paid. The journalist J. B. Atkins, who sailed to South Africa on the same ship, recalled:

He was slim, slightly reddish-haired, pale, lively, frequently plunging along the deck 'with neck out-thrust' as Browning fancied Napoleon . . . when the prospects of a career like that of his father, Lord Randolph, excited him, then such a gleam shone from him that he was almost transfigured. I had not before encountered this sort of ambition, unabashed, frankly egotistical, communicating its excitement, and extorting sympathy.[29]

Hastening to the battle front, Churchill was accompanying an armoured train on a reconnaissance mission in Natal when the train was ambushed (15 November 1899). In a display of cool courage under fire, he seized command of the situation and organized a successful attempt to free the engine, but was captured and interned with other British captives in the States Model School in Pretoria. Later it was often alleged that Churchill promised his captors not to attempt an escape, and subsequently broke his parole. This was untrue. But he did persuade Captain Aylmer Haldane and Sergeant-Major Brockie to include him in their escape plan, on the understanding that all three would leave together. In the event, Churchill climbed out first and, finding that his fellow escapees were unable to join him, set off on his own.

Jumping aboard a goods train on which he slept overnight, he spent much of the next day hiding among some trees in the company of a large vulture—later to play a starring role in almost every account of his adventures. A wanted man, deep in enemy territory, he was completely lost. 'I prayed long and earnestly for help and guidance', he wrote. 'My prayer, as it seems to me, was swiftly and wonderfully answered.'[30] At nightfall he tried his luck and knocked on the door of a bungalow. It was the only house in the district owned by an Englishman, John Howard, the manager of the Transvaal Colliery at Witbank. Howard concealed Churchill at the bottom of a mineshaft for a few days while he arranged for him to be smuggled out of the Transvaal, hidden between the bales of wool, in railway trucks bound for Lourenco

Marques in Portuguese East Africa. The Boers, who had announced a reward of £25 for the recapture of Churchill 'dead or alive', were keeping watch on the railway line. Churchill was accompanied on his journey by Charles Burnham, an English storekeeper who owned the consignment of wool, organized the transfer of the trucks between engines, and bribed or distracted Boers who might have discovered Churchill's hiding place.[31]

On 23 December 1899 Churchill disembarked in triumph at Durban. Standing out in sharp relief after the military disasters of 'black week', his escape made him the hero of the hour. His new fame enabled him to override the objections of the War Office and assume once more the dual role of officer—lieutenant of the South African Light Horse—and war correspondent. In April 1900 he joined the column commanded by his friend Sir Ian Hamilton as it advanced through the Orange Free State to the Transvaal. Galloping over the veldt with his cousin and boon companion 'Sunny', the eighth duke of Marlborough, fortified by regular supplies from Fortnum and Mason, and attended by his valet, Thomas Walden, Churchill was often in the thick of the fighting and again proved himself to be a first-class war correspondent. He turned his despatches, this time with little adaptation, into two books: *London to Ladysmith via Pretoria* (1900), which included the story of his escape, and *Ian Hamilton's March* (1900). When cigarette cards were first introduced into Britain in 1901, Ogden's of Liverpool produced a series entitled 'Leading Generals of the War'. One of the cards portrayed Winston Churchill, who was no general but almost as famous as Roberts or Baden-Powell.[32] And more capable, Churchill would no doubt have added. The lesson he drew from the war in South Africa was that war was too dangerous to be left to the generals. 'Mr Churchill', wrote the artist Mortimer Menpes, who sketched him in South Africa, 'is a man who might be unpopular because of his great cleverness. He is too direct and frank to flatter, and would never consent to efface himself in order to give added and unmerited value to the quality of others.'[33]

In the autumn of 1900, when Lord Salisbury decided to call a general election, Churchill again stood for Oldham. This was the famous 'khaki election', so called because the government was plainly seeking to capitalize upon the patriotism aroused by the war in South Africa, the divisions it had caused in the Liberal Party, and the belief, which turned out to be premature, that a decisive victory had already been achieved. Churchill concentrated on the single issue of the war, mocking the Liberals as 'a squabbling, disorganised rabble', and playing the patriotic card: 'When the troops come home you should be able to say to them—you have won your battle in South Africa and we have won our battle at home.' He had no need to stress his own reputation as a war hero, but his personal popularity tipped the balance. In a double-member constituency where every elector had two votes it was possible for electors to split them between parties. Enough Liberal voters gave their second vote to Churchill to ensure his election alongside Alfred Emmott, one of the Liberal candidates.[34]

Churchill had achieved fame and a seat in the House of Commons. But at a time when MPs were still unpaid and had to possess an independent income, he still needed to build up his investments. As there was no autumn session of Parliament, he put the time to good use with a lecture tour of the United Kingdom which earned him £3,782 for twenty-nine performances in which he told the story of his adventures with the aid of a magic lantern. He followed this up with a North American tour, organized by Major James B. Pond, which began with a lecture in Philadelphia on 11 December. Though he always spoke of the Boers with great respect, and was generally well received on the East Coast, audiences in the Midwest were more hostile. He was greeted with boos and hisses at the University of Michigan at Ann Arbor, and only managed to win over the rowdy Irish audience in Chicago by improvising a stirring tale of the heroism of the Dublin Fusiliers.[35] To his great relief, audiences in Canada were large and enthusiastic. By the time his lecture tours came to an end Churchill had made enough money to ensure that he could support himself for many years to come in the unpaid role of Member of Parliament. (Salaries for MPs were first introduced in 1911.)

In Britain Churchill's Anglo-American identity was no asset. In the United States it made him an object of pride as well as curiosity. When he spoke at the Waldorf-Astoria in New York he was introduced by the great novelist Mark Twain, the author of *Tom Sawyer* and *Huckleberry Finn*. Twain made no secret of his own opposition to the war in South Africa but finessed the topic with masterly sleight of hand into the larger theme of Anglo-American amity:

I think that England sinned when she got herself into a war in South Africa which she could have avoided, just as we have sinned by getting into a similar war in the Philippines. Mr Churchill by his father is an English-man, by his mother he is an American, no doubt a blend that makes the perfect man. England and America: we are kin. And now that we are kin in sin, there is nothing more to be desired.[36]

There was much talk on both sides of the Atlantic of the need to strengthen Anglo-American ties, and socially at least the British and American elites were more and more closely connected. By marrying an English lord, Jennie Jerome had set a trend: in the years leading up to 1914 there were more than a hundred alliances between American beauties (mainly heiresses) and British aristocrats (mainly hard up). The 19-year-old Consuelo Vanderbilt was virtually compelled by her socially ambitious mother to marry Churchill's great friend and first cousin 'Sunny', the ninth duke of Marlborough, in 1895. Another of his cousins, Frederick Guest, married the American heiress Amy Hall in 1905. Naturally enough Winston Churchill was pro-American and happy to profess his general support for Anglo-American friendship. But when his mother planned to launch a transatlantic magazine with the title 'The Anglo-Saxon' and the motto 'Blood is thicker than water', Churchill was scornful: 'Your apparent conception of a hearty production frothing with patriotism and a popular idea of the Anglo-American alliance—that wild impossibility—will find no room among the literary ventures of the day.'[37] Young Winston was eager to avoid association with an Anglo-American bandwagon. Nor, intriguingly, did he ever contemplate marriage with an American heiress.

When Queen Victoria died on 22 January 1901 Churchill was in Winnipeg on the Canadian leg of his lecture tour. 'Men felt that a great epoch had closed', wrote the historian R. C. K. Ensor;

The sky of England had been clouding for years before; what with the collapse of the country-side, the new-born social unrest in the towns, the waning of religious faith, and above all the sense of an uncontrollable transition to the unknown—the feeling that the keys of power were blindly but swiftly transferring themselves to new classes, new types of men, new nations. The queen's death focused it all.[38]

Such pessimistic views were far from the mind of Winston Churchill, nor did he rush home for the funeral: completion of the lecture tour came first. Exhilarated by youth and success, he was pleased that his mother's old friend, the grossly self-indulgent

Edward, Prince of Wales, was now King Edward VII. 'Will it entirely revolutionise his way of life?' he wondered in a letter to Lady Randolph. 'Will he sell his horses and scatter his Jews . . .?'[39]

Churchill looked forward to the new century with optimism and in so far as he reflected on the future of his country he probably imagined that the social and imperial order would continue much as before, with gradual improvements. As he was to write some thirty years later:

I was a child of the Victorian era, when the structure of our country seemed firmly set, when its position in trade and on the seas was unrivalled, and when the realization of the greatness of our Empire and of our duty to preserve it was growing ever stronger. In those days the dominant forces in Great Britain were very sure of themselves and of their doctrines. They thought they could teach the world the arts of government and the science of economics.[40]

· TWO ·

The Renegade,
1901–1911

Within four years of his election as the Conservative MP for
Oldham Churchill took a daring step that was bound to alter, for
better or for worse, the whole course of his future. He crossed the
floor of the House of Commons to join the Liberal opposition.
When the Liberals came to power he was handsomely rewarded.
The Prime Minister, Sir Henry Campbell Bannerman, appointed
him to his first ministerial office as Under-Secretary at the
Colonial Office. After this Churchill's ascent was rapid. When
Asquith took over as Prime Minister in 1908 he brought Churchill
into the Cabinet as President of the Board of Trade at the aston-
ishingly youthful age, for a politician, of 34. In 1910 he promoted
him to the Home Office and in 1911 put him in charge, as First
Lord of the Admiralty, of the most powerful navy in the world.

The glittering prizes came with a penalty attached. Churchill's
change of party placed a large and ultimately very damaging
question mark against his reputation. The Conservatives felt
betrayed and wrote him off as a shameless opportunist. When he
took up the cause of radicalism and cast himself in the role of
champion of the people against the House of Lords, they derided

him as a mountebank and a demagogue. This was a serious underestimate of Churchill, but it is not hard to see what Conservatives thought about him and why. More difficult to fathom is the response of the Liberals. The vast audiences that flocked to hear the dazzling oratory of his radical phase were proof that he stood high in the party's estimation. Nor could he have risen so rapidly to the top without a general appreciation in Liberal circles of his exceptional abilities. At the same time there was much ambivalence towards him. Mindful always that he had started out as a Tory, Liberals were never sure of his commitment to the party, and his Cabinet colleagues were disturbed by his restlessness and egocentricity.

Churchill delivered his maiden speech to the House of Commons on 18 February 1901. While strongly supporting the war in South Africa he caused some alarm on the Conservative benches when he declared: 'If I were a Boer I hope I should be fighting in the field.'[1] Having acquired a chivalrous respect for the Boers, he wished to see them offered generous peace terms, a theme he was to emphasize repeatedly over the next few years. Nor was this the only issue on which he diverged from the government. In March the Secretary for War, St John Brodrick, announced a programme of Army reform that would increase the size of the standing army by 50 per cent and substantially raise the cost. A few days later Churchill scribbled a note to the veteran Liberal politician Sir William Harcourt: 'I hate and abominate all this expediture on military armament.'[2] It was an unexpected view for an ex-soldier to adopt, but Churchill saw himself as continuing the work of Lord Randolph, whose attempts to cut spending on the armed forces had led to his resignation in 1886. Churchill, therefore, aligned himself with the Liberals. In a speech on 13 May 1901, he attacked Brodrick's proposals as unworkable and rounded out the argument with a critique of militarism. 'The wars of peoples', he declared, 'will be more terrible than the wars of kings.'[3] So impressed was the Liberal journalist W. H. Massingham that he wrote an article expressing the hope that Churchill would one day be Prime Minister—and a Liberal Prime Minister at that.[4] Coached in orthodox economics by the Permanent Secretary to the Treasury, Sir Francis Mowat, he campaigned for reductions in public expenditure and a reduction in the level of income tax, which had reached the alarming level of one shilling and twopence in the pound.

By this time Churchill had allied himself with a small and highly aristocratic group of young Tory MPs known as the 'Hooligans' or 'Hughligans' after their leader, Hugh Cecil, a devout Anglican with whom Churchill struck up a curiously close friendship that was destined not to survive the ferocious party warfare of 1910–14. The Hughligans, who spent their time creating mischief for their own party leaders, maintained cordial relations with a number of politicians on the Liberal side. Among them was the former Liberal Prime Minister Lord Rosebery, an old friend of Lord Randolph's, who had retired from the political fray but was generally thought to be planning a comeback. Churchill, who was searching for a leader to attach himself to, hoped that Rosebery would take the lead in the creation of a centre party uniting the causes of imperialism and social reform. Cecil, who feared that Churchill's imagination was running away with him, pointed out the main difficulty: 'As to joining a Middle Party', he wrote, 'that may be a very proper course when there is a Middle Party to join. Now there is none.'[5] Churchill, however, was reluctant to abandon the idea. As he wrote to Rosebery in October 1902: 'The Government of the Middle—the party wh[ich] shall be free at once from the sordid selfishness and

31

callousness of Toryism on the one hand, and the blind appetites of the Radical masses on the other, may be an ideal which we perhaps shall never attain, wh could in any case only be possessed for a short time, but which is nevertheless worth working for . . .'[6]

On those who met him, Churchill usually made a powerful impression if not always a favourable one. At five foot six and a half inches, slenderly built, with a 31-inch chest, rounded shoulders, delicate skin, ginger hair, and a pugnacious baby face with twinkling blue eyes, Churchill was striking but not handsome. Though fluent on paper he spoke with a lisp, and his speeches were the result of long and elaborate preparation. His practice at first was to deliver the whole of a speech from memory, but after an alarming experience in April 1904 in which he 'dried up' in the House of Commons, he never spoke without copious notes. Hyperactively ambitious and publicity-seeking, he was far from the ideal type of an English gentleman. To many of his fellow officers he appeared pushy and bumptious. Offspring though he was of the landed aristocracy, he belonged to a plutocratic milieu in which old and new wealth rubbed shoulders. His friends included great financiers like Cassel and Tuttie de Forest, the illegitimate son of the railway magnate Baron de Hirsch, who invited him aboard their yachts for Mediterranean cruises, or played host in magnificent villas and castles on the Continent. Churchill enjoyed fox-hunting and country-house weekends but he was equally at home at the gambling tables of the French Riviera. Meeting him for the first time in July 1903, Beatrice Webb thought him 'egotistical, bumptious, shallow-minded and reactionary, but with a certain personal magnetism, great pluck and some originality, not of intellect but of character. More of the American speculator than the English aristocrat.'[7]

In Edwardian society there was much snobbish comment on Churchill's Anglo-American identity. The King himself, though not without affection for Churchill, criticized his speeches as 'vulgar and American'.[8]

When Arthur Balfour succeeded his uncle, Lord Salisbury, as Prime Minister in May 1902, there was no place in the new government for Churchill. Unlike Joseph Chamberlain, whose son Austen was ready to follow in his father's footsteps, Balfour had no son and heir. If he had decided to adopt Churchill, who was patently in need of a patron and father figure, he would surely have won his support in the political battles that lay ahead. Chamberlain, meanwhile, had given Churchill and the Hooligans a strong hint of his intention to raise the banner of protectionism.

Since the repeal of the Corn Laws in 1846 free trade had been the ruling orthodoxy in British politics. It ensured the blessings of cheap food imported from all corners of the world to feed the growing population of the towns and cities. With the growth of competition in manufactured goods from other nations, and the introduction of tariffs against British exports, the cause of protectionism began to revive. Lord Randolph flirted with it before reverting, as Chancellor of the Exchequer, to a conventional free trade position. Winston, for his part, began his parliamentary career as a strict defender of orthodox Treasury doctrines, in which he was coached by the Permanent Secretary, Sir Francis Mowatt. Knowing that the issue was about to arise, Churchill prepared himself carefully and concluded that all the arguments pointed in favour of free trade. When Chamberlain began his campaign for 'tariff reform' in May 1903, Churchill was well briefed and leapt into the fray as one of the most active and eloquent of the 'Free Fooders', a group of about sixty Conservative MPs defending the free trade cause. The effect on the

Liberals, for whom free trade was a fundamental article of faith, was to reunite and reinvigorate them as the champions of cheap food for the masses.

At the head of a divided party Balfour himself could only procrastinate, a predicament which laid him open to the taunts of Churchill, whose platform speeches combined lucid expositions of political economy with the flinging of well-aimed political mud. Most Conservative adherents of free trade decided to remain in the party, but Churchill, after some hesitation, crossed the floor of the House and took his seat on the Liberal benches (31 May 1904). He had already accepted an invitation from the Liberal Association of North-West Manchester to contest the forthcoming general election as the free trade candidate. During the next eighteen months, as the Balfour government drifted helplessly towards the rocks, Churchill attacked his former party with an insolence that gave rise to lasting enmities.

Churchill shrugged off charges of opportunism. It was the Conservatives, he argued, who had abandoned the principle of free trade which he himself continued faithfully to uphold. For good measure he claimed that he was following in the footsteps of his father, whose life he was then writing. In the two volumes of his *Lord Randolph Churchill* (1906), he managed to disguise or explain away his father's most blatant inconsistencies by skilful selection of the evidence, and a thesis which interpreted him as a Tory with increasingly democratic sympathies who saved his party only to be rejected by it. Winston Churchill's Liberalism could therefore be construed as a continuation of Tory Democracy. Most reviewers praised both the style and the content of the book, and commended its impartiality—a remarkable tribute to Churchill's persuasiveness as a historian. One of the few hostile reactions was that of Theodore Roosevelt, who wrote of the two Churchills: 'both possess or possess [sic] such levity, lack of sobriety, and an inordinate thirst for that cheap form of admiration which is given to notoriety, as to make them poor public servants . . . a clever, forceful, rather cheap and vulgar life of that clever, forceful, rather cheap and vulgar egoist'.[9]

Churchill walked the tightrope from Conservatism to Liberalism with acrobatic skill but it stretched across a gulf that none could cross with impunity. Party passions were strong and getting stronger. The Conservatives derived their identity from the old ascendancy of land, church, and king, the Liberals from the subversive forces of religious nonconformity and urban radicalism, to which more extreme radicals—atheists, republicans, prohibitionists, and so on—were eager to attach themselves. More recently the Conservatives had established themselves as the party of ultra-patriotism, defending the Union and the Empire from a Liberal party they associated with the cause of Irish Home Rule and the feeble surrender of vital British interests. By the beginning of the twentieth century new antagonisms rooted in class divisions and the spread of socialist doctrines were entering the mainstream of politics. The Conservatives feared that the Liberals would be soft on socialism and open the door to the expropriation of wealth. The Liberals feared that the Conservatives were about to inaugurate an era of militarism abroad and reaction at home. When Churchill changed parties the consistency of his views on free trade was too fragile a shield to protect him from the tribal rage of the Conservatives, and it laid him open for decades to come to the charge that he was an opportunist, always ready to sacrifice his allies in the cause of self-advancement.

Though true in part, it was nevertheless a caricature that failed to take account of the attitudes and beliefs that shaped his ambition. Churchill's sympathies with Liberalism were genuine and pre-dated his entry into the House of Commons. How far the attraction of Liberalism stemmed from resentment against the leaders of the Conservative party for their alleged mistreatment of Lord Randolph, and how much it owed to the faith in evolutionary progress he acquired from his reading in Bangalore, would be difficult to say. But as we have seen he confessed to Lady Randolph in 1897 that he was 'a Liberal in all but name'. In describing himself as a Tory Democrat he meant that he was Tory with Liberal leanings. His ideal form of government was indeed a Coalition, provided of course that it included him. The young Churchill, therefore, was neither a Tory nor a Liberal but a cross-bench politician whose ultimate ambition was independence of party.

When at last Balfour resigned in December 1905, Campbell-Bannerman formed a government and called a general election for the following month. Churchill was returned as the MP for North-West Manchester, one of the many Tory seats captured by the Liberals in a landslide that gave them a majority of 130 over all other parties in the new House of Commons. 'Mr Winston Churchill', commented the Tory *National Review*,

is rewarded for his active apostasy by the Under-Secretaryship at the Colonies, an appointment causing unmitigated disgust throughout the Empire, which has formed a much sounder estimate of this pushful soldier of fortune, whose sword is ever at the service of the highest bidder, than the Fleet Street friends, who he so assiduously cultivates, and who repay his attentions by advertising his vulgar speeches.[10]

It was not long before Churchill aggravated the offence. Since the Colonial Secretary, Lord Elgin, was a member of the House of Lords, Churchill had the responsibility of handling colonial affairs in the Commons. In March 1906 his first important ministerial speech went badly wrong. While seeking to defend Milner from a motion of censure over the question of 'Chinese slavery' in South Africa he unwittingly gave the impression of gloating over his downfall, thus rubbing salt into Conservative wounds.

Remembered against him for years to come, the episode was an early example of a flaw in his oratorical style: an overbearing manner that seemed intended to humiliate his opponents, of whose injured feelings he was largely unaware. In July he recovered with a statesmanlike speech announcing the restoration of self-government in the Transvaal, a policy to which he had made a significant contribution. But his plea to the Conservatives to support the government and raise the issue above party fell on stony ground. 'He has no principles and no enthusiasm except egotism', declared the *National Review* in January 1907:

'Khaki' was a trump card in 1900, and he played khaki for all he was worth. He left the Unionist Party because promotion tarried. Today pro-Boer enthusiasm dominates the Liberal Party, and he is the most vociferous pro-Boer. He always plays up to the loudest gallery. He is the transatlantic type of demogague ('them's my sentiments and if they don't give satisfaction they can be changed'). There has never yet been a man of this peculiar temperament in a position of responsibility and power in British politics, and it will be interesting to see how far a politician whom no one trusts will go in a country where character is supposed to count.[11]

Enthralled by office and power, Churchill ranged inquisitively over the affairs of scores of British colonies, annotating documents with a red fountain pen. Hyperactive, and expressing his ideas in a ceaseless flow of minutes, he caused great alarm to the Permanent Secretary, Sir Francis Hopwood, who complained to Elgin: 'He is most tiresome to deal with, and will I fear give trouble—as his Father did—in any position to which he may be called. The restless energy, uncontrollable desire for notoriety, and the lack of moral perception, make him an anxiety indeed!' The historian Ronald Hyam offers a more balanced judgement. 'Churchill at the Colonial Office', he writes, 'presents a curious combination of magisterial statesman and mischievous schoolboy. He was just as capable of producing a rash and unrealistic suggestion as he was of producing a reasonable and statesmanlike one.'[12] Hyam also credits Churchill with

a generous and sensitive, if highly paternalistic, sympathy for subject peoples, and a determination to see that justice was done to humble individuals throughout the empire . . . He insisted on questioning the Colonial Office assumption that officials were always in the right when complaints were made against government by Africans or, as was more probable, by Asians. He campaigned for an earnest effort to understand the feelings of subject peoples in being ruled by alien administrators, 'to try to measure the weight of the burden they bear'.[13]

This is perhaps too generous a verdict. As a professional politician facing a Liberal House of Commons Churchill was constantly aware of the danger that abuses of colonial authority would produce protests from radical MPs. When a telegram arrived at the Colonial Office in February 1908 reporting the slaughter of Kisii tribesmen in the south-west of Kenya, Churchill growled:

I do not like the tone of these reports. No doubt the clans should be punished; but 160 have been killed outright . . . It looks like butchery, and if the H. of C. gets hold of it, all our plans in E.A.P. [East African Protectorate] will be under a cloud. Surely it cannot be necessary to go on killing these defenceless people on such an enormous scale.[14]

As a robust imperialist Churchill approved the use of force where it was essential to maintain order and authority, but like his superior, Lord Elgin, he was opposed to military operations as a means of punishing unruly tribesmen or expanding the boundaries of British authority. When Lord Lugard, the high commissioner for Northern Nigeria, proposed a punitive expedition against the Munshi, a tribe which had yet to submit to British rule, Churchill wrote: 'The chronic bloodshed which stains the West African seasons is odious and disquieting. Moreover the whole enterprise is liable to be represented by persons unacquainted with Imperial terminology as the murdering of natives and the stealing of their lands.'[15]

In the autumn of 1907 Churchill set out on a hunting expedition to east Africa that soon turned into a semi-official enquiry into colonial affairs. In Kenya he went big game hunting and investigated the conditions of African contract workers. In Uganda he visited Christian missions, had tea with Daudi Chwa II, the 11-year-old Kabaka of Buganda, and took up with great enthusiasm the project of a dam across the Ripon Falls (where a dam was eventually built in 1954). It would, he concluded,

be hard to find a country where the conditions were more favourable than in Uganda to a practical experiment in State Socialism . . . A class of rulers is provided by an outside power as remote from, and in all that constitutes fitness to direct, as superior to the Baganda as Mr Wells's Martians would have been to us.[16]

In the interludes Churchill dictated memoranda for the Colonial Office, and a series of articles for the *Pall Mall Gazette*, later published as *My African Journey* (1908).

Even in Africa he gave much thought to the future of politics at home. Indeed it was while Churchill was at the Colonial Office that he came to another turning point in his career. The Liberals had won the general election on an essentially conservative platform of maintaining free trade. But they had also concluded an electoral pact with the Labour Party and it was mainly as a result of this that twenty-nine Labour MPs now sat in the House of Commons. The rise of Labour, the propagation of socialist ideas, and the growing importance of social questions compelled party strategists to consider where the future of Liberalism lay. Ought the party to hold fast to the Liberalism of laissez-faire, or should it pursue an advanced social programme in alliance with Labour? The New Liberalism, the work of ideologues like Hobson and Hobhouse, offered a political philosophy that reconciled state intervention with Liberal principles, and a political strategy for shifting the party to the left. When it came to Churchill's ears he seized upon the New Liberalism and proclaimed it as his own. Speaking in Glasgow in October 1906, he declared that he looked forward 'to the universal establishment of minimum standards of life and labour'. There was no contradiction, he argued, between individual incentive and collective organization. Both were essential to the progress of civilization:

I do not want to see impaired the vigour of competition, but we can do much to mitigate the consequences of failure. We want to draw a line below which we will not allow persons to live and labour, yet above which they may compete with all their manhood. We want to have free competition upwards; we decline to allow free competition to run downwards.[17]

On his return from Africa in 1908 he published in *The Nation* an article entitled 'The Untrodden Field in Politics', in which he argued for a wide-ranging programme of state action including labour exchanges, minimum wages, the expansion of technical colleges and continuation schools to give young people training in a trade, and public works to counteract unemployment. 'He is full of the poor, whom he has just discovered', wrote Charles Masterman, a Liberal politician and social reformer with whom Churchill was in close touch. 'He thinks he is called by providence to do something for them. "Why have I always been kept safe within a hair's breadth of death", he asked, "except to do something like this. I'm not going to live long." '[18]

Who or what triggered Churchill's enthusiasm for state intervention? Various explanations can be given but the most significant was probably his relationship with David Lloyd George, whom he had first met when the latter congratulated him on his maiden speech. The Welshman was eleven years older, with more than a decade of parliamentary experience behind him, and a place in radical folklore as the cottage-bred boy from Llanystumdwy, raised by his uncle the village shoemaker to become the champion of Welsh nonconformity against the landlord class. Despite their very different social backgrounds, Lloyd George and Churchill shared a passion for power, a fascination with oratory, a love of risk and adventure, and (much as their opponents would have doubted it) a strong imperial patriotism. When Churchill crossed the floor of the House of Commons in May 1904, he took his seat on the Liberal benches next to Lloyd George. Here was a father figure who could give his restless ambition a new sense of direction. As Asquith's daughter Violet observed:

His was the only personal leadership I have ever known Winston to accept unquestioningly in the whole of his career. He was fascinated by a mind more swift and agile than his own . . . From Lloyd George he was to learn the language of Radicalism. It was Lloyd George's native tongue, but it was not his own, and despite his efforts he spoke it 'with a difference'.[18]

When Asquith succeeded Campbell Bannerman as Prime Minister in April 1908, he demonstrated his confidence in Churchill by introducing him into the Cabinet as President of the Board of Trade. At 34, he was the youngest Cabinet minister since the Marquess of Hartington in 1866. Since constitutional convention dictated that an MP who entered the Cabinet must resign his seat and submit himself for re-election, Churchill was compelled to stand again for North-West Manchester in a by-election, which he lost by a narrow margin. He at once accepted an invitation to stand for Dundee, where he was returned with a substantial majority at a by-election in May. In exchanging Manchester for Dundee he was moving from a prosperous middle-class constituency to an overwhelmingly working-class city blighted by poverty, unemployment, and other acute social problems. In spite of this and the fact that he was opposed by a Socialist candidate, he made no attempt to conciliate socialist voters. On the contrary, he devoted one of his great set-piece speeches to a withering attack on socialism, 'a monstrous and imbecile conception which can find no real foothold in the brains and hearts of a sensible people'. Liberalism, he declared, was the antithesis of socialism: 'Socialism seeks to pull down wealth, Liberalism seeks to raise up poverty . . . Socialism would kill enterprise; Liberalism would rescue enterprise from the trammels of privilege and preference.'[19] When it came to assaulting the Tories, however, Churchill engaged in his own version of class warfare:

We know what to expect when they return to power—a party of great vested interests, banded together in a formidable confederation; corruption at home, aggression to cover it up abroad; the trickery of tariff jungles; the tyranny of wealth-fed party machines; sentiment by the bucketful, patriotism and imperialism by the imperial pint, an open hand at the public Exchequer, an open door at the public house, dear food for the millions, cheap labour for the millionaire.[20]

Safely returned for Dundee, Churchill began to put the New Liberalism into practice at the Board of Trade. With the guidance of his Permanent Secretary, Sir Hubert Llewellyn Smith, and the support in Cabinet of Lloyd George, whom Asquith had appointed as Chancellor of the Exchequer, Churchill promoted three major reforms. The Trade Boards Act of 1909, which initially covered 200,000 workers, introduced statutory minimum wages into a number of the 'sweated trades', in which most of the workers were unionized women and the wages exceptionally low. The young William Beveridge, recruited by Churchill specifically for the purpose, devised a nationwide system of state-run labour exchanges to assist the unemployed in finding work. To help the unemployed over a longer period Churchill and his officials introduced for the first time a plan for compulsory unemployment insurance. Covering more than two million workers in specific industries, it was then handed over by Churchill to Lloyd George, who amalgamated it with his own scheme of medical insurance in the National Insurance Act of 1911. In detail the proposals were the work of civil servants, but the drive to push them through, and the vision of a more humane capitalism, were Churchill's. His motives, as he readily admitted, were mixed: 'Sometimes I want to do good in the world; sometimes I don't seem to care about anything but my own career.'[21] It was noticeable, too, that he valued social policy as an expression of the authority of a benign governing class. As he remarked to Masterman: 'I am in favour of government of the people, for the people, but not by the people.'[22]

Though none of these measures was especially controversial, Churchill's Board of Trade reforms were part of a joint political strategy which Lloyd George and Churchill pursued in Cabinet and campaigned for at great public meetings. In order to pay for social reforms they demanded reductions in expenditure on the armed forces, precipitating a Cabinet crisis over the naval estimates of 1909.

The naval rivalry between Germany and Great Britain, dating from the turn of the century, had been intensified in 1908 by the German decision to accelerate its programme of dreadnought construction. The Royal Navy had previously enjoyed a clear lead in capital ships but in the spring of 1909 the Admiralty under McKenna warned that unless the British now stepped up the pace the Germans would catch up. Demanding that six dreadnoughts be laid down in the current year, he was vigorously opposed by Churchill and Lloyd George, who insisted that four would be sufficient. Proclaiming something very like their own foreign policy of peace with Germany, they attacked the prophets of a great European war as alarmists. Edward VII's private secretary, Lord Knollys, wrote to Lord Esher: 'What are Winston's reasons for acting as he does in this matter? Of course it cannot be from conviction or principle. The very idea of his having either is enough to make anyone laugh.'[23] Asquith attempted a compromise, but the agitation in favour of naval rearmament grew and the music halls echoed with a new refrain: 'We want eight, and we won't wait!' In the event, Churchill and Lloyd George were defeated and eight dreadnoughts laid down.

In order to pay for naval rearmament, old age pensions, and other social reforms, Lloyd George was compelled to find new sources of revenue. In his budget of April 1909 he proposed a more progressive system of taxes on income and, more controversially, a range of new taxes on the value of land. When the Conservative Party threatened to employ its majority in the House of Lords to reject the budget, Churchill as President of the Budget League toured the country denouncing the peers and the Conservative party. With the exception of his broadcasts during the Second World War, the speeches he delivered in 1909–10 marked the zenith of his achievements as a popular orator. Where Lloyd George would jot down a few headings on a scrap of paper, and make up the rest of a speech as he went along, Churchill approached every major speech as though it were a literary composition. The constant repetition of his most celebrated wartime soundbites has created the impression that his speeches were full of bombast and purple prose. Churchill would generally introduce one or two passages intended to capture the headlines, together with a touch of biting wit and a flight or two of verbal fancy. But for the most part a Churchill speech consisted of carefully organized exposition and argument, expressed with clarity and economy of phrase, and supported by facts and figures obtained from officials or other expert advisers. Churchill's speeches were too carefully prepared to generate the electricity that flows from a speaker's ability to respond spontaneously to the mood of an audience, but they were more durable because they read so well. When the House of Lords finally rejected the budget in November 1909, Churchill revisted Lancashire to deliver a series of speeches on the House of Lords, free trade, and the taxation of land. Distilled and published in time for the general election under the title of *The People's Rights*, they served the Liberals as a campaign manual. 'Your speeches from first to last have reached high-water mark, and will live in history', Asquith wrote to him.[24]

Conservatives, of course, detested both Lloyd George and Churchill, but Churchill was the more despised for 'betraying' both his party and his class, and his oratory was written off as the outpourings of a demogogue. 'That Churchill is without conscience or scruple', noted a prominent Tory MP in his diary, 'without a glimmer of the comities of public reserve and deference, we all know, and all, even his closest friends, admit.'[25] To Spencer Ewart, the Director of Military Intelligence at the

War Office, the Liberal government was a harbinger of socialist revolution. 'Torrents of scurrilous and socialist oratory are being poured out upon the country by Lloyd George, Winston Churchill . . . and other demagogues', he wrote in his diary in December 1909. 'There is an ugly rumour that if the Radicals return to power Winston will come to the War Office. God forbid.'[26] Retailing the latest political gossip from London, the *Washington Post* reported that whenever Churchill entered the Turf Club, of which he had been a member for several years, he was systematically cut by the members, while the servants, Tories to a man, 'wait on him with evident disinclination'.[27]

The Liberals, though glad to have Churchill on their side, could never forget his ducal ancestry or his Tory origins. In a profile published in 1908, the editor of the Liberal *Daily News*, A. G. Gardiner, reported the remarks of one of Churchill's colleagues: 'I love Churchill and trust him . . . He has the passion of democracy more than any man I know. But don't forget that the aristocrat is still there—latent and submerged, but there nevertheless. The occasion may arise when the two Churchills come into sharp conflict, and I should not like to prophesy the result.'[28] Lloyd George, in particular, enjoyed teasing Churchill over his Tory tendencies. One day Lloyd George and Masterman began to talk in Churchill's presence, with every appearance of seriousness, of the revolutionary measures they were proposing, and the setting up of a guillotine in Trafalgar Square. 'Winston', wrote Lucy Masterman, 'became more and more indignant and alarmed, until they suggested that this would give him a splendid opportunity of figuring as the second Napoleon of the revolutionary forces.'[29] There was also some concern in Liberal circles over Churchill's egotism and apparent instability. The editor of the *Manchester Guardian*, C. P. Scott, a great admirer at first, quickly came to the conclusion that he was 'a queer emotional creature' for whom every question was a personal question.[30] Edward Grey, the Foreign Secretary, and Augustine Birrell, the Secretary for Ireland, could agree that 'the tendency in him to see first the rhetorical potentialities of any policy was growing and becoming a real intellectual and moral danger'.[31]

Doubts of this kind take on more significance in retrospect than they possessed at the time. Churchill and Lloyd George, the 'radical twins' as they were called, were heroes of the Liberal nation. 'The big thing that has happened in the past two years', wrote Beatrice Webb in November 1910, 'is that Lloyd George and Winston Churchill have practically taken the *limelight*, not merely from their own colleagues, but from the Labour Party, They stand out as the most advanced politicians.'[32]

Whether Churchill would be faithful to the Liberal party had yet to be seen. But he was faithful, both then and later, to a lifelong Liberal: his wife. A great admirer of beautiful women, but self-centred and gauche in their company, Churchill had already proposed to Pamela Plowden and Ethel Barrymore, only to be rejected by both. Then, at a dinner party early in 1908, he was reintroduced to Clementine Hozier, whom he had met briefly once before. Bowled over, he began an ardent courtship. In August he proposed, and was accepted, as they took shelter from the rain in the temple of Diana overlooking the lake at Blenheim Palace. With Hugh Cecil as best man, and Lloyd George's old friend the Bishop of St Asaph conducting the ceremony, Winston and Clementine were married at St Margaret's Westminster, on 12 September 1908.

Churchill expected his wife to be a loyal follower, but it was a role she was content to play. The unhappy child of a disastrous marriage and a financially precarious home, Clementine found in Winston a faithful husband who loved her, sustained her in material comfort, and placed her in the front row of a great historical drama. He could never be accused of marrying for money or running after other women. She, for her part, was never uncritical of her husband or afraid to express her opinions. A lifelong Liberal with a puritan streak, she never approved of his more louche Tory companions such as F. E. Smith, a close friend from 1907 onwards, or Max Aitken, later Lord Beaverbrook, introduced to Churchill by 'F. E.' in 1911. Winston, nevertheless, discussed all his political affairs with her and she often gave him sound advice, which he seldom took. Given the dissimilarities between them, it was not surprising that Winston and Clementine sometimes quarrelled furiously. She once threw a dish of spinach at him, and missed. Nevertheless they were quick to make up after a row, and their marriage was sustained by a lifelong mutual affection expressed in their pet names for each other. Winston was always 'Pug' or 'Pig', Clementine 'Kat', and the children 'the Kittens'. Their first child, Diana ('the Puppy Kitten'), was born in 1909. Randolph ('the Chum Bolly') followed in 1911, and Sarah ('Bumblebee') in 1914.

Churchill believed that a husband must be the dominant partner in a marriage. According to Clemmie, who told the story to MacCallum Scott, Churchill's cousin Freddie Guest was frequently harassed by his wife Amy, who had a habit of flying into jealous rages whenever he gave his attention to other people. One evening when Freddie stayed up playing cards after Amy had gone to bed she roused the servants, ordered a valet to remove all his clothes from his dressing-room, and locked him out of her bedroom. At about midnight Clemmie was awoken by Churchill stomping about the room:

'Clemmie', he said, 'don't you ever behave like Amy. If you do I'll leave you right away.' And he continued to walk up and down the room making speeches. 'Well', I said, 'nothing else can be done tonight. Freddie better go and sleep by himself.' 'No', said Winston, 'he won't. The honour of the family is at stake.' Then he went out and got hold of Freddie who was prepared to accept the situation. I could hear them out in the passage. 'No. You can't take a thing like that lying down', said Winston. 'If you do you are done for. You have got to spend the night in that room or I'll disown you. Go on! Hammer at the door and tell her you insist upon coming in.' Freddie gave some gentle taps and I could hear him saying in a deprecating voice, 'Amy, dear, Amy, open the door. Do you hear Amy?' 'That's not the right way to talk to her', shouted Winston, and he dealt some resounding blows on the door. 'Go on now. Tell her you'll burst the door in if she does not open it.' But Amy paid no attention and did not even answer. I heard them next by the dressing room door but it was locked also. 'Think now!' said Winston—he was acting as if he was in charge of a campaign—think, isn't there some other door to your dressing room? Can't we make a flanking attack? Are the windows practicable? Come on—set yourself to work.' Honour was satisfied when it was discovered that a third door was unlocked and Freddie got in after all.[33]

This episode from P. G. Wodehouse is of some relevance for Churchill's views on the subject of votes for women. Lord and Lady Randolph had opposed the idea and so had Winston in his Bangalore days. But if the majority of Tories were against female suffrage, the majority of Liberals were in favour, which may explain why Churchill voted in favour of a women's suffrage bill in March 1904, at a time when he was in transition from one party to the other. He reacted angrily, however, when the Women's Social and Political Union, recently founded by Emmeline Pankhurst and her daughters, began to disrupt his political meetings. 'I am certainly not going to be henpecked into a position on which my mind is not fully prepared', he wrote in November 1905, 'and if I am subjected to any further annoyance, I shall say plainly that I do not intend to vote for Female Suffrage in the next

Parliament.'[34] His temper was not improved when the WSPU ran protest campaigns against him in the Manchester North-West and Dundee by-elections. In 1909 he was arriving at Bristol railway station when a suffragette, Theresa Garnett, attempted to strike him with a dog whip. 'Take that in the name of the insulted women of England', she called out.[35] Such tepid support as Churchill still gave to the principle of votes for women seemed to evaporate altogether when he denounced a suffrage bill in the House of Commons in July 1910, but he was able to find plausible democratic reasons for doing so. The suffragists demanded votes for women on the same terms as men, but under the existing franchise the vote was exercised by heads of household. Therefore only female heads of household—widows or women living alone—would acquire the franchise and Liberals feared that most of them would be propertied women inclined to vote Conservative. And as Churchill pointed out, a prostitute would lose the vote on getting married, and regain it if she divorced. The 'democratic' case against the enfranchisement of a minority of women was, however, a convenient smokescreen for Liberals who were actually opposed to female suffrage. When in 1912 the Cabinet debated whether or not to introduce a franchise bill paving the way for universal suffrage, Churchill was strongly opposed. 'We already have enough ignorant voters', he remarked, 'and don't want any more.'[36]

After the general election of January 1910 Asquith promoted Churchill to the Home Office, where his many responsibilities ranged from the supervision of the Metropolitan Police and the maintenance of public order to the regulation of prisons, borstals, factories, coal mines, and shops. For every Home Secretary, the problem of striking a balance between liberty and order was inescapable, but Churchill's response was probably unique.

Radical in both directions, he extended the boundaries of liberty and order in a series of bold strokes.

More than any other Home Secretary of the twentieth century, Churchill was the prisoner's friend. He arrived at the Home Office with the firm conviction that the penal system was excessively harsh. Determined to reduce the number of people who were sent to prison in the first place, he was equally concerned to make life in prison more tolerable for those who had to endure it. Penal policy was not a party political or a vote-catching issue and it is a matter of conjecture why Churchill felt so strongly about it. According to his own account his experience as a prisoner of war in South Africa had left him with a loathing of prison. 'I certainly hated my captivity', he wrote in 1930, 'more than I have ever hated any other period in my whole life . . . Looking back on those days I have always felt the keenest pity for prisoners and captives.'[37] But his penal policies also reflected his wider Edwardian vision of the need for a society less oppressive of the poor, from whom the majority of prisoners were drawn.

Churchill's tenure at the Home Office was too brief to enable him to legislate for penal reform. But he stretched such powers as he did possess to the limit. The Home Secretary had the right (technically the right to advise the monarch, though the advice was never rejected) to exercise the royal prerogative of varying the sentences handed down by judges and magistrates. Previous Home Secretaries had intervened in response to pleas for clemency. Churchill went through the calendar of criminal trials, and whenever he came across a sentence he regarded as disproportionate to the crime, altered the sentence himself without consulting the judge or the magistrate concerned. In 395 cases he reduced the sentence. With the aim of setting an example over sentencing policy, he visited Pentonville gaol in October 1910 and ordered the release of a number of youths imprisoned for minor offences. It was already characteristic of Churchill that his vision extended far beyond the realm of the possible. His ultimate ambition was to impose on the judges and magistrates a uniform sentencing policy in which offences were classified according to their seriousness, and appropriate penalties prescribed.[38]

Where prison conditions were concerned, Churchill made use of his administrative powers to limit periods of solitary confinement, provide better treatment for political prisoners (mainly suffragettes), and improve recreational facilities such as concerts and libraries. He also encountered the resistance of senior officials who feared that the changes he proposed would 'weaken the deterrence of the criminal justice system and thereby lead to an increase in crime and possibly social disorder'.[39] 'He nearly drives me crazy at times', complained his Permanent Secretary, Sir Edward Troup, 'but he's the first great Home Secretary we've had since Asquith . . . Anyone can use the ideas already in the Office. He brings ideas to the Office.'[40]

Persuaded by the arguments of eugenicists, who maintained that the 'quality of the race' was degenerating due to the multiplication of the 'unfit', Churchill was briefly an enthusiast for the compulsory segregation of the 'feeble-minded', who were to be locked up in order to prevent them from having children. This draconian proposal, which had been recommended by two Royal Commissions, reflected the consensus of enlightened opinion at the time. Churchill was in favour of giving the 'feeble-minded' the option of sterilization as a condition of restoring their liberty.[41] Nothing came of this while he was at the Home Office, but he did secure the passage of a bill, much emasculated on the way to the statute book, to regulate the hours and conditions of shop assistants, and an act to improve safety in the coal mines.

Churchill's more constructive endeavours as Home Secretary were increasingly overshadowed by controversial problems of law and order. In November 1910 a suffragette rally at Westminster was met by the Metropolitan Police with extremely rough tactics in which several women were injured. Churchill was not personally responsible for 'Black Friday', but he rejected all allegations against the police and refused to institute an inquiry. Within a few days of 'Black Friday', a dispute in the south Wales coalfield led to a strike by miners employed by the Cambrian Colliery. Riots and looting broke out in the town of Tonypandy in the Rhondda Valley and one of the rioters was fatally injured in a struggle with the Glamorganshire police. The local magistrates pleaded with the Home Office to authorize the despatch of troops. Recognizing that any direct clash between troops and strikers might result in bloodshed, Churchill at first refused the request of the local authorities, and sent instead a contingent of the Metropolitan Police. But twenty-four hours later, when it was clear that the riots were continuing unabated, Churchill authorized the despatch of troops. In a bold and imaginative stroke, which may have been unconstitutional, he appointed General Neville Macready to command both troops and police, with instructions to ensure that the police acted as a buffer between the strikers and the troops. He thereby took control out of the hands of the local authorities, who might well have been tempted to employ both police and troops as strike-breakers.[42]

Churchill's conduct of the Tonypandy affair prevented further bloodshed, but he was strongly attacked by Keir Hardie for condoning brutality on the part of the Metropolitan Police. Afterwards the legend grew that Churchill had sent troops to shoot down striking Welsh miners. Although this was a gross distortion, Churchill's response to industrial unrest was not always cool and measured. During the summer of 1911, when strikes in the docks spread to the railways, he was seized by a nightmare vision of a starving community held to ransom by industrial anarchists. Overriding the local authorities, he despatched troops to many parts of the country and gave army commanders discretion to employ them. When rioters tried to prevent the movement of a train at Llanelli, troops opened fire and shot two men dead. Churchill's blood was up and when Lloyd George intervened to settle the strike Churchill telephoned him to say that it would have been better to go on and give the strikers 'a good thrashing'.[43] In a pamphlet entitled *Killing No Murder* Keir Hardie accused Asquith and Churchill of deliberately sending soldiers to shoot and kill strikers. Together with Tonypandy, these events marked a turning point in Churchill's relations with the Labour party and the trade unions. His record as a social reformer was eclipsed by his new reputation as a class warrior with a 'Prussian' love of order imposed by military force.

The perception was heightened by a tragi-comic episode in January 1911 when two criminals, alleged to be Latvian anarchists, opened fire on police surrounding them at 100 Sidney Street, a house in the east end. Churchill hastened to the scene, where his conspicuous presence in the danger zone led critics to accuse him of taking operational control from the police. The charge was mistaken. When the house caught fire Churchill did indeed confirm a police decision to let it burn down, but otherwise he was merely an enthralled spectator, playing artlessly into the hands of his political opponents.[44]

Churchill's thirst for adventure and publicity concealed the activities of an alter ego operating invisibly in the realms of the secret state. Without informing Parliament he authorized the home department of the newly established Secret Service Bureau—the ancestor of MI5—to draw up a register of thousands of enemy aliens to be arrested at the outbreak of war. His too was the unseen hand behind the Official Secrets Act, a draconian measure which made it an offence to disclose or receive without authorization any official information. Rushed through an almost empty House of Commons in half an hour on a Friday afternoon in August 1911, it was to remain in force until replaced by a new Official Secrets Act in 1989.[45]

At about the same time, there were signs that Churchill was moving to the Right. The Edwardian Liberal party was a coalition with both radical and conservative tendencies. Between 1906 and 1910 Churchill had embraced the radical tendency of the New Liberalism and the 'progressive alliance' with Labour. But the general election of January 1910 created a new political context. The Liberal government lost its overall majority and now depended upon the votes of Irish nationalist and Labour MPs. The battle between the government and the House of Lords, temporarily suspended after the death of Edward VII in May, was resumed after the collapse of a constitutional conference between the parties, and a second general election held in December 1910, but the parliamentary arithmetic was virtually unchanged. Churchill shared the Liberal party's determination to overcome the resistance of the House of Lords, which finally capitulated in August 1911 and passed the Parliament Bill restricting its own powers of veto. But he also hoped that once the struggle with the House of Lords was over, the Liberal and Conservative parties would draw closer together. In September 1910 Lloyd George had told Churchill that he had two alternatives to propose for the future: a Coalition in which the Liberals and

Conservatives reached a compromise over the issues that divided them, and a Liberal government with an advanced land and social policy. Churchill was all for a Coalition and henceforth made various efforts to find common ground with his Conservative opponents. With a view to assuaging the bitterness caused by the House of Lords crisis, Churchill and F. E. Smith in May 1911 co-founded the 'Other Club', a bipartisan dining club of which the Liberal and Conservative Chief Whips were both members.

Churchill's motives are a matter for speculation, but we may guess that he was unhappy with the prospect of a Liberal Cabinet beholden to two minority parties, Labour and the Irish nationalists, whose political agendas were not his own. His relations with Labour were deteriorating and he did not want to see the business of government and parliament subordinated to Irish quarrels. By 1910–11 there was also a new factor looming up in his thoughts: the possibility of a war between Britain and Germany.

· THREE ·

The Lilliput Napoleon,
1911–1915

Even when Churchill was immersed in welfare reforms or the struggle with the House of Lords his interest in all things military was unceasing. In 1907 he attended the annual manoeuvres of the French Army. Two years later he witnessed the manoeuvres of the German army and made his first visit to the battlefield of Blenheim. As he confessed to Clemmie after a field day with the Queen's Own Oxfordshire Yeomanry, in which he and his brother Jack both held commissions, he longed for a chance to command military forces and believed that he possessed more tactical insight than professional soldiers: 'I am sure I have the root of the matter in me—but never I fear in this state of existence will it have a chance of flowering—in bright red blossom.'[1]

Churchill at this point was not expecting a war. In August 1908 he stigmatized talk of an impending conflict with Germany as alarmism and predicted twenty years of peace in Europe. The Home Office, however, brought him into contact with the intelligence services, whose fears of German intentions were sustained by an obsession with the alleged activities—largely imaginary— of German spies in Britain. Churchill began to reflect on the implications of a major war—including the implications for himself. One weekend when he was driving down to Brighton with Lloyd George, he began to talk about the shape of things to come: 'He described how, at the climax, he himself, in command of the army, would win the decisive victory in the Middle East, and would return to England in triumph. Lloyd George quietly interposed, "And where do I come in?"'[2]

Churchill's friends and colleagues were taken aback by the frequent comparisons he drew between his own career and Napoleon's, an unusual preoccupation in a President of the Board of Trade. But as the Labour politician J. R. Clynes once wrote of him: 'Churchill was, and has always remained, a soldier in mufti. He possesses inborn militaristic qualities, and is intensely proud of his descent from Marlborough.'[3]

Between 1911 and 1915 the military leader in Churchill came to the fore, with consequences that almost destroyed his political career. Though he was largely unaware of the gathering storm, his transition from radicalism to militarism, his passion for war, and his conviction that strategy was too serious a matter to be left to the admirals and the generals all generated so much hostility that when a scapegoat was needed he was the ideal candidate.

On 1 July 1911 it was reported that a German gunboat, the *Panther*, was on its way to the port of Agadir to protect German interests in Morocco. A test of the solidarity of the Anglo-French entente, the Agadir crisis was also and quite incidentally a test of the alliance between Churchill and Lloyd George. It proved to be as strong as ever. They adopted a common position of resistance to German demands, with Churchill in the role of strategic and military adviser. He submitted to the Cabinet a paper entitled 'Military Aspects of the Continental Problem', in which he argued that the French ought not to take the counter-offensive until the fortieth day of the war, by which date the German assault would have exhausted itself. 'This was without question', writes Tuvia Ben-Moshe, 'a brilliant assessment of the initial stages of the war . . .'[4] Asquith now decided to invite Churchill to a critical meeting of the Committee of Imperial Defence, which revealed a complete lack of coordination between the plans of the Admiralty and those of the War Office. Much impressed by Churchill's interventions, and his obvious desire to take charge of the Royal Navy, Asquith appointed him First Lord of the Admiralty in October 1911.

Tradition has it that when an admiral spoke reverently to him of naval tradition, Churchill retorted: 'What are the traditions of the Navy? Rum, sodomy, and the lash!' In later years he explained that he had never said this, but wished that he had. His mission at the Admiralty was to modernize to meet the challenge of imperial Germany. Many of the reforms he proposed were inspired by the retired First Sea Lord, 'Jacky' Fisher, with whom he was in regular but secret contact. But Churchill, of course, also had great confidence in his own judgement and was ready to act boldly.

His first act was to replace three of the four Sea Lords. Sir Arthur Wilson was succeeded as First Sea Lord by Sir Francis Bridgeman, and Louis of Battenberg, a German Prince who since boyhood had lived in England, appointed Second Sea Lord. A dashing young officer, David Beatty, became Churchill's naval secretary. When Bridgeman protested against Churchill's dictatorial treatment of the Sea Lords, to whom he issued instructions as though they were officials under his command, Churchill coerced him into retirement on the grounds of ill health and replaced him, in December 1912, with Battenberg. Churchill displayed little respect for many of the senior officers of the

Royal Navy, whom he regarded as narrow-minded and hide-bound by tradition. One of his first actions, in line with Fisher's advice, was to establish a Naval War Staff of three divisions, Operations, Intelligence, and Mobilization, to prepare and coordinate war plans. With the assistance of Admiral Richmond he sought to encourage the interest of naval officers in history and strategy, and helped to launch a new periodical, the *Naval Review*. Eager to explore almost every aspect of naval affairs, Churchill set out to discover the facts for himself. Making frequent use of the Admiralty yacht, *Enchantress*—where he also entertained his political friends from time to time—he inspected ships, dockyards, and naval installations with a vigilant eye. In defiance of protocol he sometimes bypassed senior naval officers and sought information directly from junior officers or ordinary seamen.

Many of the admirals were unimpressed. According to the Second Sea Lord, Sir John Jellicoe, Churchill's fatal error was 'his entire inability to realize his own limitations as a civilian . . . quite ignorant of naval affairs'.[5] But the admirals, like so many of the experts Churchill was to encounter, were often blinkered by convention. 'In matters of technical advance', writes one historian of Churchill and the Navy, 'the First Lord was always in the van, always supporting the pioneers, always sweeping aside the obstruction of the unimaginative.'[6] Like Fisher, he favoured the construction of a Channel Tunnel, a project discussed by the Committee of Imperial Defence but turned down. Before Churchill's arrival at the Admiralty, the most powerful of the Navy's battleships were equipped with 13.5-inch guns. With Fisher's encouragement Churchill and the Admiralty engineers created a fast division of five battleships with 15-inch guns and a top speed of 25 knots: the *Queen Elizabeth*, *Warspite*, *Barham*,

Valiant, and *Malaya* were all commissioned and launched during his period as First Lord. He pressed on with converting the Fleet from coal-fired to oil-fired engines, and negotiated the purchase by the British government in 1914 of 51 per cent of the shares in the Anglo-Iranian oil company, thus ensuring a guaranteed supply of oil for the fleet.[7]

When Churchill arrived at the Admiralty the Royal Navy possessed only half a dozen aeroplanes, manned by pilots of the Royal Flying Corps. Enthralled by the military potential of aircraft, Churchill resolved to expand the Navy's air arm. In the face of resistance from the War Office, which claimed exclusive responsibility for air defence, and the Treasury, which objected to the expenditure involved, Churchill built up the naval wing of the Corps, which became known as the Royal Naval Air Service (RNAS). Mainly intended for the protection of harbours and other naval installations, the RNAS had fifty aircraft at its disposal by the outbreak of war in 1914. Churchill was also, for a time, an enthusiastic champion of the airship. In 1913, to the great alarm of Clementine, he began flying lessons. At a time when aircraft were still technologically primitive, and pilots were learning the arts of survival by trial and error, flying was extremely hazardous and Churchill had many narrow escapes. But he took to the air 150 times before a series of fatalities persuaded him, in June 1914, to stop flying—for the time being.

Churchill watched over the RNAS like a doting parent fussing over an infant prodigy. He issued instructions on everything from aircraft specifications to the uniform of the service ('naval uniform with an eagle instead of an anchor on buttons, cap badges, epaulettes and sword belt clasps') and the facilities necessary for officers ('bathrooms with hot and cold water are indispensable . . . a squash court would be better than a second lawn tennis court').[8] As in many other spheres, much of Churchill's legacy was to survive his ministerial tenure. After a brief period in which the Admiralty claimed exclusive control of the Royal Naval Service it was reunited with the Royal Flying Corps in the newly created Royal Air Force of 1918. The Fleet Air Arm, as it was now called, was to be the subject between the wars of an epic Whitehall struggle in which the Admiralty eventually regained control over the aircraft involved in naval operations.[9]

Speaking in Glasgow on 8 February 1912, Churchill argued that for Britain a large navy was a necessity whereas for Germany it was a 'luxury'—a comment which provoked much German anger. In March he announced the principle upon which naval construction would be based for the next five years: the maintenance of a 60 per cent superiority in dreadnoughts over Germany's current programme, together with two keels for every additional ship Germany laid down. When the draft of a new German naval law proposed a further increase in the size of the German fleet, he obtained the Cabinet's approval in principle for an expansion of the British naval programme. At the same time he tried to refurbish his Liberal credentials by proposing a 'naval holiday', or joint suspension of naval construction by both countries. When the Germans rejected the idea, Churchill sought a naval arrangement with France under which the British Mediterranean Fleet would be withdrawn and concentrated in home waters, leaving the French to patrol the Mediterranean. Since this would involve the British in a pledge to defend the Channel and Atlantic coasts of France, it was tantamount to a military alliance. After long and complex arguments the Cabinet agreed in July 1912.

Churchill's expansionist naval policy, and the strengthening of the Anglo-French entente, alienated the radical wing of the

Liberal party and confirmed growing speculation that he was 'moving to the right' or preparing to rejoin the Conservative Party. During the winter of 1913–14 his insistence on the construction of another four dreadnoughts, and a further increase in the naval estimates which could only be paid for by an increase in taxes, led to a crisis in which he found himself at loggerheads with Lloyd George, the majority of the Cabinet, and most of the Liberal party. Only the delaying tactics of Asquith, and a last-minute decision by Lloyd George to concede most of Churchill's demands, averted his resignation. Only Churchill, Lloyd George, and the Board of Admiralty knew that the First Lord had no intention of laying down four dreadnoughts. With the dual objective of keeping down the cost of the naval estimates, and concealing from Germany an important change in naval strategy, he had secretly abandoned the 60 per cent margin of superiority, and agreed to substitute submarines for two of the battleships. His decision, writes Andrew Lambert,

can be seen as an attempt to break the shackles on the service imposed by public and political opinion and to create a new consensus within the Navy on how naval force should be applied when it took courage and vision to do so. The endorsement of this change in policy by the professional members of the board also signified a wider acceptance among British admirals that there was an alternative to battleship strategy.[10]

When Churchill was first appointed to the Admiralty, the radical wing of the Liberal party had expected him to cut naval expenditure and pursue a conciliatory policy towards Germany. By January 1912 editor of *The Nation*, H. W. Massingham, was beginning to experience doubts:

As Liberalism does not run a war policy, so the value of its contribution to the true standard of national strength—which is the condition of the people of Great Britain—is lessened by this concentration on the fighting services.

63

Mr Churchill has his father's impressionable temper; much of his youth was spent amid the pageantry of guns and marching armies; like Faust (and most of us), he resembles the spirit which he comprehends, and which is nearest to him. Manchester made him a radical reformer. What kind of political interest will two or three years at the Admiralty develop? He has a mind of incessant activity and great acquisitive and receptive power; he likes to be at the centre of the brilliantly lighted stage that the modern statesman treads; he is a specially close and intelligent student of war. A careful director of party energies would like to see him at a safer post.[11]

By January 1914 the radicals were convinced that Churchill had deserted them. ' "Keep your eye on Churchill" should be the watchword of these days', wrote A. G. Gardiner, the editor of the Liberal *Daily News*. 'Remember, he is a soldier first, last and always. He will write his name big on our future. Let us take care he does not write it in blood.'[12]

The truth was that Churchill had changed his mind about Germany, and the likelihood of war. He had done so before he took over the Admiralty and by 1912–13 he was already thinking of the need for national unity in wartime, and the possibility of mending his fences with the Conservative party. In social policy his views were largely unchanged, but he had always been a paternalist who believed in what he was later to call 'appeasement from strength': beneficence from a position of unchallenged authority. At the Board of Trade and the Home Office he had dealt for the most part with moderate trade unionists of the Lib-Lab variety who were ready to accept the government's leadership. Seen through his eyes the industrial unrest and syndicalist propaganda of 1910–14 were an alarming spectacle which posed a genuine threat to the state. Churchill was 'moving to the Right' in the sense that his latent convictions about the social order, and the necessity of military force, were now expressing themselves more openly.

As First Lord, Churchill tended to concentrate on naval matters to the exclusion of everything else. 'You have become a water creature', Lloyd George told him in July 1912. 'You think we all live in the sea, and all your thoughts are devoted to sea life, fishes and other aquatic creatures.'[13] Nevertheless Churchill was actively involved in the greatest political issue of the day: Irish Home Rule. The Conservatives at this period were still deeply attached to the Union with Ireland, and were indeed generally known as 'Unionists'. Lord Randolph Churchill had tried to thwart Home Rule by inciting the Protestants of Ulster to resist: 'Ulster will fight, and Ulster will be right.' Under the leadership of Andrew Bonar Law, himself of Ulster Protestant descent, the Conservatives revived Lord Randolph's tactic and openly incited armed rebellion against the government. By aligning themselves with two violently opposed factions, the Conservative Opposition and the Liberal government were playing politics with the materials of an Irish civil war, an episode that injected fresh poison into the already embittered relations between the two parties.

Winston Churchill rubbed salt in Conservative wounds by attacking them for pursuing Lord Randolph's policy. In February 1912 he attempted to confront a Unionist audience in Belfast in the very same hall in which his father had spoken in 1886, but so great was the threat to his safety that the meeting had to be moved, at the last minute, to the Celtic Road football stadium. Behind the scenes, however, Churchill made persistent efforts to find a compromise. In the memorandum of August 1910 in which he had floated the idea of a Coalition government Lloyd George had written: 'The advantages of a non-Party treatment of this vexed problem are obvious. Parties might deal with it without being subject to the embarrassing dictation of extreme partisans, whether from Nationalists or from Orangemen.'[14]

One possibility, which Churchill proposed in the secrecy of the Cabinet room in March 1911, was to include Ireland in an all-round scheme of federal devolution. There would be seven regional Parliaments for England together with Parliaments for Scotland, Ireland, and Wales. The Cabinet, however, decided in favour of a single Parliament for the whole of Ireland. In September 1912 he caused something of a sensation by airing the concept of federal devolution in a speech in Dundee. By analogy with the seven kingdoms of Anglo-Saxon England, it became known as Churchill's plan to revive the 'Heptarchy'. Twice that same year Churchill urged the Cabinet, without success, to offer temporary exclusion from Home Rule to the predominantly Protestant counties. During the winter of 1913–14 he was the principal go-between in a number of secret moves to promote a bipartisan settlement. On the Conservative side his main contact was F. E. Smith, who was both a personal friend and a fervent champion of Ulster. Churchill, it was said, was threatening to quit the Cabinet if force were employed against Ulster: 'You understand that if a shot is fired I shall go out.'[15]

As the hour at which the Home Rule Bill would become law approached, the Ulster Unionists rejected out of hand a belated offer by Asquith to allow the Protestant counties to opt out for a six-year period. Churchill now changed tack, arguing that, having obtained a compromise, the Ulster Unionists must accept it. He was also eager to restore his standing in the Liberal party. In a speech at Bradford on 14 March 1914 he issued a stern warning that Ulster Unionists must agree to the government's plan or take the consequences: 'There are worse things than bloodshed, even on an extended scale', he declared.[16]

Meanwhile the Cabinet were much alarmed by police reports suggesting that the Ulster Volunteers, a force of more than

100,000 men well armed with rifles and ammunition, were planning a military coup. A Cabinet committee under Churchill authorized precautionary troop movements and Churchill himself, as First Lord of the Admiralty, ordered the third battle squadron to steam to Lamlash on the Isle of Arran, seventy miles from Belfast. In fact the squadron only got as far as the Isles of Scilly before the order was cancelled. But his actions convinced the Conservatives that the government was planning an 'Ulster pogrom' to crush the Volunteers. Their suspicions appeared to be confirmed by the notorious episode of the 'Curragh Mutiny', when fifty-seven of the seventy officers of the Third Cavalry Brigade declared that they would rather be dismissed than take part in the coercion of Ulster.

The Conservatives jumped to the conclusion that Churchill was the villain of the piece. Specifically it was alleged that a section of the Cabinet, led by Churchill and the Secretary for War, John Seely, had planned a military and naval coup intended to provoke the Ulster Volunteers into some reckless action that would justify military intervention to smash them.[17] The *Morning Post* alleged that Churchill had promised, if Belfast should fight, that the fleet would reduce the city to ruins in twenty-four hours.[18] Ministers had in fact discussed what larger operations might be needed if the Ulster Volunteers broke into rebellion: hence Churchill's remark. But there was no intention of provoking a rising. No matter: the Opposition were convinced. At a Unionist rally Lord Charles Beresford referred to Churchill as a 'Lilliput Napoleon, a man with an unbalanced mind, an egomaniac whose one absorbing thought was personal vindictiveness towards Ulster'. The Ulster Unionist leader, Sir Edward Carson, branded him as 'Lord Randolph's renegade son who wanted to be handed down to posterity as the Belfast butcher who threatened to shoot down those who took his father's advice'.[19] The Earl of Crawford, a former Conservative Chief Whip, concluded that there was 'clear evidence of an elaborate conspiracy, hatched I doubt not by Churchill, and probably not communicated to Asquith and the respectable members of the Cabinet'. He discussed with friends 'the Anglo-Mexican strains in Churchill's blood which explains the unaccountable fits of madness which recur from time to time'[20]—a confused reference to his alleged North American Indian ancestry.

In a political elite where everyone knew everyone else, rumour spread rapidly. Far away in Damascus the archaeologist Gertrude Bell received this melodramatic account of events from her sister Elsa, who was married to Sir Herbert Richmond, Assistant Director of Operations at the Admiralty:

The story is that Winston Churchill tried to make a coup d'etat. He got Seely to agree and though he (Winston) has nothing to do with the army, he was in and out of the War Office the whole time hatching his plot presumably. Warrants for the arrest of Carson and of 200 others were prepared and the troops, without Asquith's knowledge, secretly ordered to move on Ulster. Then all the Ulster leaders were to be arrested and the troops to be (unexpectedly) on the spot to quell in a moment the uprising of the Ulster volunteers that would of course result immediately from the leaders' arrest. Thus suddenly all would have been settled, Ulster cowed, and Winston the man who had done it all. He also ordered a squadron of battle ships to go to Belfast, but stopped them by wireless when the plot was found out.[21]

Churchill often employed provocative language on the public platform while pursuing relatively conciliatory policies behind the scenes. But a belligerent style inevitably aroused fears of belligerent intent and Churchill was partly to blame for Tory suspicions. The 'plot that failed' had never been attempted, but the story of the 'Ulster pogrom' was destined to live on as one of the more potent of anti-Churchill myths. Bonar Law, who led the

Conservative Party (apart from one short break) from 1911 to 1923, 'always accepted the "Pogrom" theory of the Ulster crisis, blaming Churchill as the real leader'.[22] There was even a echo on the day of Churchill's funeral in 1965, when a minute's silence was observed at football grounds throughout the country. The historian Ian S. Wood was present at the Easter Road ground in Edinburgh for the match between Hibernian and Rangers. As he recalls: 'The Glasgow club's famously Protestant support included one man who called out that Churchill would have "given Ulster to the Fenians"'.[23]

While attending the German army manoeuvres of 1909 Churchill had written to Clementine: 'Much as war attracts me & fascinates my mind with its tremendous situations—I feel more deeply every year—& can measure the feeling here in the midst of arms—what vile & wicked folly & barbarism it all is.' As war loomed in July 1914 Churchill confessed to her that his passion for war was now in the ascendancy: 'Everything tends towards catastrophe and collapse. I am interested, geared up and happy. Is it not horrible to be built like that?'[24] When Austria declared war on Serbia two days later, Churchill, acting with Asquith's approval, ordered the fleets to their battle stations. In the critical Cabinet discussions over the next few days Churchill, Grey, and Haldane were consistently in favour of British intervention while others, including Lloyd George, wavered.

On 3 August, the day German troops invaded Belgium, the Cabinet decided on a British ultimatum to Germany to expire at midnight on 4 August. Asquith awaited a reply in his room at 10 Downing Street but the fatal hour arrived with no response from Berlin. 'As I was passing at the foot of the staircase', Margot Asquith recalled, 'I saw Winston Churchill with a happy face striding towards the double doors of the Cabinet room.'[25]

At the outbreak of war the Royal Navy began to impose a long-distance blockade on Germany. The German merchant marine was driven from the high seas while routine searches of neutral vessels diverted essential war supplies bound for Germany into British hands. There were strong protests in the United States against British interference with American trade, but the German riposte to the blockade, the declaration in February 1915 of unrestricted submarine warfare against merchant shipping, led to the sinking by a German U-boat on 7 May of an American passenger liner, the *Lusitania*, with the loss of 1,200 lives. Much to the advantage of Britain, American outrage compelled Germany to suspend the U-boat campaign. Unknown to the passengers on board, however, the *Lusitania* had also been carrying a consignment of rifle ammunition and shells ordered by the British government. Conspiracy theorists have alleged that Churchill deliberately employed the ship as bait with the aim of embroiling the United States in the war against Germany, but the argument does not withstand detailed scrutiny.[26]

In the long run the blockade was to prove a very effective strategy, but it failed to satisfy Churchill's desire for dramatic and decisive operations. 'Churchill', one historian writes, 'took a more active part in the day-to-day running of the war than any First Lord in history. His were many of the ideas for action; it was he who drafted many of the signals to the ships. He studied and analysed each operation with great care . . .'[27] Churchill's interventionism, which he scarcely bothered to conceal, was a double-edged sword. Though he stood to gain the credit from successful actions by the Royal Navy, he was sure to get the blame when things went wrong.

The day after the outbreak of war Churchill authorized the creation within the Admiralty of a cryptography department which became known, from the room in which it was housed, as Room 40. Within a few months a series of coups delivered into the Admiralty's hands the Imperial German code and cypher books and the capacity to read German naval signals. Enthralled by the flow of intercepts, and the power conferred by the possession of top-secret information, Churchill confined the circulation of intelligence to an inner circle of Admiralty officials and the Prime Minister: Cabinet colleagues, like naval commanders at sea, were excluded—a system described by one historian as 'over-centralised and inefficient'.[28] Over the longer run, Room 40 evolved into the Government Code and Cypher School, established in 1919 with the support of Churchill among others.

In spite of Room 40 the Germans achieved a number of early naval successes for which Churchill was strongly criticized. In August two German battleships, the *Goeben* and the *Breslau*, escaped from the Adriatic through the Dardanelles to Constantinople. On 21 September Churchill boasted that if the German fleet did not come out and fight they would be 'dug out like rats in a hole',[29] but the following day the Germans sank three British cruisers, with the loss of 1,459 officers and men, off the Dogger Bank. Two more British cruisers were sunk at the Battle of Coronel, off the coast of Chile, on 1 November. On 16 December German battlecruisers shelled Scarborough and other east coast ports, killing or injuring 500 civilians. Criticism of the Admiralty mounted and was only partially offset by successful actions off the Falkland Islands (8 December) and the Dogger Bank (24 January).

Enthralled by all aspects of the fighting, Churchill was eager to play a part in the land war and ingenious in stretching the Admiralty's responsibilities. He converted the Naval Reserve into the Royal Naval Division, an infantry force of some 15,000 men, in which many of his friends were commissioned as officers. Although Churchill promised that the Division would later be transferred to the control of the War Office, he now had at his disposal something very like a private army. He also established what soon became known as his 'Dunkirk circus', three squadrons of aircraft which bombed German defences from airfields in northern France, protected by a force of Rolls Royce cars with armour plating.

For three and a half days in October 1914 Churchill found himself in virtual command of a land battle. As they advanced into Belgium and France the Gemans were threatened by the presence on their right flank of the Belgian field army, which had taken refuge with the Belgian king and government in the coastal fortress of Antwerp. At the end of September the Germans began to bombard the city and the Belgians appealed to the allies for help. Asquith and the Cabinet agreed that everything possible should be done to save Antwerp but the Belgian government, concluding that allied reinforcements would arrive too late, announced that it was about to leave the city. Summoned by Kitchener and Grey to a meeting to discuss the crisis, Churchill offered to go to Antwerp in person to report on the situation and stiffen Belgian resistance.

Arriving in Antwerp on 3 October, Churchill persuaded the Belgian government to postpone a decision for three days. No sooner was he on the spot than he took personal charge of the defence of the city, calling in as reinforcements the Royal Marine Brigade and the bulk of three battalions of the Royal Naval Division then in training. It was not Churchill's fault that both the British and French War Offices were unprepared, and unable to send the promised reinforcements in time. He failed to prevent the fall of the city, which capitulated on 9 October, but according to the military historians he delayed it long enough to ensure that the Battle of Ypres was won and the Channel ports saved from the Germans.[30]

There was much criticism in the press of Churchill's actions, with his opponents contending that the whole episode was a futile adventure which he had imposed on all concerned, the Belgians included. One of the key indictments against him was set out by the Conservative *Morning Post*, which had recently crossed swords with him over Ulster:

When Mr Churchill became First Lord he set himself more directly to undermine the power of the Board and to establish himself as Dictator . . . In plain language, Mr Churchill has gathered the whole power of the Admiralty into his own hands, and the Navy is governed no longer by a Board of experts, but by a brilliant and erratic amateur.[31]

Whenever the Royal Navy suffered a reverse, the *Morning Post* returned to the charge that Churchill was superseding the authority of the admirals. Constitutionally speaking, Churchill was entitled to do this under Orders in Council obtained by Gladstone in 1869 and 1872, but he was nevertheless infringing the custom and practice of the Admiralty.[32] And as Geoffrey Best observes of the Antwerp affair, 'something unbalanced does seem to have happened'.[33] After two days in the city Churchill become so enthralled by the exercise of command that he fired off a telegram offering to resign his Cabinet post in return for a high-ranking command in the field. When Asquith read out the telegram to his colleagues there was a roar of laughter and Churchill was ordered home.[34]

The laughter illuminated in a flash the gulf between Churchill and most of his fellow politicians. Although they were ultimately responsible for the conduct of the war, they knew little of military matters and generally deferred to the judgement of the men in

73

command. But inside Churchill was a generalissimo struggling to get out. The admirals and the generals, inevitably, were alarmed. 'It is a tragedy that the Navy should be in such lunatic hands at this time', wrote Admiral Richmond in his diary on 4 October. 'The man must have been mad to have thought he could relieve [Antwerp] . . . by putting 8000 half-trained troops into it', wrote Vice-Admiral David Beatty, the Commander of the Battle Cruiser Squadron, to his wife.[35] Churchill, however, seemed quite oblivious of the storm gathering around him. On his return from Antwerp he implored Asquith 'in a ceaseless cataract of invective and appeal' to relieve him of the Admiralty and entrust him with a command in the field. 'His mouth waters at the sight and thought of K's [Kitchener's] new armies', reported Asquith to Venetia Stanley. 'Are these "glittering commands" to be entrusted to "dug-out trash", bred on the obsolete tactics of 25 years ago—"mediocrities who have led a sheltered life mouldering in military routine" &c &c'. More generous than most in his opinion of Churchill, Asquith called him as 'a wonderful creature with a curious dash of schoolboy simplicity (quite unlike Edward Grey's) and what someone said of genius:—"a zigzag streak of lightning in the brain".'[36] But Antwerp was the moment at which Churchill first became associated with disastrous military adventures. 'Winston', Lloyd George declared, 'is becoming a great danger . . . Winston is like a torpedo. The first you hear of his doings is when you hear the swish of the torpedo dashing through the water.'[37] The leader of the Conservative Party, Bonar Law, wrote to a correspondent: 'I agree with the estimate you have formed of Churchill. I think he has very unusual intellectual ability, but at the same time he seems to have an entirely unbalanced mind which is a real danger at a time like this.'[38]

In January 1915 Lieutenant Colonel Ernest Swinton presented the War Office with an ingenious plan for a 'machine gun destroyer', an armour-plated vehicle with ten men inside, mounted on caterpillars and armed with machine guns. With its crew shielded from enemy fire, the machine would advance at a speed of four miles an hour to capture the German trenches. Both Churchill and Hankey, the Secretary to the War Council, were much taken with the idea and persuaded the War Office to give it a trial. When the protoype machine fell into a trench and could not get out the War Office abandoned the experiment, but Churchill meanwhile was pursuing an alternative plan, submitted to him by Major Hetherington of the Royal Naval Air Service, for a 1,000-ton armoured vehicle to transport infantrymen. In February 1915 Churchill appointed an Admiralty Landships Committee, under the Director of Naval Construction, Tennyson d'Eyncourt, to explore the idea. The following month he took the constitution-ally dubious step of authorizing the expenditure of £70,000 on a project which could not possibly be regarded as Admiralty business—the construction of eighteen prototypes.[39] Churchill later claimed that the tank, which made its debut on the Somme on 15 September 1916, was the direct descendant of the Admiralty's 'landship'. But the prototype landship was an armoured infantry carrier intended to transport fifty men across no man's land. Except for the fact that it also advanced very slowly, at two miles per hour, the first tank was a very different type of weapon which evolved out of the failure of the landship and the introduction of new War Office specifications. Churchill was far-sighted in the support he gave both to the landship and the tank, but he was not alone in this: Haig, the Commander-in-Chief, took note of Churchill's ideas and pressed strongly for the development and large-scale production of the tank.[40]

When anti-German prejudice compelled the first Sea Lord, Prince Louis of Battenberg, to resign in October 1914, Churchill decided to recall from retirement an old sea dog whose buccaneering spirit matched his own: 'Jacky' Fisher. 'Those who knew them both', wrote Edgar Williams, 'realized that the arrangement involving such domineering characters, each used to having his own way, fond as they were of each other, would not work . . .'[41] At first both Churchill and Fisher were excited by the possibility of a naval operation to capture the island of Borkum in the Baltic. But the entry of Turkey into the war in alliance with Germany and Austria-Hungary in November 1914 had meanwhile opened up an alternative theatre of operations in the Balkans and the eastern Mediterranean. When the Russian government appealed urgently for action to relieve Turkish pressure in the Caucasus, Kitchener, the Secretary for War, urged Churchill to undertake a naval demonstration at the Dardanelles, the narrow stretch of water, forty-one miles long and four miles across at its widest point, which gave access by sea to the Turkish capital of Constantinople. The Dardanelles were guarded on both sides by forts and guns mounted on the Gallipoli peninsula to the west and the coast of Asia Minor to the east.

Churchill replied that a naval attack alone would be insufficient: a combined operation would probably be more effective. If he had stuck to this position he might have become the hero of 1915, but Kitchener declared that he could not spare any troops, and again pressed the First Lord to mount a naval demonstration. Churchill now despatched a telegram to Admiral Carden, the commander of the Mediterranean squadron, seeking his opinion on whether it would be possible to force the Dardanelles with the aid of a number of obsolete battleships that were surplus to requirements in home waters. Carden replied that he thought the Dardanelles might be forced by extended operations with a large number of ships. Churchill became captivated by the vision of a fleet sailing through the Dardanelles, bombarding and destroying the Turkish forts and gun batteries on both sides of the Straits, and provoking by their appearance in front of Constantinople a revolution and the withdrawal of Turkey from the war. The supply lines to and from Russia through the Straits would be opened up, and the Balkan states rallied to the cause of the allies: at a stroke the military balance would be transformed.

Such was the vision. The outcome was a disaster. Both Kitchener and Churchill wavered between the concept of an operation carried out by ships alone, with troops landing subsequently as an occupation force, and a combined naval and military operation. A naval attack was finally launched on 18 March under the command of Admiral de Robeck. Whether it could ever have succeeded against the dual threat of minefields and gunfire from the Turkish forts remains a subject for debate. After the loss of three battleships de Robeck halted the attack and in spite of Churchill's pleas and injunctions refused to renew it. The War Council now came down definitely in favour of a combined operation and the purely Churchillian phase of the action was over. After many delays and hesitations, a combined British, Australian, and New Zealand expeditionary force under the command of Churchill's friend Sir Ian Hamilton landed on the tip of the Gallipoli peninsula on 25 April. Within a few days it was clear that the troops were pinned down on a narrow stretch of beach with the Turks shelling them from the commanding heights above. The War Council authorized further reinforcements, but there was no disguising the fact that the news was bad. Sensing a fiasco in the making, the *Morning Post* argued that the attack by ships alone ought never to have been attempted, and singled out Churchill for blame: 'We assert that the first lord of the admiralty acted against the opinion of the experts. We assert further that he led the cabinet to believe that he had behind him the opinion of Lord Fisher . . . The truth is that Winston Churchill is a danger to the country.'[42]

Fortune now deserted Churchill. From the start, Fisher had blown hot and cold about the Dardanelles. Increasingly overwrought and unstable, and fearful of losses, he suddenly cracked when Churchill, without consulting him, added two submarines from home waters to a list of reinforcements for the Mediterranean. On 15 May Fisher offered his resignation and fled into hiding. The news put a knife in the hands of Churchill's enemies. Churchill, a civilian amateur strategist who had never risen above the rank of junior officer in the Army, had overridden the judgement of the most famous Admiral in the Royal Navy on a strictly naval issue. Ironically, as a handful of insiders knew, it was Fisher whose judgment was unbalanced. In a state bordering on megalomania, he tried to compel Asquith to appoint him naval dictator, with absolute power over the disposition of all ships, the naval construction programme, and the appointment of all officers of all ranks. The press, however, was strongly biased in favour of Fisher. In his post-war memoirs Churchill complained in a scathing passage of the idolization of military leaders at the expense of the politicians:

The foolish doctrine was preached to the public through innumerable agencies that Generals and Admirals must be right on war matters, and civilians of all kinds must be wrong. These erroneous conceptions were inculculated billion-fold by the newspapers under the crudest forms.[43]

Churchill's actions were thought to be all the more heinous because it was the third time he had committed the offence in the space of just over twelve months. As that politically minded soldier Sir Henry Wilson wrote to Bonar Law: 'A man who can plot the Ulster Pogrom, plan Antwerp and carry out the Dardanelles fiasco is worth watching.'[44]

Churchill might have weathered the storm but for the fact that Asquith, beset by a crisis over munitions, chose this moment to invite the Conservatives into a Coalition. Fearful of his military ventures, seething with resentment over Ulster, and eager to punish a renegade, the Conservatives insisted on his removal from the Admiralty and the War Council. Asquith appointed him Chancellor of the Duchy of Lancaster, a post that was largely honorific, together with a place on the new Dardanelles Committee.

'Both afloat and ashore', wrote the historian Arthur Marder, 'the Navy received the news of Churchill's retirement from Whitehall with a feeling of relief.'[45] The political world in general viewed Gallipoli as conclusive proof of Churchill's egotism, his warmongering mentality, and the dangerous amateurism of his pretensions as a strategist. 'It is the Nemesis', Lloyd George told his mistress, Frances Stevenson, 'of the man who has fought for this war for years. When the war came he saw in it the chance of glory for himself, & has accordingly entered on a risky campaign without caring a straw for the misery and hardship it would bring to thousands . . .'[46] Lloyd George, it must be added, was not only a friend and admirer of Churchill but a jealous rival. The suggestion that in preparing for war Churchill had somehow contrived to precipitate the conflict was mischievous. The allegation that he was indifferent to the suffering involved took no account of his belief (however misplaced) that Gallipoli would dramatically shorten the war.

The Gallipoli affair dragged on through the summer and autumn. Though casualties mounted and there was little sign of progress, Churchill continued to champion the operation with unquenchable enthusiasm. By October the majority of the Dardanelles Committee had come to the conclusion that the operation should be abandoned and when at last the Cabinet decided in favour of withdrawal Churchill was left with no alternative but to resign from the government. One of the few redeeming features of the Gallipoli affair was the brilliant evacuation with which it was brought to a close in January 1916. By that time, however, some 46,000 allied troops, including 8,700 Australians and 2,700 New Zealanders, had been killed.

Churchill never ceased to believe that Gallipoli was a brilliant conception which could have struck the enemy a mortal blow but for the incompetence with which it was carried out. Military historians have generally been more sceptical. An attack by ships alone was unlikely to force the Straits. A properly planned amphibious attack might have led on to the capture of Constantinople, but what then? 'The balance of probability', writes one authority,

is that even if Turkey had been knocked out of the war in 1915, it would have contributed little to defeating Germany, at least in the short term. The seizure of Constantinople *might* have led to a pro-allied Balkan confederacy, which *might* have opened up a viable new front against the Central Powers. But politics, geography and logistics would have made it immensely difficult to press home the advantage accrued from a victory on the periphery of the Central Powers by a direct advance into Austria-Hungary.[47]

It was certainly unfair that Churchill should be the scapegoat. It was Kitchener who first pressed for a naval operation and Asquith who authorized it. Fisher concealed his early doubts and subsequently expressed great enthusiasm. Nor did Churchill's responsibility extend much beyond the naval attack on 18 March.

The land campaign which began on 25 April was primarily the responsibility of the War Office. Nevertheless Churchill's own egotism and impetuosity were factors in his downfall. He was overconfident of success, trumpeting victory in advance and passionately supporting the operation long after most people had written it off. Gallipoli was a cross to which he nailed himself.

As Martin Gilbert has argued, one of Churchill's greatest mistakes on the road to Gallipoli was his failure to listen to the advice of his wife:

She alone of those closest to him told him of his faults . . . she stressed the danger to his career of the impatience and scorn which he often showed towards those who disagreed with him. She rebuked his tendency to take provocative or unexpected measures without regard to the likely reaction of others. She stressed how much he harmed himself by acting upon ideas which he had not given others time to accept, or which he failed adequately to explain.

Churchill's greatest weakness, Gilbert concludes, was his desire always to be at the centre of affairs, and to be known to be at the centre.[48] Churchill, however, was incapable of reforming himself, and hindsight enables us to see that his overpowering egotism was the source of his greatest achievements as well as his biggest failures.

· FOUR ·

The Winstonburg Line,
1915–1924

Churchill was devastated by his fall from grace in May 1915. 'Like a sea-beast fished up from the depths', he wrote, 'or a diver too suddenly hoisted, my veins threatened to burst from the fall in pressure.'[1] Nothing could wholly fill the void, but his family did their best. Clemmie was a loyal supporter in times of trouble, as was Churchill's brother Jack, currently serving at Gallipoli, and his sister-in-law Gwendeline ('Goonie'). When the Winston Churchills had to leave Admiralty House, they went to live with Goonie and her two children, John and Peregrine, at 41 Cromwell Road. At the weekends the two families would gather at a weekend retreat: Hoe Farm, near Godalming.

Here Churchill discovered a powerful antidote to depression. He took up oil-painting and was shown by Hazel Lavery, the wife of Sir John Lavery, how to daub the canvas with bold strokes and bright colours. Soon he was haunting Lavery's studio and painting alongside him. Churchill never claimed to be a professional artist, let alone a great one, but in the course of a lifetime he greatly enjoyed himself painting hundreds of pictures. Whenever he went on holiday he took his easel and paints with him, and even managed to complete one canvas during the Second World War—a view of Marrakesh, which he presented to President Roosevelt. In the aftermath of Gallipoli, however, even the brightest colours could not efface the blot of Gallipoli, and contrary to the idea that he was indifferent to the loss of life, he was haunted by a sense of guilt. One day in August 1915 his old friend W. S. Blunt arrived at Hoe Farm to find Churchill painting a portrait of Clemmie's sister, Nellie Hozier. Churchill said: ' "There is more blood than paint upon these hands . . . All those thousands of men killed. We thought it would be a little job, and so it might have been if it had been begun in the right way . . ." '[2]

After his resignation in November 1915 Churchill sought emotional relief in active service and obtained from Sir John French a promise of the command of a Brigade. In the interim he joined the second battalion of the Grenadier Guards at Laventie for training. To Churchill's dismay, Asquith then vetoed his promotion to Brigadier-General and ordered that he be given the command of a battalion instead. On 4 January 1916 Lieutenant-Colonel Winston Churchill was placed in command of the 6th battalion of the Royal Scots Fusiliers. He arranged for his friend 'Archie' Sinclair, a Highland laird and aspiring Liberal politician, to join him as second-in-command. Towards the end of January the battalion moved up to the front line, near the Belgian village of Ploegsteert, close to the Franco-Belgian frontier.

Churchill's arrival, and his unorthodox methods of command, caused much astonishment, and some resentment at first among the junior officers. But he proved a good commanding officer, combining leadership and inspiration with a great solicitude for the welfare of the rank-and-file, who were mainly industrial workers from the west of Scotland. He organized concerts and sporting activities, and mitigated punishments for disciplinary offences, in a microcosm of his Home Office prison reforms. When the battalion moved into the trenches he divided his time between his HQ, about 500 yards away, and his dugout, from which he made regular night-time forays into no man's land. The sector of the front on which he was served was relatively quiet but Churchill and his HQ were frequently under fire and there were several occasions on which he narrowly escaped death.[3]

Much as Churchill enjoyed soldiering, his military ambitions were thwarted by his modest rank, and he feared that a prolonged absence from Westminster would deny him the chance to restore his fortunes. In March 1916 he returned home on leave to speak in the House but destroyed the effect of an otherwise powerful attack upon Balfour's conduct of the Admiralty with an ill-judged appeal for the return of Fisher as First Sea Lord. In May 1916 the amalgamation of his battalion with another led to the extinction of his command and gave him a presentable excuse for resigning his commission and coming home. Churchill had spent only a hundred days at the front, but the experience had served to confirm his critical estimate of the British high command. To replenish his income, while keeping his name in the public eye, he began to write war commentaries for the press. He also made a number of speeches, critical of the conduct of the war, in the House of Commons. Eagerly awaiting the downfall of Asquith, he planned to ally himself with a victorious combination of Lloyd George, Bonar Law, Curzon, and Carson. They, however, were not planning to ally with him.

In the political crisis of December 1916 Asquith was replaced by Lloyd George, but the Conservatives under Bonar Law insisted that Churchill should be excluded from the new govern-ment. As Lloyd George explained in his war memoirs, they claimed to be acting from patriotic motives:

They admitted he was a man of dazzling talents, that he possessed a forceful and a fascinating personality. They recognised his courage and that he
was an indefatigible worker. But they asked why, in spite of that, although
he had more admirers, he had fewer followers than any prominent public
man in Britain? Churchill had never attracted, he had certainly never
retained, the affection of any section, province or town. His changes of
party were not entirely responsible for this. Some of the greatest figures in
British political life had ended in a different Party from that in which they
commenced their political career . . .

Here was their explanation. His mind was a powerful machine, but there
lay hidden in its material or its make-up some obscure defect which prevented it from always running true. When the mechanism went wrong,
its very power made the action disastrous, not only to himself but to the
causes in which he was engaged and the men with whom he was co-
operating. That was why the latter were nervous in his partnership. He
had in their opinion revealed some tragic flaw in the metal. They thought of
him not as a contribution to the common stock of activities and ideas in the
hour of danger, but as a further danger to be guarded against.

Although Lloyd George took a more generous view of Churchill's
abilities, he emphasized that he would only be useful as the
member of a War Cabinet in which 'his more erratic impulses
could have been kept under control . . . Men of his ardent temperament and powerful mentality need exceptionally strong
brakes.'[4]

Churchill fought back. His main achievement during the
period in which he was out of office was the partial rehabilitation
of his reputation. His first biographer, MacCallum Scott, rewrote
his life to include the Admiralty years and a detailed defence of
Antwerp and Gallipoli. Briefed by Churchill himself, MacCallum
Scott was at pains to deny the charge that the First Lord had overridden the advice of the admirals. His conclusion is a reminder
that even in Churchill's darkest hours there were always a
handful of Churchillians prepared to declare their faith in him:

Those who believe that Churchill's public career is ended have not learned the lessons of history, and have no understanding of human nature, of the power of genius, and of the craving of the mass of the people for leadership. The men of destiny do not wait to be sent for; they come when they feel their time has come. They do not ask to be recognised, they declare themselves; they come like fate; they are inevitable.[5]

One of his few Conservative allies, J. L. Garvin, the editor of *The Observer*, wrote: 'He is young. He has lion-hearted courage. No number of enemies can fight down his ability and force. His hour of triumph will come.'[6] Another admirer was the anonymous author of an editorial in the *Washington Post* who declared roundly: 'Half a dozen Winston Churchills in the British cabinet prior to the European war would have saved England from the folly for which she is now paying a frightful toll.'[7]

In June 1916 Asquith agreed to the appointment of a Commission to enquire into the responsibility for the Gallipoli. Though handicapped by Asquith's refusal to allow him access to the official records, Churchill devoted much of his time to preparing a very eloquent and plausible defence. The first report of the Dardanelles Commission, published in March 1917, made it clear that Churchill was not solely or even principally responsible, and paved the way for his restoration to office. It could not prevent his enemies from repeating the old charges or interrupting his meetings with the cry: 'What about the Dardanelles?'

After the Battle of the Somme Churchill had come to the conclusion that great offensives on the western front were far more costly to the allies than to the enemy, and ought to be avoided until new methods of attack were devised or overwhelming numerical superiority achieved. In a secret session of the House of Commons on 10 May 1917 he argued the case in a powerful speech. Here was one of the perennial sources of his survival in British politics. No one else could match his ability, on a good day, to sway the House of Commons by the force of his argument. Difficult though he might be as a ministerial colleague, he could be more dangerous on the outside. Fearing that Churchill might emerge as the new leader of the Opposition, Lloyd George took him aside and promised to restore him to office. When rumours of his return began to circulate, leading Conservatives protested furiously. The Chairman of the Conservative Party, George Younger, wrote to Lloyd George warning him that the party might revolt against Churchill's appointment:

His unfortunate record, the utter futility of his criticisms of your War Policy in the last Secret Session, and his grave responsibility for two of the greatest disasters in the War have accentuated the distrust of him which has prevailed both in the House and outside of it for a long time past, and I feel certain that his inclusion in the Government would prove disastrous to its fortunes.

After some hesitation Lloyd George took the plunge and appointed Churchill as Minister of Munitions. Since his new post was outside the War Cabinet, this appeared to meet Bonar Law's demand for the exclusion of Churchill from all part in the conduct of the war. Nevertheless 100 Conservative MPs signed a motion deploring his appointment and the Conservative press frothed with rage. 'Lloyd George's throne tottered', as Beaverbrook wrote. 'But it did not fall.'[8]

Accompanied by his bust of Napoleon, Churchill moved into the Ministry's quarters in the former premises of the Metropole Hotel in Northumberland Avenue. Created by Lloyd George in 1915, it was already in full swing with a staff of 12,000 officials, two and a half million workers employed in its factories, and the output of guns and shells running at record levels. Churchill's brief was to ensure a continuous and increasing flow of production.

He began by reorganizing the Ministry itself, compressing fifty separate divisions into ten, and creating a Munitions Council which met daily to coordinate and determine policy. The next priority was the reduction of industrial unrest. Production was threatened by strikes and Churchill took action to redress some of the most prominent grievances. He abolished the 'leaving certificate' which prevented workers in the munitions trades from moving from one employer to another. More controversially he authorized a 12 per cent bonus for skilled workers on time rates, unwittingly setting off a train of inflationary wage demands as unskilled workers struggled to catch up. Churchill, however, was ready to employ the stick as well as the carrot. In the summer of 1918 he put an end to a strike of engineers in Coventry by threatening to conscript them into the Army.

Although Churchill was excluded from the War Cabinet, he displayed all the dynamism of a war leader. He seized the opportunity of renewing his campaign for the production of tanks and gave a powerful impetus to the development of mustard gas, which had first been introduced by the German Army in September 1917.[9] Determined to investigate for himself the needs of the armies on the western front, he made frequent visits to France for consultations with his French opposite number, Louis Loucheur, and the British Commander-in-Chief, Sir Douglas Haig. In spite of Churchill's past criticisms of the high command, he managed to convince Haig that he was doing everything in his power to assist him. In May 1918 Haig reciprocated by placing a French country house, the Chateau Verchocq, at Churchill's disposal on his visits to France. 'I managed to be present', Churchill wrote, 'at almost every important battle during the rest of the war.'[10] Churchill also struck up a firm friendship with Haig's aide-de-camp, Major Desmond Morton, in later years his most important contact in the world of secret intelligence.

In the autumn of 1917 Churchill attempted to recruit a well-known opponent of the war to the Ministry of Munitions. He had been captivated by *Counter-attack*, a recently published volume of poems in which Siegried Sassoon depicted the horrors experienced by soldiers in the trenches and the folly of the generals who sent them into battle. Churchill's appreciation of the poems was a measure of his disenchantment with allied strategy, but unlike Sassoon he was not in the least disillusioned with war itself. Sassoon describes how Churchill tried to argue him out of his anti-war position:

Pacing the room, with a big cigar in the corner of his mouth, he gave me an emphatic vindication of militarism as an instrument of policy and stimulator of glorious individual achievements, not only in the mechanism of warfare but in the spheres of social progress. The present war, he argued, had brought about inventive discoveries which would ameliorate the condition of mankind. For example, there had been immense improvements in sanitation.[11]

Having disagreed with everything Churchill said, Sassoon declined the offer of a job at the Ministry.

However much Churchill deplored the bloodbaths on the western front, they made no fundamental difference to the social Darwinian views of war which he had acquired as a subaltern in the 1890s. They were indeed to endure into the Second World War, according to a memorandum in the FBI's file on Churchill. In an off-the-record discussion with American newspapermen in 1943, a source who had been 'intimately associated' with Churchill reported that someone had asked him how it was that

God could make such a beautiful sunrise and then permit so much misery in the world?

Churchill made a lengthy statement that there was no peace on earth save in death; that all life is war, a struggle for survival; that the best in men comes out in time of war; that in times of war the real improvements are achieved, and that under the stress of war tremendous progress is made for the good of living. Churchill stated that when war ends, men settle down to taking things easy, to complacency, and only war will compel more progress.[12]

To many people war was never more than a tragic necessity. To Churchill it was never less than a school of virtue.

As Minister of Munitions Churchill continued to differ from Haig over strategy. He argued that the British and French armies allies should remain on the defensive until 1919, by which date the build-up of American forces, together with an overwhelming superiority in tanks, aircraft, gas, and machine guns, would ensure an allied victory. Lloyd George rejected this advice, but during the crisis of March 1918, when the German offensive in the west threatened to break through the allied lines, he turned to Churchill, despatching him on an urgent mission to Paris to coordinate action with the French premier, Georges Clemenceau.

Churchill's own links with France dated back to the days when Mrs Everest had wheeled him up and down the 'Shams Elizzie'. At school he had acquired a fluent but ungrammatical command of French with the vowels pronounced in an emphatically English accent. But his love affair with France seems to have begun in 1907 when he first set eyes on the French Army at its annual manoeuvres: 'When I saw the great masses of the French infantry storming the position, while the bands played the "Marseillaise", I felt that by those valiant bayonets the rights of man had been gained and that by them the rights and liberties of Europe would be faithfully guarded.'[13] Both Clemenceau and his great rival, Marshal Foch, made an abiding impression on Churchill. They represented for him, he explained, the dual nature of France: Clemenceau its anti-clerical, revolutionary, and republican past, Foch its more ancient, aristocratic heritage of Joan of Arc and the Palace of Versailles.

The Great War came to an end sooner than expected. On 8 August 1918 the British Fourth Army under Rawlinson broke through the German front line near Amiens in an offensive in which the infantry attack was reinforced by seventy-two tanks. So began the victorious advance of the allied armies which led to the outbreak of revolution in Germany, the abdication of the Kaiser, and the armistice of 11 November 1918. As one of the originators of the tank, and the head of the Ministry which built and supplied the tanks for Haig's army, Churchill could claim to have played a part in the breakthrough and the victories that followed. He had also established—contrary to the notion that he was usually at odds with the 'brasshats'—an amicable working relationship with Haig.

As the war drew to a close Churchill's thoughts turned towards the political future at home. Since the replacement of Asquith by Lloyd George in 1916 the Liberal party had split. The Lloyd George Liberals, of whom Churchill was one, had collaborated with Bonar Law and the Conservatives in a Coalition government which had 'won the war'. Both parties to the Coalition were in favour of extending it into the peace, and agreed to fight the next general election on a common platform. The Asquith Liberals, meanwhile, retained their independence, but it had yet to be seen whether there was room for a party occupying the space between the Coalition on the Right and the Labour party on the Left. The Labour Party had made great advances during the war, evolving from a parliamentary pressure group into a potential governing party. So too had the industrial wing of the labour movement, the trade unions, whose rank and file were increasingly militant. All this led Churchill to predict in the autumn of 1918 that politics would polarize between a bourgeois party of Tories and Radicals, 'democratic and progressive but based on the existing social order', and a Labour party fighting for a new social order.[14] There was no doubt which side Churchill would be on, but he campaigned in Dundee on a platform of social and constitutional reform little changed from the Edwardian era. He declared himself in favour of the taxation of war profits, the forty-hour week, the nationalization of the railways and electricity, and a scheme of federal devolution for Scotland, Ireland, Wales, and four English regions.[15]

In the general election of December 1918 the Lloyd George Coalition won a stupendous victory with 478 out of the 707 seats in the House of Commons. It was an exceptional moment in electoral history when Lloyd George's unrivalled prestige as the 'man who won the war', combined with anti-German hysteria (which Churchill avoided) and pledges of social reform, joined to give the Coalition an overwhelming but temporary ascendancy. Churchill, who was returned with a massive majority in Dundee, now hoped to return to the Admiralty, but Lloyd George insisted that he accept the twin posts of Secretary for War and Air. He was immediately faced with a crisis over demobilization. There was much resentment in the ranks against existing arrangements because they took no account of the length of time a man had served. So great was the anger that a mutiny broke out at Calais and riots broke out at home. Acting with great speed and decision, Churchill introduced a new scheme, based on the principle of 'first in, first out', which defused the discontent.

From the War Office Churchill looked out on a world transformed by the Great War. Everywhere the social and imperial
order in which he had grown up was under threat or disinte-
grating. The Liberal party was deeply divided and the Labour
Party advancing to replace it as the main alternative to the Conservatives. Industrial unrest at home increasingly took the form
of 'direct action' intended to coerce the government into the
acceptance of workers' demands. In Ireland the Home Rule
party had been swept away by Sinn Fein, which proclaimed an
independent republic and embarked on a campaign of civil disobedience. In India the Congress movement, led by Mahatma
Gandhi, launched in 1920 a campaign of civil disobedience in
support of *swaraj*—self-government. The Bolshevik revolution
in Russia cast menacing shadows over Europe and Germany was
on the brink of chaos. The whole world, Churchill remarked at a
Cabinet meeting, was in the melting pot.[16]

His reaction was one of pugnacious resistance to radical or
revolutionary change. This resulted in frequent clashes between
Churchill and Lloyd George, who still retained something of his
pre-war radicalism. 'Don't you make any mistake', Churchill told
him. 'You're not going to get your new world. The old world is a
good enough place for me, & there's life in the old dog yet. It's
going to sit up and wag its tail.'[17] Churchill was haunted by the
spectre of the Bolshevik Revolution. Soviet communism, he concluded, was the worst tyranny in history and Lenin and Trotsky
more dangerous enemies than the Kaiser's Germany. He loathing
of communism found expression in the nightmare imagery
with which he depicted 'the foul baboonery of Bolshevism' as
'a plague bacillus', a 'cancer', and a 'horrible form of mental
and moral disease'.[18] His greatest fear was that Bolshevism would
conquer both Russia and Germany, thus creating a hostile and

aggressive bloc stretching from Europe to the Pacific. He therefore urged the victors to adopt a policy of magnanimity and
friendship towards Germany: 'Kill the Bolshie, Kiss the Hun', as
he put it to Asquith's daughter Violet.[19]

The Bolshevik revolution of 1917 resulted in a civil war
between the Bolsheviks, who made peace with Germany, and the
white armies of Kolchak and Denikin. In 1918 the allied powers
sent troops and supplies to aid the white armies with the aim of
bringing Russia back into the war, but the defeat of Germany
removed the main purpose of allied intervention. When the War
Cabinet decided to withdraw from Russia the 14,000 British
troops which remained there at the end of the war, Churchill
promised to carry out the government's policy. But at a meeting of
the Supreme Allied War Council in Paris, in February 1919,
he argued passionately in favour of a concerted allied attempt to
send additional troops to support the white armies. Although he
managed to persuade the War Cabinet (which remained in being
until September 1919) to furnish extra money and supplies, Lloyd
George and his colleagues rejected his pleas for continued military intervention. Having agreed to implement the War Cabinet's
policy, Churchill withdrew British troops in the summer of 1919,
but he remained optimistic about the prospects for overthrowing
the Bolshevik regime. His candidate for the leadership of the new
Russia was General Denikin, the leader of the white Russians
in the south. In October 1919, with Bolshevik Russia encircled
on all fronts by white Russian forces, Churchill proclaimed that
Bolshevism was about to collapse. He was looking forward to
going to Moscow to advise Denikin on the drawing up of a new
constitution. Within a few months, however, Denikin's army was
in full retreat and Churchill's hopes were shattered. When Lloyd
George came out in favour of opening trade negotiations with

the Bolsheviks, he was furious, and hovered on the brink of resignation when the Anglo-Soviet trade treaty was approved by the Cabinet in November 1920.

Churchill's perceptions of the brutal and repressive nature of Soviet communism have been vindicated by the passage of time. Military intervention along the lines he proposed might have spared Russia many horrors, though a white Russian Empire maintained by military force would probably have been brutal in its own fashion. But after the bloodbath of the Great War no British government could have mobilized the manpower or the money that intervention required. Churchill's policy, which his rhetoric inflated to the point where it began to sound alarmingly like the prelude to another great war, damaged him not only in the eyes of radicals and socialists, but also in the minds of ministers and officials who thought him unbalanced.

Churchill was also concerned about developments at home. The intelligence services supplied him with intercepts of messages from Moscow authorizing Soviet agents in Britain to distribute Russian gold to organizations like the British Communist Party, and left-wing Labour groups, that were campaigning against the war. Churchill in turn denounced Bolshevik subversion and threw in for good measure the charge that the Labour party was a prey to the manipulation of extremists. It was, he announced in January 1920, 'quite unfitted for the responsibility of government'.[20]

Preoccupied by the 'red peril', Churchill did not appreciate until the beginning of 1920 that Ireland was sliding into chaos. The Chief of the Imperial General Staff, Sir Henry Wilson, pressed for the introduction of martial law. Churchill, like the rest of the Cabinet, was against this, but strongly supported Lloyd George's policy of recruiting two paramilitary forces, the 'Black and Tans' and the 'Auxis', who carried out unofficial reprisals against the IRA and also murdered some innocent civilians. When Lloyd George appointed him chairman of a Cabinet committee on Ireland, in June 1920, Churchill was full of rash ideas for intensifying the conflict, including raising a force of 30,000 Ulstermen to maintain British authority throughout Ireland. But as he also explained to the Cabinet, his aim was to achieve a position of strength from which constitutional concessions could be granted.

By May 1921, as Colonial Secretary, he was urging the Cabinet to enter into negotiations on the grounds that British forces now had the upper hand. Two months later Lloyd George called a truce and Churchill was drawn once more into the Prime Minister's confidence. During the negotiations which led to the Anglo-Irish treaty of 6 December 1921 Churchill was a member of the British delegation and determined to drive a hard bargain. He was chiefly responsible for the military clauses of the treaty, which reserved for Britain three naval bases: the 'treaty ports' as they were later called. His opposite number in the military negotiations was Michael Collins, the leader of the IRA, with whom he established a good working relationship. With the granting of Dominion status to the Irish Free State, Churchill as Colonial Secretary became responsible for Anglo-Irish relations during an extremely tense period in which there was violence along the border between North and South, and the South itself was descending into civil war. Collins feared that in signing the Treaty he was signing his own death warrant, and so it proved. But shortly before his assassination in August he sent Churchill a message to thank him for all the support he had given to the precarious government of the Irish Free State during the first few troubled months of its existence: 'Tell Winston that we could never have done anything without him.'[21] Churchill felt a sense of paternity towards the Irish Free State and was greatly affronted when De Valera came to power in 1932 and began to abrogate the constitutional terms of the Treaty. He was even more incensed when Neville Chamberlain returned the 'treaty ports' to Ireland in 1938.

Churchill's reputation as a militarist was often at odds with his record in cutting defence expenditure. In the aftermath of the Great War the pressures to reduce public spending were overwhelming. In August 1919 the Cabinet adopted, without dissent from Churchill, the 'Ten-Year Rule', whereby military expenditure was to be based on the assumption that there was to be no major war for the next ten years. Churchill himself chafed at the expense involved in the British occupation of the former Ottoman territories of Palestine and Mesopotamia (Iraq), regions which, he told the House of Commons in the summer of 1921, were 'unduly stocked with peppery, pugnacious, proud politicians and theologians, who happen at the same time to be extremely hard up'.[22] He recommended that the League of Nations mandate for Palestine be given to the United States: it was Lloyd George who insisted that it should go to Britain.

Churchill's drive for a settlement of the Middle East led him to urge that both Palestine and Iraq should be run by a new Middle East Department of the Colonial Office with the power to coordinate a settlement of Britain's relations with the Arabs. In February 1921 Lloyd George took the logical step of appointing Churchill himself as Colonial Secretary (until April 1921 he also retained the Air portfolio), and the new Middle East Department was established, with a staff which included T. E. Lawrence.

The situation Churchill inherited in the Middle East was highly confused and explosive. In order to encourage an Arab revolt against Ottoman rule, the British government in 1915 had promised Sherif Hussein of Mecca that it would support the creation of an independent state uniting most of the Arab territories under Turkish rule. The assurances he was given seemed plain enough to Hussein, but 'were so ambiguously expressed and subject to such provisos and reservations as would, on subsequent detailed examination, relieve most consciences in Britain'.[23] When the Arab revolt broke out in 1916 Lawrence, together with Hussein's son the Emir Feisal, conducted a guerilla war in the desert from which his later fame as 'Lawrence of Arabia' was to spring. But that same year Britain's promise to the Arabs was compromised by the secret Sykes-Picot agreement whereby the French and the British reserved for themselves post-war spheres of influence in Syria and Mesopotamia respectively. It was further undermined by the Balfour Declaration of November 1917 which declared that the British government 'view with favour the establishment in Palestine of a national home for the Jewish people, and will use their best endeavours to facilitate the achievement of this object, it being clearly understood that nothing shall be done which may prejudice the civil and religious rights of the existing non-Jewish communities in Palestine or the rights and political status enjoyed by Jews in any other country'. The San Remo conference of April 1920 duly awarded France the mandate to govern Syria and Britain the mandate to govern Palestine, with the terms of the Balfour Declaration enshrined in the mandate, and Mesopotamia. The Emir Feisal's brief reign as King of an independent Syria was terminated when the French drove him out. In Mesopotamia the British stamped out a full-scale rebellion in the summer and autumn of 1920, while Palestine was the scene of Arab riots in protest against the Balfour Declaration and the beginnings of Jewish immigration.

With the aid of his advisers in the Middle East Department Churchill briefed himself thoroughly on the issues and summoned in March 1921 a conference in Cairo attended by authorities on the region including the British High Commissioner, Sir Percy Cox, his political secretary, Gertrude Bell, and Lawrence. 'We covered more work in a fortnight than has ever been got through in a year', wrote Gertrude Bell. 'Mr Churchill was admirable, most ready to meet everyone half way and masterly alike in guiding a big meeting and in conducting the small political committees into which we broke up.'[24] It was decided that Mesopotamia should be transformed into the kingdom of Iraq with the Emir Feisal as the first monarch.

Churchill had been personally sympathetic to Zionism ever since his contacts with Manchester Jews before the First World War. But whereas the prominence of Jews in the Bolshevik movement intensified the anti-Semitism of the more paranoid elements on the Right, Churchill believed that Zionism would serve as an antidote to Bolshevism by offering the persecuted Jews of Russia and eastern Europe a homeland and a 'national idea' of their own. 'If, as may well happen', he wrote in February 1920, 'there should be created in our own lifetime by the banks of the Jordan a Jewish State under the protection of the British Crown, which might comprise three or four millions of Jews, an event will have occurred in the history of the world which would, from every point of view, be beneficial and would be especially in harmony with the truest interests of the British Empire.'[25]

At the time Churchill wrote these words, the Jews in Palestine numbered about 80,000, the Palestinian Arabs about 600,000. But he was then Secretary for War. Once he was in charge of the Colonial Office, he was compelled to recognize the importance of retaining Arab goodwill and the necessity of performing a delicate balancing act between Zionists and Arab nationalists. Much to the disappointment of the Zionist leader Chaim Weizmann, who had pressed Churchill to extend the boundaries of the 'Jewish national home' to include territory to the east of the river Jordan, he ruled that the whole of 'eastern Palestine' should become a second Arab kingdom of Transjordan under Feisal's brother, the Emir Abdullah. It would therefore be closed to Jewish immigration. On a visit to Palestine after the Cairo conference Churchill offered further reassurance to a delegation of Palestinian Arabs: 'The establishment of a national home does not mean a Jewish government to dominate the Arabs. The British Government is the greatest Moslem State in the world, it is well disposed to the Arabs and cherishes their friendship.'[26] Lloyd George and Balfour privately assured Weizmann that they had always understood the Balfour Declaration to mean an eventual Jewish state; Churchill, who was present, spoke up in defence of the more limited pledges of the White Paper.[27]

In retrospect he put a very different construction on his intentions in the evidence he gave to the Peel Commission on Palestine in 1937. Here Churchill was speaking off the record in extremely frank terms unsuitable for public consumption. The Palestinian Arabs, he said, were a conquered people who had fought against the British in the Ottoman armies, and the British had the right to impose on them the policy of the Balfour Declaration. Asked to define his conception of 'the Jewish National Home' he replied:

The conception undoubtedly was that, if the absorptive capacity over a number of years and the breeding over a number of years, gave an increasing Jewish population, that population should not in any way be restricted from reaching a majority position ... As to what arrangement would be made to safeguard the rights of the new minority, that obviously remains open, but certainly we committed ourselves to the idea that some day, somehow, far off in the future, subject to justice and economic convenience, there might well be a great Jewish State there, numbered by millions, far exceeding the present inhabitants of the country and to cut them off from that would be wrong.[28]

It seems that as a Colonial Secretary confronted by a tense situation in Palestine, Churchill felt obliged to give assurances to the Arabs that were incompatible in the long run with his personal preference for a strong Zionist policy.

The Cairo conference also had a military dimension. In his determination to cut the defence budget, Churchill grasped eagerly at a proposal by Trenchard, the founder of the RAF, who argued that Mesopotamia could be controlled more effectively, and far more cheaply, by a handful of RAF squadrons. There was more at stake here than the fate of Iraq. Trenchard was struggling to ensure the continuing independence of the RAF in the face of opposition from the War Office and the Admiralty, who were seeking to split up and divide the air force between them. At the Cairo Conference Churchill ensured the acceptance of Trenchard's proposals for 'air control' in Mesopotamia. In May 1921 Churchill obtained the agreement of the Cabinet, and in spite of much resistance from the War Office air power was gradually substituted for ground forces.

It was uncertain at the time whether Churchill's decisions would survive a change of government, but in the event the consequences were long-lasting. By drastically cutting the cost of the British military presence, Churchill made it possible for the British to remain in Mesopotamia as imperial guardians of a highly artificial state that might not have held together without them. He also ensured the continuing independence of the RAF and the widespread use of air power between the wars to 'police' or 'control' rebellious movements within the Empire. The bombing of armed rebels, however, could easily degenerate into the use of terror against a civilian population. In his days as a cavalry subaltern Churchill had reacted strongly against brutalities for which there was no military necessity, and quite apart from his more chivalrous sentiments he was ever mindful of the damage that could be done to ministers by revelations in the House of Commons. In July 1921 he drew Trenchard's attention to a horrific episode in Mesopotamia in which aircraft had fired on women and children taking refuge in a lake. 'I am surprised', he wrote, 'that you do not order the officers responsible for it, to be tried by court martial. If such a thing became public it would ruin the air project which you have in view. By doing such things we put ourselves on the lowest level.'[29] Though Churchill rejected such methods, he nevertheless recommended the use of gas against 'uncivilised tribes' in Mesopotamia. 'Gases can be used', he wrote, 'which cause great inconvenience and would leave a lively terror and yet would leave no serious permanent affect on most of those affected.' As Colonial Secretary he continued to support the use of chemical warfare by the RAF, maintaining that it was a humane and scientific expedient for saving life.[30] At the time of the Iraq war of 2003 the allegation spread like wildfire that Churchill had anticipated Saddam Hussein's use of poison gas against the Kurds.[31] But the gas employed by the Iraqi dictator was a deadly weapon with which 5,000 Kurds were massacred at Halabja in 1988. The gas to which Churchill was referring was tear gas, a means of crowd control available to most police forces in our own day.

Churchill's Middle East settlement, like his handling of the crisis over demobilization in 1919, was a demonstration of one of his greatest skills: his ability to cut through an administrative tangle by assembling the people involved and obtaining a set of clear-cut decisions. But although he could point to fresh achievements, Lloyd George kept him firmly under control. Churchill was furious when the Prime Minister ignored his claims to the Treasury in April 1921 and appointed Robert Horne as Chancellor in succession to Austen Chamberlain. But Lloyd George was under no pressure to promote Churchill and could probably have sacked him with impunity.

Confiding his views to a colleague in October 1921, the CIGS, Sir Henry Wilson, described Antwerp, the Dardanelles, and the 12.5 per cent bonus for munitions workers as 'experiments which cost this country hundreds of millions, thousands of lives, and the loss not only of territory but of prestige ... I admire Winston in many ways but in truth he is too expensive for any purpose that I can see that he can serve.'[32] Wilson spoke for many who appreciated Churchill's abilities but questioned his motives and judgement. As one commentator put it in 1920:

Unhappily for himself, and perhaps for the nation, since he has many of the qualities of real greatness, Mr Churchill lacks the unifying spirit of *character* which alone can master the discrepant or even antagonistic elements in a single mind, giving them not merely force, which is something, but direction, which is much more. He is a man of truly brilliant gifts, but you cannot depend upon him. His love for danger runs away with his discretion; his passion for adventure makes him forget the importance of the goal.[33]

Perceptions of Churchill as unstable and unreliable may have had something to do with the knowledge that he was not wholly English. His colleague Edwin Montagu described him in 1921 as 'English, American, Red Indian'. A few years later Lloyd George remarked: 'Winston undoubtedly had nigger blood in him. Look at his build and slouch. The Marlboroughs were a poor type physically, but Winston was strong. Another characteristic of Winston is that when he gets excited he shrieks: again the nigger comes out.'[34]

A glimpse of the kind of tittle-tattle about Churchill circulating in Tory circles is provided by the historian Charles Carrington, who in 1922 had just graduated from Oxford and taken up a teaching post at Haileybury. There he was befriended by H. L. Elford Adams, a temporary master at the school and a relation of the Percies, the family of the dukes of Northumberland. One evening they were talking politics and got on to the subject of Churchill. '"Why, of course you know the truth about him", said Adams, "everyone in Society knows this. He killed Earl Percy in a duel about a woman! They went over to Boulogne, fought with pistols, and Percy was severely wounded. He died in hospital in Paris."'[35] Churchill had certainly known Percy, a contemporary and a junior minister in the Balfour government who had died in December 1909. But the story was pure fiction.

For the Labour Party, which was rapidly emerging as the main opposition to the government, Churchill was a *bête noire*. The voice of the Labour Left at this time was the *Daily Herald*, edited by the pacifist George Lansbury, with Siegfried Sassoon as literary editor. Setting out the case against Churchill in May 1919, the *Herald* accused him of militarism at home and abroad. Tonypandy and 'Black Friday' were cited in evidence alongside Antwerp and Gallipoli. In a few years, the paper prophesied, it would be necessary to decide the future of the social order. 'With Churchill in command at the War Office we shall approach the decision a conscript and militarised nation, we shall have within our own borders repression and violent revolt, we shall be despatching all over the world the armies of imperialist aggression.'[36]

Among those who wrote for the *Herald* was Osbert Sitwell, a youthful poet and aesthete who had served in the Grenadier Guards but loathed war as the ultimate expression of philistinism. Outraged by Churchill's anti-Bolshevik campaign, he contributed verses satirizing the views of 'a certain statesman':

> As I said in a great speech
> After the last great war
> I begin to fear
> That the nation's heroic mood
> Is over
> Only three years ago
> I was allowed to waste
> A million lives in Gallipoli
> But now
> They object
> To my gambling
> With a few thousand men
> In Russia![37]

As Sitwell recalled, three of his verses were published as a pamphlet entitled *The Winstonburg Line* by 'an elderly Scottish Socialist in a brown tweed suit, with a flaming red tie, spectacles, and a Trotsykite beard'. They sold in large numbers at 'hands-off-Russia' meetings. Both Sassoon and Sitwell lived to see the Second World War, by which time they were both famous men of letters. But where Sassoon supported the war and gave three cheers for Churchill, Sitwell was anti-war and irreconcilably opposed, as his biographer puts it, to 'the bloodstained demagogue whose natural habitat was war'.[38]

Of all the the criticism directed against Churchill from the Left, the most enduring was the work of the cartoonist David Low, a New Zealander who had arrived in Britain in 1919. In his early cartoons, published in *The Star*, Churchill often featured as a warmonger. But instead of depicting Churchill as menacing or sinister, Low recognized his comic potential. Churchill could be pompous, and Low with his exact observation of body language and facial expression could exaggerate the pomposity just sufficiently to create a ludicrous impression. He also captured the element of mischief that often appeared in Churchill's face: the twinkle in the eye, and the sly grin of the schoolboy about to let off a stink bomb. Low disapproved strongly of Churchill's politics but the accuracy and humour with which he portrayed him trembled on the brink of affection. In a cartoon of 1922 entitled 'The Winstonoceros and Prey', Churchill appears as a rhinoceros gripping in his mouth a socialist bogey on a stick. 'This interesting pachyderm', reads Low's caption, 'has the appearance of being armourplated, but is sensitive to tickling at the joints of the harness. Reports of its savage nature are probably exaggerated but it has been known to destroy imaginary enemies with great fury.'[39] Low was satirizing Churchill, but up to a point Churchill was disarming Low.

Low frequently portrayed the Coalition as a double-headed ass. It was essentially an alliance between Lloyd George himself and the Conservative party, a temporary arrangement which left the Coalition Liberals insecure. Both Lloyd George and Churchill sought a way out of the problem by advocating 'fusion'—an amalgamation of the two wings of the Coalition to form a new Centre Party based on resistance to socialism. Churchill campaigned strongly for this during the first half of 1920, at a time when the Conservatives might have accepted the idea, but it foundered on the opposition of many Coalition Liberals. After this, Lloyd George and Churchill could only hope to find some means of prolonging the life of the Coalition.

In 1920, with the enthusiastic support of Lloyd George, but

much against the will of Churchill, the allies had imposed on the Turks the draconian Treaty of Sèvres. In response Turkish nationalists under the leadership of Mustapha Kemal rose up against the Treaty and began to force the Greeks into retreat. Up to this point Churchill had taken a robustly pro-Turkish line. But in August 1922 Turkish forces drove the Greeks into the sea and advanced towards the British garrison at Chanak on the eastern shore of the Dardanelles. For about a fortnight it looked as though the garrison might be attacked or overrun, and the Cabinet decided on 29 September to instruct Sir Charles Harington, the British commander on the spot, to deliver an ultimatum to the Turks. Churchill, by this time, was an excitable member of the war party in the Cabinet: he did not mean to suffer a second humiliation at the Dardanelles. When Harington decided not to deliver the ultimatum the Chanak crisis petered out, but the government's warlike stance was highly unpopular and helped to seal the fate of Lloyd George's tottering regime. At the Carlton Club meeting on 19 October Conservative MPs voted to bring down the Coalition and fight the general election as an independent party.

Churchill, who was recovering from an operation for appendicitis, was too ill to take part in the opening stages of the election. Clementine bravely stood in for him at Dundee but quickly discovered that the mood of the electorate had turned ugly. When a pale and fragile Churchill at last arrived he had to be carried to the platform on a makeshift sedan, and address the audience seated. He was howled down. He and his fellow Liberal candidate were defeated by the Labour candidate, E. D. Morel, and the veteran prohibitionist Edwin Scrymgeour. 'In the twinkling of an eye', Churchill was to write, 'I found myself without an office, without a seat, without a party, and without an appendix.'[40]

Churchill had also been going through a troubled phase in his family life. In April 1921 Clementine's brother, William Hozier, shot himself in a hotel in Paris. The following June Lady Randolph died suddenly after the amputation of a leg. The most shattering blow for Winston and Clementine was the death from septicaemia in August of their youngest daughter, Marigold ('the Duckadilly'), aged 2 years 9 months. At the end of 1921 Clementine collapsed from nervous exhaustion. 'What changes in a year!', Churchill wrote to her, 'What gaps! What a sense of fleeting shadows! But your sweet love and comradeship is a light that burns. The stronger as our brief years pass.'[41] Before long there was cause for rejoicing after all. On 15 September 1922 Clementine gave birth to their fifth and last child, Mary.

After the fall of the Coalition Churchill withdrew to the south of France. Ever since 1918 hecklers had been interrupting him at public meetings with the cry of 'What about Gallipoli?' Determined to confound the critics, he set to work with astonishing speed and energy on a mammoth history of the Great War. The first volume of *The World Crisis*, published in April 1923, was devoted mainly to his pre-war reorganization of the Royal Navy, and the opening months of the war, including Antwerp. In the second, which appeared six months later, he concentrated on Gallipoli and the argument that it was a strategically sound concept flawed by errors and tricks of fate for which he was not responsible. The main theme of the third volume, published in two parts in March 1927, was his measured critique of Haig's strategy on the western front. A fourth volume on the crises of the immediate post-war period, *The Aftermath*, appeared in March 1929, and a fifth, *The Eastern Front*, in November 1931.

Although parts of *The World Crisis* were highly autobiographical, drawing on documents from Churchill's private

papers, the book as a whole was a stupendous narrative of the
war in Europe featuring masterly set-piece accounts of major
battles. Dictated to secretaries as he strode up and down the
room, it exhibited his passionate interest in war and his romantic
conception of the 'true glory' of the troops who perished on the
Somme. Yet Churchill could not write of the bloodbaths on the
western front without sombre reflections on the growing destructive power of modern warfare: 'Mankind has never been in this
position before. Without having improved appreciably in virtue
or enjoying wiser guidance, it has got into its hands for the first
time the tools by which it can unfailingly accomplish its own
extermination.'[42] Churchill's world-view was pessimistic and he
never succumbed to the illusion that the 'war to end wars' had
removed the sources of conflict in Europe. The causes of war,
he wrote in 1924, had not been removed but aggravated by the
peace treaties, and the dominance of France over Germany was
unlikely to endure. Meanwhile military science was remorseless
in the invention of ever more destructive weapons: 'Might not a
bomb no bigger than an orange be found to possess a secret power
to destroy a whole block of buildings—nay to concentrate the
force of a thousand tons of cordite and blast a township at a
stroke?' Poison gas and chemical warfare, he observed, were still
at an early stage of development, and methods of spreading
deadly disease were under investigation in the laboratories of the
great powers.[43]

The critical response to *The World Crisis* was mixed. A number
of authorities on military history banded together to attack its
alleged inaccuracies and, by implication, Churchill's lack of
judgement in military affairs.[44] On the literary Left the critic
Herbert Read seized on a passage from the book as an example
of bogus style. 'Such eloquence is false', he wrote, 'because it is

artificial . . . the images are stale, the metaphors violent, the whole passage exhales a false dramatic atmosphere . . . a volley of rhetorical imperatives'.[45] In his novel *The Shape of Things to Come*, H. G. Wells wrote satirically of *The World Crisis* seen from the perspective of a utopian future in which nation states had been superseded by world government:

There one finds all the stereotyped flourishes and heroisms of nineteenth-century history from the British point of view; the 'drama of history' in rich profusion, centred upon one of the most alert personalities in the conflict. He displays a vigorous naive puerility that still gives his story an atoning charm. He has the insensitiveness of a child of thirteen. His soldiers are toy soldiers and he loves to knock over a whole row of them. He takes himself and all the now forgotten generals and statesmen of the period with a boyish seriousness . . . He not only measures for us the enormous gulf between the mentality of his times and our own, but he enables us to bridge that gulf with an amused and forgiving sympathy.[46]

The writing of *The World Crisis* coincided with the restoration of Churchill's political fortunes. In May 1923 his old opponent Bonar Law was succeeded as Prime Minister and leader of the Conservative party by the more accommodating Stanley Baldwin. Churchill's hopes of reunion with the Conservatives were temporarily blocked when Baldwin declared in favour of protection and called a general election in December 1923. Standing for the last time as a Liberal, at Leicester West, Churchill was defeated by the Labour candidate. When the Liberals decided to support a minority Labour government under the leadership of Ramsay MacDonald Churchill seized the chance of putting himself at the head of the many right-wing Liberals who would have preferred an anti-socialist alliance. He issued a statement declaring: 'The enthronement in office of a Socialist Government will be a serious national misfortune such as usually has befallen great states only on the morrow of defeat in war.'[47] In the Westminster (Abbey) by-election of March 1924 Churchill entered the fray as an 'Independent Anti-Socialist', and almost beat the Conservative candidate. Having served notice that he was still a force to be reckoned with, he was shortly afterwards adopted by the local Conservative association as the 'Constitutionalist' candidate for the safe Conservative seat of Epping.

In the ensuing general election of October 1924 the Conservatives were returned with a substantial overall majority. To Churchill's astonishment Baldwin—whose aim was to detach him from Lloyd George—asked him whether he would accept the Treasury. 'I should have liked to have answered, "Will the bloody duck swim?"', Churchill recalled, 'but as it was a formal and important conversation I replied, "This fulfils my ambition. I still have my father's robe as Chancellor. I shall be proud to serve you in this spendid office." '[48]

· FIVE ·

Respectability Won and Lost,
1924–1939

Churchill's appointment as Chancellor of the Exchequer opened up for him a new and unexpected prospect. He had shaken off the Liberals, the disreputable embrace of Lloyd George, and the turbulent folk of Dundee, and entered a party where the tone was set by suburban middle-class voters of the kind who had now returned him as the MP for Epping. He had left behind the violent aftermath of the Great War for the hush of the Treasury corridors and problems of monetary and fiscal policy. The Treasury was not only the most powerful of Whitehall departments, but the headquarters of all that was most orthodox and proper in the government of Britain. Here was an opportunity for Churchill, entering his fifties and balding rapidly, to make amends for the political wild oats of his youth and settle down to a life of worthy endeavour in Baldwin's England. The road to respectability lay before him.

Would he take it? 'There are', warned Ian Colvin of the *Morning Post*,

a good many Conservatives—including some of the staunchest and the least self-seeking—who are disappointed and almost estranged by this

112

appointment. They allege that Mr Churchill has made at least one capital blunder in every one of the offices he has held; that—what is worse—he has never shown any sign of political principle; and that his only consistency has been in the pursuit of his own political fortunes. They argue that the leopard does not change his spots nor the Ethiopian his skin . . .'[1]

Churchill, however, delighted the Conservative Party, the Treasury, and the Bank of England with his first major decision, the most respectable he had ever taken. In the budget of April 1925 he announced the restoration of the gold standard at the pre-war parity of $4.86 to the £.

Warned of the dangers by Beaverbrook and Keynes, Churchill had approached the decision with great caution. In January 1925 he invited his Treasury officials, and the Governor of the Bank of England, Montagu Norman, to reply to an 'Exercise' in which he set out possible objections to an early return to gold. It was essential, Churchill explained, that they should be prepared to answer any criticisms which might be made of their policies— though he may also have been trying to gauge the strength of the case. He certainly experienced doubts. Impressed by an article which Keynes had published in *The Nation*, he fired off a letter to his Controller of Finance, Otto Niemeyer, which, in the words of Keynes's biographer, 'contains perhaps the most savage indictment of the Treasury and the Bank ever penned by a Chancellor of the Exchequer'. The Treasury, Churchill wrote, had never faced the profound significance of what Keynes termed 'the paradox of unemployment amidst dearth'. The Governor of the Bank 'shows himself perfectly happy in the spectacle of a Britain possessing the finest credit in the world simultaneously with a million and a quarter unemployed . . . The seas of history are full of famous wrecks. Still if I could see a way I would far rather follow it than any other. I would rather see Finance less proud and Industry more content.'[2]

Churchill's Treasury advisers tried to convince him that a return to gold would reduce unemployment. Torn between rival opinions, Churchill arranged a dinner party at which two protagonists of the return to gold, Niemeyer and Bradbury, argued the case against two of its critics, Keynes and McKenna. Keynes and McKenna argued that it would involve substantial deflation and unemployment, but when Churchill asked McKenna what decision he would make as a politician he replied: 'There is no escape. You will have to go back; but it will be hell.'[3] Keynes had lost the argument, but he soon returned to the fray in a pamphlet entitled *The Economic Consequences of Mr Churchill*. Keynes argued that a return to gold at the pre-war parity involved an overvaluation of sterling as a result of which export industries would attempt to reduce their costs by cutting wages. The consequences would be particularly severe for the miners. His judgement was vindicated when the coal owners attempted to force through wage cuts and a national coal strike threatened. In order to avert it Churchill agreed at the end of June 1925 to a subsidy of miners' wages for a nine-month period during which proposals for a settlement could be worked out.

Although the title of Keynes's pamphlet suggested that Churchill was to blame for the situation, he argued that the Chancellor had been 'gravely misled' by his advisers—the Treasury officials and the Governor of the Bank. 'Keynes never blamed Winston Churchill personally for the return to gold', writes Robert Skidelsky. 'Nor did Churchill take Keynes's attack personally.' On the contrary, Keynes was elected in 1927 to the Other Club.[4] Churchill in later years came to think of the return to gold as a great mistake, but the person he blamed more than anyone else was the Governor of the Bank of England, Montagu Norman.

In financial policy Churchill was in principle a Gladstonian committed to free trade, strict economy in public expenditure, and balanced budgets. In practice he was a little more flexible, employing ingenious forms of accountancy that enabled him to present a deficit as a surplus. But Churchill was broadly orthodox in both outlook and policy. He was engaged in a battle to restore the Edwardian political economy, or what remained of it after the heavy burden of war debts and interest payments incurred between 1914 and 1918. Free Trade, the cause for which he had stood for so long, remained the central pillar of Churchillian economics. But it was under siege now from socialists on the Left and protectionists on the Right.

On free trade he demonstrated some flexibility, accepting the relatively minor instalments of protectionism that had already been introduced, but rejecting the demands of tariff reformers like L. S. Amery for protective duties on iron and steel. There were no concessions to socialism. On the contrary, one of his first initiatives as Chancellor was an extension of the system of national insurance which he and Lloyd George had pioneered before 1914—an alternative to the socialist policy of redistributing wealth through taxation. Neville Chamberlain, the Minister of Health, had prepared a scheme of contributory old age and widows' pensions. He was surprised and a little suspicious when an enthusiastic Churchill approached him with a proposal to finance the measure and announce it in his first budget.

Churchill's aim was a budget that balanced (or appeared to balance) the interests of the middle and the working classes. In his budget of April 1925 he cut the income tax, which at that time was paid mainly by the middle classes, by sixpence (2.5 pence) in the pound. But he coupled this with the extension of national insurance, which covered manual workers only, to protect working-class widows and orphans. Churchill's own way of life, based on extravagant habits of expenditure that invariably plunged him into the red, had nothing in common with bourgeois prudence. But as a politician he displayed an astute concern for the interests of the middle-class taxpayer and a consequent determination to curb public spending. Fortunately for Churchill, this was a period when international tensions were low and he could argue for strict limits in expenditure on the armed forces. He outraged the Admiralty by compelling reductions in its cruiser programme, and refused to finance the construction of a naval base at Singapore. For what, he asked in a letter to Baldwin (15 December 1924) were the Admiralty preparing? 'A war with Japan! But why should there be a war with Japan? I do not believe there is the slightest chance of it in our lifetime.'[5] In Europe, meanwhile, this was the era of Locarno, a relatively tranquil interlude. Even Churchill judged that the prospects of war were remote. In June 1928 the Cabinet accepted Churchill's proposal that the Ten Year Rule should be placed on a permanent basis, advancing day by day until such time as a decision was taken to revise it.

In September 1922 Churchill had paid £5,000 for a new home: Chartwell Manor, near Westerham in Kent. A dilapidated house on a hilltop overlooking the Weald of Kent, it came with eighty acres of land including a valley and a lake. Captivated by the view, Churchill bought the house in defiance of Clementine, who disliked Chartwell but subsequently worked hard to make the best of it. After hiring the architect Philip Tilden, Churchill began to pour a fortune into the renovation, redesign, and extension of Chartwell. By the spring of 1924 it was ready for occupation.

Chartwell was Churchill's first permanent home. Here he could enjoy family life and the company of his friends in a more spacious and hospitable setting, but the house was also his political headquarters. Among his more frequent visitors were F. E. Lindemann ('the Prof'), Professor of Experimental Philosophy (Physics) at Oxford, and Brendan Bracken, a youthful Irish adventurer, mistakenly rumoured to be Churchill's illegitimate son, who gatecrashed high society and turned himself by the age of 30 into a press magnate. The 'Prof' would arrive at Chartwell in a chauffeur-driven Rolls Royce, Bracken at the wheel of his yellow Hispano-Suiza. Both were romantic reactionaries who rejoiced in Churchill's swashbuckling politics, and both tended to reinforce perceptions of Churchill as a buccaneer at odds with the respectable classes. In Churchill himself, Chartwell brought out a hitherto unsuspected love of the land. He experimented with the raising of pigs, chickens, and other livestock, investing large sums with very little return. He took up bricklaying and was recruited by a local branch official as a member of the Amalgamated Union of Building Trade Workers, but the Union's executive, failing to share the joke, ruled that he was ineligible for membership.

Churchill's expansionism was confined to Chartwell. On the national scene his hopes of boosting trade and employment were thwarted. Like previous Chancellors, he tried hard to unravel the tangle of war debts and reparations left over from the Great War, but found the United States unwilling to cancel the debts incurred by Britain and France. He also complained about the strict monetary policies of the Bank of England under its Governor, Montagu Norman. Even more alarming was the prospect of the harm that might be done to the economy through industrial strife. The nine months' subsidy on miners' wages, to

117

which Churchill had agreed in June 1925, expired at the end of April 1926 with no settlement of the dispute in sight. When the General Council of the TUC threatened to call a general strike in support of the miners, Churchill was determined that the strike would be broken.

So were Baldwin and his colleagues. On the evening of 2 May 1926, the Cabinet were unanimous in breaking off negotiations with the General Council of the TUC. Baldwin, however, was fearful that Churchill would break loose and commit some outrage against the strikers. With a view to diverting him he gave Churchill an ill-defined role in charge of the production of an emergency government newspaper, the *British Gazette*. When other press proprietors hesitated to cooperate, the editor of the *Morning Post*, H. A. Gwynne, offered to put the newspaper's plant at the governnment's disposal.

As we have already seen, the *Morning Post* had long been the headquarters of the paranoid Conservative Right and as such extremely hostile to Churchill over Irish Home Rule, Antwerp, and Gallipoli. It was a remarkable sign of the times that Churchill and Gwynne were now on the same side and applauding one another's patriotism. In spite of this Gwynne found Churchill's attempts to run the paper extremely tiresome. The *Gazette* was established with a clear chain of command in which Sir Malcolm Fraser was in charge of production and distribution, and David Caird, with the assistance of Gwynne, of the editorial content. Both were responsible, through Baldwin's aide J. C. C. Davidson, to the Cabinet. Churchill, who was meant to exercise a general oversight, disrupted the process by descending on the office and trying to organize the staff himself. 'So long as he does not come to the *Morning Post* offices tonight', wrote Davidson to Baldwin, 'the staff will be able to do what it is there to do, viz. organise the printing, the production and distribution of the *Gazette*. I must depend on you, and the staff are relying on me, to find some means of preventing his coming.'[6] Gwynne was also alarmed because Churchill was engaged in a struggle with Davidson for the control of editorial policy. Davidson, who insisted on the right to censor Churchill's contributions, could rely if necessary on the support of Baldwin and the Cabinet, but as he wrote in his memoirs, 'a good deal of Winston's pugnacious spirit penetrated the *Gazette* and brought storms of questions in the House of Commons'.[7]

Churchill was also a turbulent presence, with his friend and ally Birkenhead, on the Supply and Transport Committee. 'Birkenhead', Davidson recalled, 'was absolutely mad, and so was Winston, who had it firmly in mind that anyone who was out of work was a Bolshevik; he was most extraordinary, and never have I listened to such poppycock and rot.' They were restrained by the chairman of the committee, the Home Secretary Joynson-Hicks. There was a striking divergence of opinion when Churchill demanded that a convoy of food from the London docks should be accompanied by a big display of military force. He was overruled and the convoy was cheered through the streets.[8] Churchill was also eager to commandeer the British Broadcasting Company (not yet a nationalized corporation), a proposal resisted by its managing director, John Reith, with Baldwin's support. Reith and Churchill met for the first time, the beginning of a lifelong mutual antipathy between two mighty egotists re-enacting the quarrels of roundheads and cavaliers. 'He was really very stupid', Reith confided to his diary.[9]

After nine days the General Strike petered out, but the dispute in the coal industry lingered on, with very little attempt by Baldwin to resolve it. Churchill had always distinguished clearly between the General Strike, which he regarded as a challenge to the constitution, and the coal dispute, which he regarded as purely industrial. In the autumn, while Baldwin was away on holiday, Churchill intervened and tried to put pressure on the coal owners to settle, but was thwarted by powerful interests in the Conservative party.

The General Strike confirmed yet again the notion of Churchill as a trigger-happy extremist. Among those who jumped to the conclusion that the strike was Churchill's fault was the Canadian Prime Minister, Mackenzie King. On the first day of the strike he wrote in his diary:

Baldwin did splendidly till the last moment, he has been influenced by Winston Churchill against his better judgment . . . Churchill may be shot, anything may happen & a revolution greater than anything England has ever known brought on . . . I feel sorry for Baldwin, for the King, & many others—for Churchill I feel a scorn too great for words. He has been the evil genius in this.[10]

Within a fortnight of the end of the strike, the *New Statesman* published an article claiming that Churchill had led the 'war party' which had precipitated the strike by breaking off negotiations with the TUC on 2 May. 'Mr Churchill was the villain of the piece', the paper reported. 'He is reported to have remarked that he thought "a little blood-letting" would be all to the good.'[11] This version of the origins of the strike passed at once into labour tradition and lasted for decades. In a history of the Labour party published in 1948 G. D. H. Cole wrote: 'A considerable section of the Cabinet, headed by Churchill, was intent on a show-down . . . The next day, May 2, this section of the Cabinet got its way and procured the breaking off of negotiations by the Government.'[12] On this particular point, Labour tradition was mistaken. But it was true that Churchill had been bellicose and excitable during the strike, lacking Baldwin's faith in the essential moderation of the British working class. Among those who spread the tale was his most persistent gadfly, H. G. Wells. In his novel *Meanwhile* (1927), one of the characters describes the General Strike in a letter to a friend:

As might be expected Winston has gone clean off his head. He hasn't been so happy since he crawled on his belly and helped snipe in Sidney Street. Whatever anyone else may think, Winston believes that he is fighting a tremendous revolution and holding it down, fist and jaw. He careers around staring, inactive, gaping, crowded London, looking for barricades.[13]

In the eyes of Labour, Churchill compounded the offence by his prominent support for the Trade Disputes and Trade Union Act of 1927, which made general strikes illegal, prohibited civil servants from joining trade unions affiliated to the Labour Party, and reduced the political funds available to trade unions by compelling union members to 'contract in' to the fund instead of 'contracting out'.

The antipathy of Labour did Churchill little harm in the Conservative Party. The second of his biographers, Carl Bechhofer Roberts, who wrote under the pen name 'Ephesian', could point in 1927 to a remarkable new twist in the Churchillian plot:

Thus it is that the seemingly impossible has happened; the deep breach between Churchill and the Conservative Party has been healed. Today the Conservatives have no more favourite spokesman; and no one seems conscious of any incongruity. Even when opponents rake up his old speeches against him, their missiles pass over his head. The past is expunged.[14]

Churchill was also orthodox in his view of employment policy. He set his face firmly against the radical programme of public works advocated by Lloyd George and the Liberals as the solution to unemployment. Nevertheless he brought to the annual budget a showmanship reminiscent of the 'Welsh Wizard'. In 1927 he was captivated by the idea of 'derating'—the abolition of local authority rates on industry—which he hoped would act as a powerful stimulus to trade and industry. But his proposals led to prolonged battles with Chamberlain. The final scheme, announced by Churchill in the budget of 1928, was a compromise. Industry and the railways were to be freed of 75 per cent of local authority rates, and agriculture of 100 per cent, but a new tax of 4 pence in the pound on petrol was introduced as partial compensation for the loss of revenue. Derating proved to be a damp squib and was subsequently abandoned by the second Labour government.

Churchill was on the brink of respectability as a Conservative, but whether he would be acceptable as a future leader had yet to be seen. His roots in the party were shallow and the protectionists were frustrated by his continued adherence to free trade. The more obvious candidate for the succession was Neville Chamberlain, the Minister of Health. Chamberlain's reputation has never entirely recovered from the policies of appeasement which he pursued with such vigour in the late 1930s. But in the 1920s he was the most vigorous and substantial of Tory ministers in home affairs. He arrived at the Ministry of Health in 1924 with a list of twenty-five measures he wished to put on the statute book. By the time he left the ministry in 1929, twenty-one had become law.[15]

Like so many of the politicians and officials who had worked with Churchill in the past, Chamberlain recognized his exceptional qualities but was alarmed by the rapid intuitive processes of his mind and his imaginative leaps from the possible to the impossible. Writing to his friend Lord Irwin, the Viceroy of India (who was later to become Lord Halifax), he set out an analysis of Churchill's strengths and weaknesses:

One doesn't often come across a real man of genius or, perhaps, appreciate him when one does. Winston is such a man and he has *les défauts de ses qualités*. To listen to him on the platform or in the House is sheer delight . . . I have often watched him in Cabinet begin with a casual comment on what has been said, then as an image or simile comes into his mind proceed with great animation, when presently you see his whole face suffused with pink, his speech becomes more and more rapid and impetuous until in a few minutes he will not hear of the possibility of opposition to an idea which only occurred to him a few minutes ago. In the consideration of affairs his decisions are never founded on exact knowledge, nor even on careful or prolonged consideration of the pros and cons. He seeks instinctively for the large and preferably the novel idea such as is capable of representation by the broadest brush. Whether the idea is practicable or impracticable, good or bad, provided he can see himself recommending it plausibly and successfully to an enthusiastic audience, it commends itself to him . . . He is a brilliant wayward child who compels admiration but who wears out his guardians with the constant strain he puts on them.[16]

Almost everyone in the ministerial ranks of the Conservative Party between the wars would have agreed with this verdict, and the conclusion was plain: Churchill could be an asset to a government provided he was strictly under control, but he was not a team player.

Unlike most Cabinet ministers, Churchill was seldom content to mind his departmental business. To the alarm of the Foreign Office he continued to keep a close watch on the international scene. He was still viscerally anti-Bolshevik and rejoiced when diplomatic relations with the Soviet Union were broken off after the Arcos raid. On Britain's relations with Europe, he was isolationist. When the Foreign Secretary, Austen Chamberlain, proposed an Anglo-French alliance, Churchill came out strongly against the idea. According to Sir Eyre Crowe, he was all for letting France 'stew in her own juice'.[17]

If Churchill's love affair with France was in abeyance, so too were his hopes of a worldwide partnership between Britain and the United States, the 'two great branches' (in Churchillian parlance) of 'the English-speaking peoples'. Churchill's concept of the 'English-speaking peoples' dated back to the late Victorian era when politicians and publicists on both sides of the Atlantic began to argue that as the British and American peoples were kith and kin, they should combine together in a civilizing mission to dominate the twentieth-century world. On the British side, the appeal of the idea was also grounded in calculations of great power politics. 'If one were to put it in the most brutal fashion possible', Max Beloff has written,

one would have to say that ever since the 1890s the dominant element in the British 'establishment' has known in its heart that the world order dependent on British sea-power ... could no longer be sustained by British power alone. It was therefore the intended lot of the United States, perhaps its moral duty, to take over an increasing share of this burden and to use its new strength to further Britain's original purposes.[18]

The fact that Churchill had an American mother was certainly a part of the story. In May 1898, while still a subaltern in India, he wrote to her: 'As a representative of both countries the idea of an Anglo-American rapprochement is very pleasant. One of the principles of my politics will always be to promote the good understanding between the English-speaking communities.'[19] Possibly his tuition in naval affairs at the hands of Admiral Fisher, a strong supporter of Anglo-American friendship, also had its effect. At any rate Churchill's first public declaration of faith in an Anglo-American future appears to date from December 1911 in the introduction to a pamphlet on Irish Home Rule:

It must always be a guiding star of British statesmanship, not only to federate the Empire, but to draw nearer in bonds of friendship and associ- ation to the United States ... The road to the unity of the English-speaking races is no doubt a long one, and we cannot see the end of it. But it is an open road, and an Irish Parliament, loyal to the Crown, and free to make the best of the Emerald Isle, is assuredly the first milestone upon it.[20]

The entry of the United States into the war in April 1917 prompted Churchill to reaffirm his almost mystical faith in Anglo-American unity. On 4 July 1918 he spoke of a shared constitutional heritage in which the origins of the Declaration of Independence could be traced back to Magna Carta and the Bill of Rights. The cost of the war, he declared, had been 'far more terrible than our most sombre expectations', but the British people were about to obtain a 'priceless and utterly unhoped for' reward:

Deep in the hearts of the people of these islands . . . lay the desire to be truly reconciled before all men and all history with their kindred across the Atlantic Ocean, to blot out the reproaches and redeem the blunders of a bygone age, to dwell once more in spirit with them, to stand once more in a battle at their side, to create once more a union of hearts, to write once more a history in common. That was our heart's desire. It seemed utterly unobtainable, but it has come to pass . . . One feels in the presence of a Great Design of which we can only see a small portion, but which is developing and unfolding swiftly, and of which we are the necessary instruments. No event since the beginning of the Christian era is likely to strengthen and restore man's faith in the moral governance of the universe.[21]

No sooner was Germany defeated than Churchill discovered a new and even more deadly enemy of Anglo-American values: Bolshevik Russia. But contrary to Churchill's hopes Britain and the United States began to drift apart as the United States withdrew into isolationism. He seems genuinely to have hoped that the Irish Treaty would remove an important obstacle to Anglo-American understanding, a point he emphasized in recommending it to the House. As Chancellor of the Exchequer, however, he soon found himself at odds with the United States over the question of war debts.

At the end of the First World War, Britain owed the United States some four thousand million dollars; but Britain in turn was owed seven thousand million dollars by its European allies. The Lloyd George government had proposed in 1922 an all-round cancellation of war debts, but the United States insisted on the repayment in full of Britain's debt, thus compelling Britain to exact payments from its allies and continued reparations from Germany. American policy, Churchill was later to write, was 'a recognisable factor in the economic collapse which was presently to overwhelm the world, to prevent its recovery and inflame its hatreds'.[22]

The deeper source of Churchill's alienation was the American policy of naval expansion after 1918. The former First Lord of the Admiralty was determined to maintain Britain's naval supremacy. As a member of the Lloyd George government, he had accepted the Washington Naval Treaty of 1922, whereby Britain accepted parity with the United States in capital ships. But Churchill maintained that owing to its predominance in auxiliary warships, notably cruisers, Britain retained its naval predominance and must continue to do so. The issue came to a head in the summer of 1927 when the Coolidge administration submitted a proposal for parity between Britain and the United States in all classes of ship to the disarmament conference in Geneva. The British delegates at Geneva were ready to acquiesce, but Churchill submitted a paper to the Cabinet expressing dissent. 'There can really be no parity', he wrote, 'between a power whose navy is its life and a power whose navy is only for prestige . . . It always seems to be assumed that it is our duty to humour the United States and minister to their vanity.

They do nothing for us in return but exact their last pound of flesh.'[23]

With the aid of his friend Birkenhead, Churchill orchestrated a Cabinet revolt against concessions to the United States. In a memorandum on 20 July he adopted an even more anti-American tone:

We do not wish to put ourselves in the power of the United States. We cannot tell what they might do if at some future date they were in a position to give us orders about our policy, say, in India, or Egypt, or Canada, or on any other great matter behind which their electioneering forces were marshalled. Moreover, tonnage parity means that Britain can be starved into obedience to any American decree. I would neither trust America to command, nor England to submit. Evidently on the basis of American naval superiority speciously disguised as parity immense dangers overhang the future of the world.[24]

Churchill's tactics succeeded in wrecking the Geneva conference, provoking the resignation from the Cabinet of Lord Robert Cecil. Nor was this an isolated outburst. In September 1928 a Conservative politician recorded Churchill's thoughts on the United States: 'He thinks they are arrogant, fundamentally hostile to us, and that they wish to dominate world politics.'[25] In a Cabinet memorandum two months later, Churchill recalled the various attempts Britain had made to conciliate the United States since 1918 and concluded: 'Whatever may have been done at enormous cost and sacrifice to keep up friendship is apparently swept away by the smallest little tiff or misunderstanding, and you have to start again and placate the Americans by another batch of substantial or even vital concessions.'[26]

In the general election of May 1929 the Baldwin government lost its overall majority and was succeeded by a second minority Labour government, dependent for office on the support of the Liberals. For a time Churchill sought to construct a parliamentary alliance between the Liberals and the Conservatives, but the proposal was vetoed by the Protectionists in the Shadow Cabinet. Leaving behind him the frustrations of Westminster, Churchill set sail across the Atlantic with his 19-year-old son Randolph, his brother Jack, and Jack's son John, for a sightseeing tour of North America. The party traversed the whole of Canada from Quebec to Vancouver in a luxurious private railway car provided by an American steel tycoon, Charles M. Schwab, with whom the Ministry of Munitions had placed contracts in the First World War. When they visited the oilfields of Calgary, and Randolph spoke slightingly of the oil magnates' lack of culture, his father rebuked him: 'Cultured people are merely the glittering scum which floats upon the deep river of production!'[27]

Crossing the border into the United States, Churchill entered a country where Prohibition was still in force. This was not a state of affairs of which he approved, but he was too diplomatic to say so when he met the American press. He did, however, remark: 'We [in Britain] realize £100,000,000 pounds sterling a year from our liquor taxes—which I understand you give to your bootleggers.' The British, he explained, had a 'deep-rooted prejudice against compulsion'.[28] Prohibition seems never to have been enforced in the vicinity of the Churchills. With liberal supplies of whisky and brandy concealed in Randolph's luggage they travelled down the West Coast from Seattle to California, where they were the guests of the press and movie magnate William Randolph Hearst in his castle at San Simeon. Hearst was a strong critic of Britain and its naval policies, but as fellow adventurers touched by megalomania he and Churchill had much in common and soon struck up a cordial relationship. Hearst entertained him to lunch at the studios of MGM, introduced him to a galaxy of Hollywood stars including Charlie Chaplin, and arranged a lucrative contract for Churchill to contribute regular articles to the Hearst Press. From California the Churchills were then transported by Schwab's private rail car to Chicago, and Baruch's private rail car to New York.

The welcome Churchill received in the United States was not only lavish but warm. Travelling more widely than on his previous visits, he was profoundly impressed by the country's spectacular scenery, its vast natural resources, and the immense productive power of its industry. By the time he reached the end of his American journey, the hostility he had so recently expressed towards the United States had given way to expressions of Anglo-American amity and a desire to put an end to the naval dispute. On 25 October he was the guest of the Iron and Steel Institute at a dinner in New York. 'We don't want all the good people in the world to disarm', he declared, 'while the bad ones remain heavily equipped for war. You are the friends we would like to see most strongly armed. We welcome every growth and development of each arm of the American navy.'[29] Churchill's visit proved to be a turning point in his view of Anglo-American relations. In later years he occasionally expressed a residual suspicion of American intentions, but after 1929 he was consistently pro-American.

Churchill happened to be in New York on 29 October 1929, 'Black Tuesday', when the stock market collapsed. 'Under my very window', he recalled, 'a gentleman cast himself down fifteen storeys and was dashed to pieces, causing a wild commotion and the arrival of the fire brigade.'[30] The sequel to the Wall Street Crash was the Great Slump of 1929–32, in the course of which the volume of world trade fell by two-thirds and the industrial areas of Britain and the United States were blighted by mass unemployment. On the Left it was argued that the capitalist system was doomed or in need of drastic reform, but Churchill was convinced it would recover. Although he lost more than £10,000 in the Wall Street crash, he invested his prodigious literary earnings in British and American stocks and shares, and his prescription for international economic recovery was joint action by Britain and the United States. As he told the House of Commons in November 1932, there was hardly any difficulty in the world that could not be solved by Anglo-American co-operation, though it was not going to happen tomorrow: 'It is not in our power to anticipate our destiny.'[31]

The time was right for Churchill to revive his vision of Anglo-American destiny. In December 1931 he returned to the United States to deliver the message—and earn a small fortune—in a series of lectures entitled 'The Pathway of the English-Speaking Peoples'. His visit began with a disaster when he was hit by a taxi and seriously injured while trying to cross Fifth Avenue. But he recovered sufficiently to resume his tour, lecturing to packed halls in New York, Hartford, Springfield, Chicago, Cleveland, Toledo, Detroit, Rochester, and Washington—striking proof of his celebrity status in the United States. Whether he succeeded in persuading his audiences is another matter. 'Winston Churchill', wrote the *Washington Post*,

is in the United States for the general purpose of trying to hitch the British wagon to the American star . . . Not many years ago political and economic unity with the Yankees would have been repulsive to British statesmen . . . Now the tables are turned and Mr Churchill is trying to flatter the United States into taking over some of Britain's liabilities.[32]

While Churchill addressed American audiences on global themes, his political prospects at home were uncertain. One of the effects of the Slump had been a revival of the protectionist cause in the Conservative Party. In 1930 Baldwin was almost driven from the leadership by Beaverbrook's campaign for 'Empire Free Trade', and it was Joseph Chamberlain's son and heir, Neville, who now appeared to be his most likely successor. Churchill, who had stood consistently for free trade ever since 1903, began to stage a dignified retreat. Invited to give the annual Romanes lecture at Oxford, he spoke in June 1930 on the subject of 'Parliamentary Government and the Economic Problem'. Churchill admitted that the doctrines of classical economics which had prevailed in his youth had been superseded by a widespread belief in state intervention. No longer did anyone believe that wages should be determined 'by the higgling of the market'. Few would agree that private enterprise was 'the sole agency by which fruitful economic undertakings can be launched or conducted'. But the challenge posed by the Slump, Churchill argued, was too complex for the party system, with its partisan interests and vote-catching slogans, to resolve. He proposed the creation of an Economic sub-Parliament, 'debating day after day with fearless detachment from public opinion all the most disputed questions of Finance and Trade'. It would consist of 'persons of high technical and business qualifications', chosen by the political Parliament in proportion to its party groupings. It would possess no powers but its conclusions, Churchill argued, might form the basis of a cross-party consensus in the House of Commons.[33]

Among the audience for the lecture was the historian H. A. L. Fisher, who had been Churchill's Coalition Liberal colleague in the days of the Lloyd George government. 'I imagine', he wrote, 'that he is feeling very uncomfortable as a Free Trader in the Conservative Party, which is now leaning more heavily in the direction of tariffs, and that it would be a great relief to his mind to have the whole economic problem taken out of the political arena and discussed by a body of economic technicians.'[34] There was to be no such relief. The Conservatives pressed on towards protectionism and Churchill was eventually to accept the whole programme, including the food taxes he had denounced in 1903. But whereas in 1903 his ambitions and convictions had marched together, in 1930 his ambitions overrode his convictions. In his heart of hearts he remained a free trader, but he could scarcely abandon the Conservatives for a second time, and the Liberals themselves were split over the issue. As we can also see in retrospect, Churchill's Romanes lecture was more than a farewell to free trade. It was a farewell to the social and economic questions he had tackled with such confidence in the Edwardian era, and with much bafflement as Chancellor of the Exchequer. Unlike Lloyd George, he no longer believed in radical solutions, and piecemeal reforms lacked the drama and excitement he craved. He was sorely in need of a rallying-cry to restore him to the front line of the political battle. He found it in the defence of British rule in India.

On the authority of Ramsay MacDonald's Labour government the Viceroy, Lord Irwin, issued in October 1929 a declaration that the ultimate goal of British rule in India was 'Dominion Status'. To Churchill's dismay Baldwin endorsed the Declaration, and supported a Round Table Conference of British and Indian representatives to discuss constitutional reform. Although Churchill was prepared to accept a measure of self-government at the provincial level he was passionately opposed to the idea of an All-India Federation with an element of self-government at the centre. After months of tension the final break between Churchill and Baldwin came in January 1931, when Gandhi and other Congress politicians were released from gaol to enable them to attend the Round Table Conference. Resigning in protest from the shadow Cabinet, Churchill began a campaign to mobilize the Tory backbenches and the constituency activists against Baldwin. 'It is alarming and also nauseating', he declared on 23 February 1931, 'to see Mr Gandhi, a seditious Middle Temple lawyer, now posing as a fakir of a type well-known in the East, striding half-naked up the steps of the Viceregal Palace, while he is still organising and conducting a campaign of civil disobedience, to parley on equal terms with the representative of the King-Emperor.'[35] The young R. A. Butler, a great admirer of Baldwin, thought that Churchill's speech had touched the hearts of the British public.[36]

In October 1930 Churchill published *My Early Life*, a witty and elegiac account of his youth and a lament for the social and imperial order which had passed away with the Great War. Parliamentary politics, Churchill believed, were now in the hands of lesser men drifting on the fickle currents of a mass electorate. What was needed was strong leadership both at home and in India. As Baldwin wrote in November 1930: 'He wants . . . the Tory party to go back to pre-war and govern with a strong hand. He has become once more the subaltern of Hussars of '96.'[37] When Baldwin and MacDonald joined forces in the National government of August 1931, Churchill's views on India ensured his exclusion from office.

Churchill was now the leader of a group of about sixty Tory MPs opposed to the Baldwin–MacDonald line on India. The Diehards, as one historian has pointed out, were 'a collection of long-serving but largely inarticulate backbenchers, of no ministerial experience and little debating or platform skill'.[38] Although they had the support of a number of Tory peers, they were desperately short of leadership in the House of Commons, and compelled to accept Churchill because no other senior politician was prepared to take on the role. The Diehards, however, represented the type of Tory who had loathed and despised Churchill as a radical demagogue in the Edwardian era. They valued his firepower in debate but did not trust him. As Baldwin's ally and confidant, J. C. C. Davidson, recalled, 'the diehard Tories who opposed us over India never regarded Churchill as a Conservative at all, but as a renegade Liberal who had crossed the Floor. He was regarded as being unstable politically . . . He was a brilliant man, but it was considered that this very brilliance denoted instability of principles and judgment.'[39] Brigadier J. H. Morgan, a barrister who acted as constitutional adviser to the Diehards, later gave this account of their relations with Churchill:

All of them, Salisbury, Wolmer (now Selborne), Lloyd, Danesfort, Gretton, Page Croft, among others, were friends of mine and confided in me pretty freely. *All* of them distrusted Churchill; their attitude to him was summed up by Wolmer when, dining with me at the Reform one night, he said: 'We don't want Winston with us, he has forced himself upon us.' I replied, 'Why not?' Wolmer said: 'He *discredits* us; *we* are acting from conviction but everybody knows Winston has no convictions; he has only joined us for what he can get out of it.'[40]

Opinions of Churchill were perhaps more uniformly dismissive in the 1930s than at any previous time. Stripped of the dignity of office, ageing and restless and full of apocalyptic warnings about the end of Empire, he looked less like a statesman than a ham actor whose melodramatics were out of date. His campaign for rearmament contradicted the pacific outlook of the National Government and the League of Nations idealism of the young men of the Oxford Union, who in February 1933 passed a famous resolution 'that this House will not fight for King and Country'. His views on India were generally regarded as disreputable or worse. In March 1933 a cartoon by Will Dyson in the *Daily Herald* depicted him as a Nazi stormtrooper carrying a pamphlet inscribed 'Thoughts on Gandhi by Adolf Churchill'.[41] The following month Samuel Hoare wrote to the Viceroy of India: 'I believe at the back of his mind he thinks that he will not only smash the Government but that England is going Fascist and that he, or someone like him, will eventually be able to rule India as Mussolini governs north Africa.'[42] 'As for Winston', wrote Neville Chamberlain in March 1935, 'he makes a good many speeches considerably fortified by cocktails and old brandies. Some of them are very good speeches in the old style, but they no longer convince. His following tends to shrink rather than to increase.'[43] His so-called friends were scarcely more charitable. 'He has been everything in every Party', wrote Beaverbrook. 'He has held every view on every question . . . he is utterly unreliable in his mental attitude.'[44] Lloyd George remarked: 'He would make a drum out of the skin of his own mother to sound his own praises.'[45]

Most observers believed that Churchill's aim was to seize the leadership of the Conservative Party from Baldwin. Whether or not this was the case, there is no reason to doubt the strength of his convictions on India. In 1922 he told a conference of ministers:

An idea was prevalent among many people, both in India and at home, that we were fighting a rearguard action in India, and that the British *raj* was doomed, and that India would gradually be handed over to Indians. He was strongly opposed to that view of the situation . . . He believed that opinion would change soon as to the expediency of granting democratic institutions to backward races which had no capacity for self-government.[46]

Between 1924 and 1928 Churchill could rely on his boon companion Lord Birkenhead, the Secretary of State for India, to resist demands for constitutional change. Birkenhead confidently predicted that in the year 2030 India would still remain 'a loyal and integral part of the British Empire'. British rule could be justified by the need to prevent ethnic and religious conflicts, and sustained by the classic technique of divide and rule. 'I have always placed my highest and most permanent hopes', he explained, 'upon the eternity of the Communal situation. The greater the political progress made by the Hindus the greater, in my judgment, will the Moslem antagonism and mistrust become.'[47] In 1918 a promise had been made to appoint in ten years' time a commission to report on the workings of the constitution. Fearful that a Labour government would take office and appoint a body sympathetic to nationalist demands, Birkenhead appointed Sir John Simon, a Liberal with conservative views on India, to head a Commission carefully packed (with no Indian members) to ensure a harmless outcome. Simon lived up to expectations and delivered a report proposing an extension of self-government in the provinces while the Viceroy and his Council retained absolute power at the centre. This was a prescription Churchill could and did accept, but by the time the report was published in 1930 it had been overtaken by events. When the Irwin Declaration was issued in October 1929, Birkenhead was furious, declaring that Indians would not be fit for self-government in a hundred years.[48]

Churchill was left to carry the torch without his old friend, whose death in October 1930 caused him deep and lasting grief. Self-government, he predicted, would lead to exploitation, corruption, and communal strife between Muslim and Hindu. Unlike the Viceroy and his officials, who were in touch with the political realities, he failed to appreciate the strength of the nationalist movement. The Congress leaders, he imagined, could be swept aside in a vigorous display of imperial will: attempts to appease them would only increase their appetite for power. Underlying Churchill's policies were racial attitudes and stereotypes that were commonplace at the time, but have since become wholly unacceptable. Hence, when giving evidence in 1937 to the Peel Commission on Palestine, Churchill could argue that more advanced races had the right to expand at the expense of the less advanced:

I do not admit, for instance, that a great wrong has been done to the Red Indians of America, or the black people of Australia. I do not admit that a wrong has been done to these people by the fact that a stronger race, a higher grade race, or at any rate, a more worldly-wise race, to put it that way, has come in and taken their place.[49]

In April 1933 Churchill turned down an invitation to join the Joint Select Committee appointed to examine and report on the government's proposals for constitutional reform. Though the Diehards were a minority in the House of Commons it was a different story in the constituency parties, where they organized a highly effective campaign of subversion through the India Defence League. At the annual party conference they won a third of the vote in October 1933 and nearly a half in October 1934. The battle reached a climax in the 1934–5 session of Parliament, as the Secretary for India, Samuel Hoare, struggled to pilot the Government of India Bill through the Commons. Churchill, however, could rejoice in a last-minute stroke of luck. Though the India bill reached the statute book the Indian Princes refused to participate, thereby postponing indefinitely the plan for a federal government at the centre. Provincial self-government was introduced in 1937, but the All-India Federation envisaged in the bill was never to materialize.

Driven as much by financial need as by political motives,

Churchill devoted much of the 1930s to literary endeavours. In 1929 he began work on the life of his ancestor, the first duke of Marlborough. Churchill had the advantage of exclusive access to the Blenheim archives, and the services of the young Maurice Ashley as his research assistant. But the book owed its force to Churchill's deep knowledge of high politics and military operations, his mastery of the source materials, and his passionate desire to vindicate his ancestor's character from the charges levelled against him by Macaulay. Published in four volumes between October 1933 and September 1938, *Marlborough: His Life and Times* took its place at once among the classics of historical writing. Coinciding with the rise of Nazi Germany, and telling the story of his ancestor's leadership of a Grand Alliance to prevent the domination of the Continent by a single power, it was also a source of inspiration to Churchill in his campaign against appeasement. In 1932 he signed a contract for another multi-volume work, *A History of the English-Speaking Peoples*, for which Cassell agreed to pay an advance of £20,000. Setting himself a target of 1,000 words a day, he began work on the book on 1 August 1938. By the outbreak of war in September 1939, when plans for publication had to be suspended, there were 530,000 words in proof and the book was almost finished. In the intervals between writing history and making it, he poured out a stream of articles for the press, including a series of biographical profiles later collected and published as *Great Contemporaries* (1937). His weekly commentaries in the *Evening Standard* were syndicated throughout Europe by a Hungarian Jew, Emery Reves, and were published in book form as *Step by Step* (1939).

Churchill was probably the most highly paid English author of his day, but his earning powers were rarely sufficient to meet the bills resulting from his extravagant spending habits. 'To run his estate efficiently', writes one of his biographers, 'Churchill was helped by eight or nine indoor servants, a nannie or governess, two secretaries, a chauffeur, three gardeners, a groom, and a working bailiff.'[50] In the spring of 1938 losses on the stock market compelled him to put Chartwell up for sale, but he was rescued by the generosity of the financier Sir Henry Strakosch, who agreed to cover his share losses and take control of his American investments.

Churchill's marriage to Clemmie endured but there were many storms as the children grew up. The uncontrollable Randolph veered between adoration of his father, drunken escapades, and rash political initiatives, like his intervention in the Liverpool Wavertree by-election of January 1935, when he stood without his father's permission as a rebel Tory candidate, splitting the Conservative vote and handing the seat to the Labour party. Meanwhile Diana's marriage in 1932 to John Bailey had ended in a divorce, though she then married Duncan Sandys, a Conservative MP who became one of the few loyal supporters of Churchill in the late 1930s. Both Winston and Clemmie were horrified when Sarah Churchill, by that time a successful actress, defied them by marrying a divorced Viennese entertainer, Vic Oliver. 'He did not impress me with being a bad man', wrote Churchill after their first encounter, 'but common as dirt.'[51] Later he grew fond of his son-in-law and was distressed when the marriage broke up.

* * *

Churchill's India campaign distracted attention from his simultaneous warnings over the rise of Nazi Germany. In September 1932, when Churchill was in Munich on a tour of Marlborough's battlefields, Randolph contacted Ernst 'Putzi' Hanfstaengl, Hitler's press secretary, to suggest a meeting between his father and the Nazi leader, who had not yet come to power. Hanfstaengl, who spoke excellent English, introduced himself to Churchill, who invited him to dine and listened with great interest to his account of Hitler. But Churchill also had a message for Hitler: 'Tell your boss from me that anti-semitism may be a good starter, but it is a bad sticker.' This appears to have put Hitler off. At any rate Hanfstaengl told Churchill the next day that Hitler would not, after all, be coming to see him.[52] Fortunately for Churchill, who was much swayed by personal contacts, the two men were never to meet.

By January 1933 Hitler was Chancellor of Germany and within a few months the apparatus of a one-party police state was in place. Churchill was horrified by the brutally repressive character of the Nazi regime and repelled by its anti-Semitism, which he frequently condemned in his speeches. 'I remember', Attlee recalled, 'the tears pouring down his cheeks one day before the war in the House of Commons, when he was telling me what was being done to the Jews in Germany.'[53] But it was the external ambitions of the Nazis, not their internal policies, that caused Churchill most alarm. With fascism as such—a loose term which covered a variety of regimes—he had no quarrel. In February 1933 he praised Mussolini, at that time a potential ally of Great Britain, as 'the greatest lawgiver among living men'.[54] While recognizing Germany's legitimate grievances over the Treaty of Versailles, Churchill argued that it would be folly for the victors to disarm before the grievances of the vanquished were redressed. He therefore condemned the attempts made by the British Government and the International Disarmament Conference in Geneva (1932–4) to reduce Britain and France's armed forces to the level of Germany's. If Germany were to obtain military equality with her grievances unredressed, he warned, 'so surely should we see ourselves within a measurable distance of the renewal of a general European war'.[55] Following the withdrawal of Germany from the League of Nations and the Disarmament Conference in the autumn of 1934, he was critical of unilateral British concessions like the Anglo-German naval agreement of 1935, which allowed Germany to build a Navy of up to one-third of the size of the British. When the agreement was put to the vote in the House of Commons, Churchill nevertheless voted with the government.

Diplomacy, Churchill argued, must be backed by military force. From 1934 onwards he campaigned for rearmament in the air with the aim of restoring parity of front-line strength between the RAF and the Luftwaffe. It was a campaign in which Churchill was both a protagonist and the agent of disaffected civil servants and officers who supplied him with information in breach of the Official Secrets Act. Among his informants were his old friend Desmond Morton, whose work as Director of the Industrial Intelligence Centre gave him access to secret intelligence data, and two Foreign Office officials, Michael Creswell and Ralph Wigram. In the House of Commons Churchill gathered around him a formidable body of Conservative supporters and pressed the government hard in powerful speeches, full of detailed allegations, that sent shock waves through the Cabinet.

Although he was out of office Churchill was no outsider. As a Privy Councillor and elder statesman he always had access to the inner circle and was often consulted on matters of defence. In September 1934, when Baldwin was on holiday at Aix-les-Bains, Churchill and Lindemann called in to see him and urged the establishment of a high-powered committee to enquire into the problems of defence against air attack. Their initiative led to the setting up of the Air Defence Research Committee of the Committee of Imperial Defence. When Baldwin succeeded MacDonald as Prime Minister in June 1935 he invited Churchill to serve on the Air Defence Committee, of which he remained a member up to the outbreak of war in 1939. Churchill was therefore well briefed on the development of radar and Fighter Command's plans to combat the Luftwaffe.

On some aspects of defence the information Churchill received was misleading. In calculating the front-line strength of the Luftwaffe he failed to allow for the inferiority of the aircraft types produced during the early stages of German rearmament. 'Until 1939', writes Richard Overy, 'the German air force was no real threat to Britain.'[56] In spite of the part he had played in the invention of the tank, Churchill was unaware of the revolutionary doctrines of tank warfare adopted by the German army, and his faith in the French Army was unshakeable.[57] Consequently he paid comparatively little attention to the state of the British Army, expecting that it would be built up gradually after the outbreak of war, while the French held the line. He accepted too readily the Admiralty's over-optimistic assessments of the ability of warships to defend themselves against attack from the air, and the effectiveness of the Asdic detection device in reducing the menace posed by submarine warfare. In January 1938 he declared: 'The air menace against properly armed and protected ships at sea will not be of a decisive character.' Eight months later he spoke of 'the undoubted obsolescence of the submarine as a decisive war weapon'.[58] Churchill prophesied war, but not the kind of war the British were compelled in the end to fight.

In Churchill's view, all other threats were eclipsed by the danger from Nazi Germany. Acts of aggression by other nations might therefore have to be tolerated or appeased. When Italy attacked Abyssinia in October 1935 he was torn between revulsion against an act of aggression which undermined the League of Nations, and the desire to maintain friendly relations with Italy as a potential counterweight to Germany. The following month Baldwin called a general election in which he combined a commitment to rearm with a solemn pledge to uphold the League of Nations and the principle of collective security against aggression. The Labour Party, which had long championed the cause of the League, was outmanoeuvered and defeated at the polls. But whereas Labour believed in the subordination of British foreign policy to League principles, most Conservatives were pragmatists who supported the League only to the extent that it served British interests. Churchill, from this point of view, was a mainstream Conservative. He spoke up in favour of the abortive Hoare–Laval plan of December 1935, which proposed to reward Mussolini's aggression with territorial concessions at Abyssinia's expense.

By 1936 the India question was out of the way, the government was pressing on with rearmament, and there were large areas of foreign policy on which Churchill agreed with the Cabinet. His reaction to Hitler's remilitarization of the Rhineland (7 March 1936) was muted and instead of calling for military retaliation he commended the French for taking the issue to the League of Nations. 'What is the real problem, the real peril?' he asked the House of Commons. 'It is not the reoccupation of the Rhineland, but this enormous process of the rearmament of Germany. There is the peril.'[59] There had been rumours before the Rhineland crisis that Baldwin was about to appoint Churchill to the new post of Minister for the Co-ordination of Defence. In the event Baldwin appointed a lawyer, Sir Thomas Inskip, with whom

Churchill's relations proved to be remarkably cordial. Underlying differences between Churchill and the government remained. The Cabinet increasingly recognized the need to give priority to the air defence of Great Britain, but Churchill argued that, however essential, measures to defend the homeland were no substitute for the re-establishment of a military balance of power on the Continent.

Both in public and in private he expressed grave forebodings about the growing might of Germany. On 6 October 1936, while visiting Oxford to unveil a memorial to T. E. Lawrence, he dined at All Souls. 'Mr Churchill', someone asked, 'is there going to be war?' 'Certainly', Churchill replied, 'a very terrible war in which London will be bombed and Buckingham Palace will be razed to the ground, and the lions and tigers will escape from the zoo and roam through the streets of London attacking people.'[60] England, he told the Canadian Prime Minister Mackenzie King a fortnight later, had never been in greater danger. Inside five years she might become a 'vassal state' of Germany:

She was down, down, down relatively in the matter of her prestige. She was drifting terribly. It was all drift, drift drift. Germany was like a great vessel of millions of tons that was near a reef. She would swing from side to side and would seek to hold back but was driving on to the reef.[61]

In the spring of 1936, with the assistance of a secret cross-party organization known as the 'Focus', Churchill began to call for Britain to adopt a foreign policy based on collective security under the League of Nations. By implication this would include the Soviet Union, whose admission to the League he had welcomed in 1934. Parting company with the Tory Right, with whom he had been collaborating over India, he extended the hand of friendship to Leon Blum's Popular Front government in France, which came to power in May 1936. More remarkable was his readiness to reach out to the regime he had tried so hard to strangle in its cradle. As recently as 1931 Churchill had addressed a public meeting called to protest against the slave labour camps in the Soviet Union—the 'Gulag Archipelago'. But with the rise of Hitler Churchill fell silent on the atrocities committed by the Stalinist regime against its own subjects. The collectivization of agriculture was enforced by a campaign of ruthless brutality in which some ten million kulaks were murdered or imprisoned.[62] Then came the Great Terror of 1934–9 in which first of all the Communist Party and then the Red Army fell victim to Stalin's purges. Half a million members of the party were executed, up to five millions imprisoned. Out of an officer corps of 80,000, 35,000 were liquidated, including 110 out of the 195 divisional commanders.[63] In his anti-Bolshevik mood of 1919 Churchill would readily have believed the tales of horror trickling out of the Soviet Union, and he may well have believed them in the 1930s. But from 1933 his anti-communism was subordinated to the conviction that Nazi Germany was the more important danger, a military rather than an ideological judgement from which it followed that Britain and the Soviet Union shared a common interest in resisting Hitler. By 1936 he was in regular contact with Ivan Maisky, the Soviet ambassador in London.[64]

Churchill's rapprochement with the Soviet Union, a theme handled with great discretion in his speeches—there were Tories listening—was threatened for a while by the outbreak of the Spanish Civil War in July 1936. As Churchill saw it, Spain was in the grip of a struggle between Fascism on the one hand, and Communism and Anarchy on the other. Like most Conservatives, he inclined at first to the side of General Franco and the nationalists. The atrocities by the Communists and Anarchists on the Republican side, he maintained, were worse than those of their opponents, and he blamed the Soviet Union for helping to create revolutionary conditions in Spain. When the Spanish ambassador in London offered to shake hands he recoiled, muttering: 'Blood, blood, blood'.[65] As the Civil War dragged on, however, Churchill began to fear that a nationalist victory would result in a Spain heavily under the influence of Nazi Germany. Perhaps he also recognized that Stalin had employed the Communist Party in Spain to curb and suppress the social revolution. By the end of 1938 he was persuaded that 'the British Empire would run far less risk from the victory of the Spanish Government than that of General Franco'.[66]

Churchill's campaign for collective security was interrupted in December 1936 by the Abdication crisis. The new king, Edward VIII, was determined to marry an American divorcee, Wallis Simpson. In the eyes of the respectable, the King and his mistress were the leaders of a frivolous and irresponsible set, half-American and wholly undesirable, which threatened to undermine the moral authority of the monarchy. Edward's refusal to behave himself had long been a cause of anxiety and the guardians of the Victorian state were in no mood to tolerate any more nonsense. Baldwin told the King that he must either abandon his plan to marry Mrs Simpson or abdicate. Churchill, who had long been a friend of the King's, hoped that he could be persuaded to see the error of his ways: why give up an Empire for a mistress? He therefore pleaded in the House of Commons for the King to be given more time to come to a decision. Whispering in his ear was the incorrigibly mischievous press lord, Beaverbrook, who detested Baldwin and wanted to form a King's Party to overthrow him. It is unlikely that Churchill, who acted throughout with Baldwin's knowledge and consent, was engaged in a plot to seize the premiership, but even his friends concluded that he was. 'George Lloyd told me', the Earl of Crawford recorded,

that he, Austen C[hamberlain], and Horne had protested to Winston at the dangerous course he was pursuing, but Churchill was already coining his phrases, and though expressing warm personal friendship for the King and ascribing all action to these sentiments, he none the less saw the fruits of office temptingly close before his eyes. His judgment is nearly always wrong however resonant his prose—he is an evil counsellor . . .[67]

When Baldwin finally departed in May 1937, Churchill welcomed his successor, Neville Chamberlain, and warmly seconded his nomination as leader of the Conservative Party. Churchill respected Chamberlain as the driving force behind rearmament and hoped that he would take a firmer line with Germany. No doubt he also hoped that the new Prime Minister would restore him to office, but Chamberlain, who recalled him as a turbulent colleague in the Baldwin Cabinet of 1924 to 1929, had no intention of doing so. Chamberlain also intended to run his own foreign policy, a determination which led to the resignation of the Foreign Secretary, Anthony Eden, on 20 February 1938. Eden, who had just turned 40, was the rising hope of Conservatives who supported the League of Nations against the dictators. A diplomat of great skill, whose masculine beauty and impeccable tailoring made him the most photogenic of Cabinet ministers, his capacity for the more brutal aspects of politics had yet to be proved. When he resigned, it was in protest against Chamberlain's appeasement of Italy, not Germany.

Churchill praised Eden, criticized Chamberlain for making concessions to Mussolini, and warned against a policy of appeasing the demands of the totalitarian powers. But in the month following Eden's resignation, Churchill's name was fourth on a list of 150 MPs who signed a declaration assuring Chamberlain of their wholehearted support.[68] When German troops marched into Austria in March 1938, Churchill expressed in private his sympathy for Chamberlain. Never, he remarked, had a Prime Minister inherited a more ghastly situation, the blame for which rested entirely with Baldwin. The British were faced with an appalling dilemma: 'We stand to lose everything by failing to take strong action. Yet if we take strong action, London will be a shambles in half an hour.'[69] For their part Eden and his small band of supporters in the House of Commons were careful to keep their distance from Churchill. 'Don't be worried my darling', Harold Nicolson assured his wife, Vita Sackville-West: 'I am not going to become one of the Winston brigade.'[70]

Czechoslovakia, now clearly marked out as the next victim of a German assault, posed an alarming problem for British policy-makers. Both France and the Soviet Union were pledged to assist Czechoslovakia in the event of a German attack, and if they were to do so Britain would be compelled to join them. The Chiefs of Staff, however, advised that it would be impossible to prevent the Germans from overruning Czechoslovakia. Chamberlain was convinced that in the event of war neither the United States nor the Soviet Union could be relied upon to give any effective support. There was, however, a danger that a war between Britain and Germany would encourage both Italy and Japan to join in an attack on the British Empire. The moral justification of a war for Czechoslovakia was also in doubt. Under the Treaty of Versailles three million German speakers in the Sudetenland, former inhabitants of the Austro-German Empire, had been included without their consent in a state dominated by seven million Czechs and three million Slovaks. Many of the Sudetenlanders were fervent supporters of the local Nazi movement, led by

Konrad Henlein, which demanded autonomy for the German-speaking population, a proposal strongly resisted by the Czech government. Had Britain and France the right to deny self-determination to the Sudetenlanders?

On this particular question there was very little difference between Chamberlain and Churchill. In the spring of 1938 both hoped that a German attack could be averted by putting pressure on the Czechs to concede autonomy to the Sudetenland. But Churchill in the meantime urged the government to collaborate with France in gathering together as many European states as possible—the Soviet Union included—for mutual defence under the banner of the League of Nations. At a great public meeting in the Manchester Free Trade he asked his listeners to consider the alternative:

Undoubtedly our government could make an agreement with Germany. All they have to do is to give her back her former colonies, and such others as she may desire; to muzzle the British press and platform by a law of censorship, and to give Herr Hitler a free hand to spread the Nazi system and dominance far and wide through Central Europe . . . We should be the helpless, silent, gagged, apparently consenting spectators of the horrors which would spread through Central Europe. The Government that enforced such a policy would be swept away. The mere instinct of self-preservation would make it impossible for us to purchase a fleeting and precarious immunity at the cost of the ruin and enslavement of Europe.[71]

By the beginning of September 1938 hopes of an internal solution to the Czech question were fading fast and there were many signs that Hitler intended to march his troops into the Sudetenland. Determined to avoid war at almost any price, Chamberlain flew three times to Germany in an attempt to find some diplomatic formula that would enable Hitler to obtain by agreement what he was threatening to obtain by force. After the second meeting at Godesberg he came back with terms so humiliating that they were rejected by the Cabinet. War appeared to be imminent, the paths of Chamberlain and Churchill converging. But the Munich conference of 29 September, convened at the last possible moment by Mussolini, enabled Chamberlain and his French opposite number Daladier to act out a charade of negotiations while agreeing to the immediate transfer of the Sudetenland to Germany. In the course of the crisis Churchill had warned Chamberlain and Halifax on three different occasions to stand firm.

Chamberlain returned home to a hero's welcome. His bold initiative, so it seemed at the time, had spared the nation the horrors of war. 'He was deluged with letters of praise', wrote the historian C. L. Mowat, 'from people at home and abroad, high and low, from the King, from General Smuts, from the kitchen-maid of the Chamberlain family.'[72] Carried away by euphoria, he told the cheering crowd outside Number 10 that it was 'the second time in our history that there has come back from Germany to Downing Street peace with honour. I believe it is peace in our time.'[73] But Munich had opened up a chasm between Chamberlain and Churchill, who was appalled by the shame of a humiliating surrender and the loss of a strategic bastion. Throwing caution to the winds he denounced Chamberlain's policy root and branch: 'I will begin', he said, 'by saying what everybody would like to ignore or forget but which must nevertheless be stated, namely that we have suffered a total and unmitigated defeat . . .' The course of the negotiations between Hitler and Chamberlain were summarized with biting sarcasm: '£1 was demanded at the pistol's point. When it was given, £2 were demanded at the pistol's point. Finally, the dictator consented to take £1 17s. 6d. and the rest in promises of good will for the future.' Churchill ended with a prophecy: 'This is only the first sip, the first foretaste of a bitter cup which will be proffered to us year by year unless by a supreme recovery of moral health and martial vigour, we arise again and take our stand for freedom as in the olden time.'[74]

The House, thought Leo Amery, was 'really impressed' by Churchill's speech. Even Chips Channon, a devoted Chamberlainite, acknowledged that it 'discomforted the Front Bench'.[75] But the more effective Churchill's attacks, the stronger the backlash that followed. Apart from Duff Cooper, who had caused a sensation by resigning from the government in protest, Churchill was by far the most prominent and outspoken of the small band of Tory MPs who had abstained in the division at the end of the Munich debate. He was now subjected to a pincer attack in which he was denounced by Goebbels on the one hand and Chamberlainite Conservatives on the other. The winter of 1938–9 was the true period of his exile in the wilderness. Ostracized by his own party he narrowly survived a vote of confidence in his constituency association. When he spoke in favour of a motion to establish a Ministry of Supply, in November 1938, only two Conservative MPs voted with him: Brendan Bracken and Harold Macmillan.

Most Conservatives shunned Churchill, and he inspired little confidence on the Labour side. Three weeks after Munich Robert Fraser, a leader-writer on the *Daily Herald*, warned the Labour politician Hugh Dalton against the idea of making common cause with Churchill:

There is only one danger of Fascism, of censorship, of the unification of parties, of national 'discipline', and that will come if Chamberlain is overthrown by the Jingoes in his own party, led by Winston, who will then settle down, with his lousy and reactionary friends, to organise the nation on Fascist principles for a war to settle scores with Hitler.[76]

The most powerful of the trade union leaders, Ernest Bevin, General Secretary of the Transport and General Workers' Union, was a root-and-branch opponent of appeasement. But he too denounced the idea of cooperation with Churchill:

Those who made this suggestion do not understand the Trade Unions, nor do they give us credit for memory. Winston Churchill restored the gold standard and upset every wage agreement in the country. He was the chief protagonist in starving the miners into submission when he was Chancellor. He was the sponsor of the Trade Disputes and the Trade Union Act of 1927 . . . Is it any wonder that he makes no appeal to us![77]

Paradoxically Churchill's most important assets in the winter of 1938–9 were his isolation and his unique record as a Cassandra prophesying doom. They might turn out to be the last will and testament of a bankrupt politician. But as Churchill himself was well aware, they might just be the title deeds of a man of destiny.

· SIX ·

The Making of a Hero, 1939–1945

On 15 March 1939 German troops marched into Prague and the Czechoslovak state ceased to exist. The moral case for the Munich agreement—that Hitler's aims were limited to the incorporation of Germans in the Reich, that a just grievance against the Treaty of Versailles was being redressed, that appeasement would bring 'peace in our time'—collapsed overnight. By the same token Churchill's analysis of Munich was vindicated. The argument which had been employed so often to justify his exclusion from office—that he lacked judgement—began to rebound against Chamberlain and his colleagues. Was it not they who had lacked judgement? Had not Sir Samuel Hoare, speaking a few days before the invasion of Prague, conjured up the prospect of a new Golden Age of prosperity for the world? At long last Churchill was in a position where, assisted by the tide of opinion now flowing against appeasement, he could begin to turn the tables on his critics.

Shifting his ground, Chamberlain authorized a British guarantee to Poland, but his estimate of Churchill was unchanged and he had no wish to include him in the government. His views were shared by the King. During his North American tour of June 1939 George VI, who had served in the Navy as a midshipman when Churchill was at the Admiralty, confided his thoughts to the Canadian prime minister, Mackenzie King:

He told how prior to the Dardanelles attack, Churchill had been told over and over again not to make the attack too soon, to wait some time, but was determined to go at it. At the time he had made up his mind, he had still to study the maps. The King indicated he would never wish to appoint Churchill to any office unless it was absolutely necessary in time of war. I confess I was glad to hear him say that because I think Churchill is one of the most dangerous men I have ever known.[1]

There was, however, nothing Chamberlain or the King could do to prevent the reinvention of Churchill as a respected elder statesman. Since he had been in the public eye for decades it is likely that he already possessed some kind of popular following, but the absence of opinion polls before the late 1930s makes it hard to detect and impossible to measure. Then in May 1939 a Gallup poll put the question: 'Are you in favour of Mr Winston Churchill being invited to join the Cabinet?' 56 per cent replied 'Yes', 26 per cent 'No', and 18 per cent were undecided.[2]

There was also much boosting of Churchill in the anti-appeasement sections of the press. Even before Prague, *Picture Post* ran a feature in which Wickham Steed, a former editor of *The Times*, interviewed him at Chartwell. 'Should some great emergency arise', he wrote, 'his qualities and experience might then be national assets; and the true greatness, which he has often seemed to miss by a hair's breadth, might, by common consent, be his.'[3] On the other side of the Atlantic, Barnet Nover of the *Washington Post* discussed the question of whether or not Chamberlain would bring Churchill into the government: 'To do so would mean his own eclipse. Churchill is a man of such

brilliance as inevitably to throw the present collection of mediocrities in the British Cabinet into deep obscurity. But no step
could be more salutary for Great Britain and for Europe's peace
than that.'[4]

In July 1939 Chamberlain was disturbed when Lord Camrose,
the owner of the *Daily Telegraph*, launched a campaign for
Churchill's return to office. An editorial described him as

a statesman not only schooled in responsibility by long and intimate contact with affairs of state, but possessing an unrivalled peacetime knowledge
of the crucial problems which war presents, especially in the higher
strategy. With vision and energy he unites a conspicuous gift of exposition
and popular appeal, and in this strait pass the nation cannot prudently
dispense with the great services which he is so capable of rendering.[5]

Churchill's old ally, J. L. Garvin, the editor of the *Observer*,
lent his support, and the pro-Labour *Daily Mirror* hired him as a
columnist with the announcement that he was 'the most trusted
statesman in Britain'.[6] Chamberlain found it hard to appreciate
that a reassessment of Churchill was in progress. In his view
the campaign to restore him to office was simply a conspiracy
involving Maisky, the Soviet ambassador, and Churchill's son
Randolph. Camrose's participation was vexing, but 'since his
illness Camrose is a changed man'.[7]

Chamberlain's principal motive in excluding Churchill was to
leave the door open for another round of appeasement. To give
Churchill office, he thought, would be to signal that Britain was
now determined to fight. When the German invasion of Poland
on 1 September made the inclusion of Churchill unavoidable,
Chamberlain drew up a plan for a War Cabinet of six members in
which Churchill would have no departmental responsibilities.
None of the three service ministers—the First Lord of the
Admiralty, the Secretary for War, and the Secretary for Air—was

to be included. Within hours someone—it is not clear who—
revived all the old anxieties about Churchill and the plan was
changed. Churchill was to go to the Admiralty and all three
service ministers into the War Cabinet. As the Chief Whip, David
Margesson, explained to Sinclair, the leader of the Liberal party,

the reason why Mr Churchill had been sent to the Admiralty was the feeling
that he would be a very dangerous member of the Cabinet if he were left to
roam over the whole field of policy, and it would be much safer to give him a
job of work to get his teeth into. It was largely for the same reason that Lord
Hankey had originally been included in the Cabinet, because it was felt
that he was a man whose experience and authority Mr Churchill would
respect, and who would therefore be able to keep him in order.[8]

Churchill was thrilled to return to the very same post he had
occupied in August 1914. 'Winston is back', the Admiralty signalled to the Fleet, or so tradition has it—no record of the signal
has ever been found. Accompanying Churchill to the Admiralty
were Brendan Bracken, who became his Parliamentary Private
Secretary, and Professor Lindemann, his scientific adviser. In
October 1939 Churchill asked Lindemann to form a statistical
branch to collect naval and other statistics which were usually
presented to Churchill in the form of graphs and charts.

The overall direction of the war was now in the hands of
Chamberlain and the War Cabinet, acting on the advice of a
Military Co-ordination Committee chaired by Lord Chatfield.
Chamberlain, who was fearful at first of Churchillian intrigues,
was surprised to discover that the First Lord of the Admiralty
was a remarkably loyal colleague. For the first and only occasion,
Mr and Mrs Churchill and Mr and Mrs Chamberlain dined
together. Nevertheless the two politicians were rivals, both of
whom wanted to run the war. Chamberlain, however, seemed ill at
ease as a war minister. Churchill's beaming face and exuberant

style threatened to eclipse him and within a few weeks there was talk of a change of Prime Minister. On 26 September he gave the House of Commons a review of the war at sea, the first time he had spoken from the despatch box for more than a decade. Harold Nicolson wrote in his diary:

The effect of Winston's speech was infinitely greater than could be derived from any reading of the text. His delivery was really amazing and he sounded every note from deep preoccupation to flippancy, from resolution to sheer boyishness. One could feel the spirits of the House rising with every word. It was quite obvious afterwards that the Prime Minister's inadequacy and lack of inspiration had been demonstrated even to his warmest supporters. In those twenty minutes Churchill brought himself nearer the post of Prime Minister than he has ever been before.[9]

Churchill followed up his success with a world broadcast on 1 October in which he surveyed the state of the war in Europe and the progress of the British war effort—an even more prime ministerial performance. Hamilton Fyfe, a journalist on the left-wing *Reynolds News*, noted in his diary that the broadcast sounded like a bid for the premiership. The main topic of conversation the following week, he wrote, was how soon Churchill would take Chamberlain's place. In the pro-Labour *Daily Herald*, Maurice Webb predicted that if the Conservatives remained in power, Churchill was the clear favourite to succeed Chamberlain. 'It is hardly premature to say', wrote William Connor in the *Daily Mirror*, 'that in popular imagination Churchill has already ousted Chamberlain as the dominant war figure.'[10] These were, of course, comments by long-standing enemies of Chamberlain with a vested interest in undermining him, but the enthusiasm for Churchill was genuine. 'Winston Churchill', reported James Reston in the *New York Times*, 'has emerged from the first five weeks of the war as the most inspiring figure in Great

Britain and ultimate successor to the 71-year old Neville Chamberlain ... He has been condemned as a Russophobe and a Teutophobe, as an irresponsible genius, but even his old critics now seem to agree that he will make a great wartime leader.'[11]

When U-47, the German U-boat commanded by Gunther Prien, sank the battleship *Royal Oak* at Scapa Flow on 14 October, Churchill quite rightly escaped the blame. But he shared in the reflected glory of Admiral Harwood's victory at the Battle of the River Plate (13 December 1939), and the scuttling of the *Graf Spee* a few days later. In February 1940 there was a thrilling sequel. Churchill personally ordered the interception in Norwegian territorial waters of the *Altmark*, a ship which contained British prisoners of war captured by the *Graf Spee*. It was Chamberlain who reported the news of the release of the prisoners to the House, but Churchill who was patted on the shoulder and congratulated by MPs.[12]

Though Churchill's popularity was growing, there was no sudden collapse in Chamberlain's support. Gallup reported in October that 65 per cent were satisfied with Chamberlain as Prime Minister, and when at the end of 1939 respondents were asked: 'If you had the choice between Mr Chamberlain and Mr Churchill, which would you have as Prime Minister?' 52 per cent were for Chamberlain, 30 per cent for Churchill, and 18 per cent undecided.[13] The public, in any case, had no means of making Churchill Prime Minister. More ominous, from Chamberlain's point of view, was the decline of opposition to Churchill within the political elite. Few had been more critical of him than the Conservative elder statesman the Earl of Crawford. But in February 1940, in the final entry of the diary he had kept ever since 1892, he wrote:

People say Churchill is tactless, that his judgment is erratic, that he flies off at a tangent, that he has a burning desire to trespass upon the domain of the naval strategist—all this may be more or less true but he remains the only figure in the cabinet with the virtue of constant uncompromising aggressive victory. He delivers the massive killing blow, encourages the country, inspires the fleet—the more I see and hear of him the more confident I become that he represents the party of complete totalitarian victory![14]

Churchill's dynamism was certainly making a mark at the Admiralty. He ordered that all naval vessels should be fitted with radar and all merchant ships armed. Confident that the U-boat menace would rapidly be overcome, he announced figures for German losses which his advisers knew to be greatly exaggerated. When Captain Talbot, the Director of Anti-Submarine Warfare, queried the figures Churchill telephoned him to say: 'There are two people who sink U-boats in this war Talbot. You sink them in the Atlantic and I sink them in the House of Commons. The trouble is that you are sinking them at exactly half the rate I am.' In April 1940 Talbot was dismissed on Churchill's instructions.[15]

Churchill sought a daring role for the Navy. Apparently oblivious of the danger posed by bombers to ships without fighter cover, he repeatedly pressed the naval staff to adopt Operation Catherine, a hair-raising plan, eventually thwarted by the First Sea Lord, Admiral Pound, to send a naval force into the Baltic. Another idea that captured his imagination was the mining of Norwegian coastal waters to prevent the transport of Swedish iron ore to Germany. After the Russian invasion of Finland on 30 November 1939, he urged the despatch of an expeditionary force to Narvik to seize the Swedish ore fields, under the pretext of going to the aid of Finland. Not until the end of March 1940 did the Supreme Allied War Council authorize the mining of the leads, by which time Hitler had decided to pre-empt an allied occupation. On 9 April German forces marched into Denmark and Norway.

Chatfield having resigned a few days before, Churchill at Chamberlain's request now took the chair of the Military Co-ordination Committee and began to dominate operations. An expeditionary force under the command of Admiral Cork was despatched to Narvik but a few days later Churchill decided to open up a second front around Trondheim, and the rear half of the convoy was diverted to central Norway. When Churchill suggested a naval bombardment of Narvik, the land commander, General Mackesy, protested that it would be shameful to bombard thousands of Norwegian men, women, and children. Churchill signalled to Cork: 'If this Officer appears to be spreading a bad spirit through the higher ranks of the land forces, do not hesitate to relieve him or place him under arrest.'[16] After further rapid changes of plan on Churchill's part the forces sent to the Trondheim area were overwhelmed and evacuated.

Churchill's critics began to murmur that the Norway fiasco was a second Gallipoli, but this time the deeper political currents were in Churchill's favour. Chamberlain and his colleagues had been in office since 1931. They could no longer escape the blame when disaster struck. On 8 May 1940, the second day of the parliamentary debate on Norway, Churchill wound up with a strong fighting speech in defence of the government. But when the House divided, the government's majority fell from its normal level of more than 200 to 81, a decisive moral defeat.

Chamberlain realized that a Coalition government was now inevitable, and that in the likely event of Labour refusing to serve under him he would have to resign. But who was to be the successor? The alternative leader preferred by the 'Establishment' was the Foreign Secretary, Lord Halifax, and there is some evidence to suggest that initially Churchill was prepared to serve under him. At 4.30 p.m. on 9 May Chamberlain called a meeting to discuss the succession, the others present being Churchill, Halifax, and the Conservative Chief Whip, David Margesson. Chamberlain and Margesson raised the question and waited for the others to speak. Churchill, however, had been urged by Kingsley Wood, and possibly Brendan Bracken as well, not to disclaim the succession. Churchill therefore said nothing, and after a brief silence Halifax explained the reasons why he did not think a member of the House of Lords should be prime minister. Churchill had won the premiership with scarcely a hint of intrigue or disloyalty.

When Chamberlain awoke next morning to the news that Germany had invaded Belgium, he imagined at first that he could stay on, but his fate was sealed by a message from the Labour Party reiterating its refusal to serve under him. On Chamberlain's advice Churchill was summoned to the Palace and at 6 o'clock that evening he accepted the King's invitation to form a government. 'It was the irony, or fatality of history', wrote Liddell Hart, 'that Churchill should have gained his opportunity of supreme power as the result of a fiasco to which he had been the main contributor.'[17] In ruling circles his appointment as Prime Minister was generally regarded as a gamble, and a dangerous one at that, but Churchill himself was confident. 'I felt', he wrote, 'as though I were walking with destiny and that all my past life had been a preparation for this hour and for this trial.'[18]

Churchill at once invited the Labour and Liberal parties to join a Coalition government. Three days earlier Attlee had told Bracken that Labour would not accept Churchill as Prime

Minister because they had never forgiven him for Tonypandy, but in the event the crisis was so compelling that old scores were swept aside.[19] The party's National Executive approved Labour's participation and the Labour party conference endorsed the decision by 2,413,000 votes to 170,000. Churchill now set up a War Cabinet of only five members consisting of himself and the leaders of the two main parties: Chamberlain and Halifax for the Conservatives, Attlee and Greenwood for Labour. Although he found room in his administration for non-party figures like Woolton and Anderson, the government he established was based firmly on the party system, with a balance maintained between Conservative and Labour, and a Whips' Office staffed jointly by the two parties. The leader of the Liberals, his old friend 'Archie' Sinclair, came in as Secretary for Air. To begin with the War Cabinet was based on the Lloyd George model of 1916, with four out of its five members free of departmental responsibilities. But Churchill gradually moved away from this: by January 1941 there was a War Cabinet of eight, of whom four were departmental ministers.

While avoiding a purge, Churchill began to disperse the inner circle of the 'men of Munich'. Sir Horace Wilson, the head of the Treasury and *eminence grise* of the Chamberlain regime, was banished from 10 Downing Street. Hoare was sent into exile as ambassador to Madrid, and Simon removed to the Lords as Lord Chancellor. Chamberlain, however, stayed on as Lord President, retaining the leadership of the Conservative Party, and Halifax continued as Foreign Secretary. Churchill brought in Ernest Bevin, the General Secretary of the Transport and General Workers' Union, as Minister of Labour, to mobilize the trade unions behind the war effort. And in fulfilment of his long campaign for rearmament in the air, he stripped the Air

Ministry of its responsibility for the manufacture of aircraft and transferred it to a Ministry of Aircraft Production under his old friend Beaverbrook.

Like most incoming Prime Ministers, Churchill arrived with his own 'kitchen cabinet' of personal advisers, consisting principally of Bracken, his Parliamentary Private Secretary, Lindemann, his scientific adviser, who became head of the Prime Minister's Statistical Section, and Desmond Morton, his liaison officer with the intelligence services. Their arrival on the scene was an additional cause for alarm. 'The gangsters will shortly be in complete control', remarked Halifax—the only man who could have kept them out.[20] John Colville, one of Chamberlain's private secretaries, stayed on and was converted, within a few weeks, into a fervent Churchillian whose diary, kept in defiance of civil service regulations, gives us the most intimate portrait we have of Churchill as Prime Minister. At the request of the War Cabinet, the Harley Street physician Sir Charles Wilson, later Lord Moran, was appointed in May 1940 to watch over the Prime Minister's health. When Churchill crossed the Atlantic in December 1941 he took his doctor with him, and subsequently Wilson accompanied the Prime Minister on all his travels. He supplied Churchill with sleeping pills and other prescriptions, and summoned the appropriate consultants whenever the Prime Minister fell seriously ill. 'To his unfailing care', Churchill wrote after the war, 'I probably owe my life.'[21] The notes Moran took of conversations with his patient, including confidential details of his medical history, later formed the basis of a controversial book, *Winston Churchill: The Struggle for Survival, 1940–1965* (1966).

Addressing the House of Commons for the first time as Prime Minister, on 13 May 1940, Churchill said: 'You ask, what is our aim? I can answer in one word: it is victory, victory at all costs, victory in spite of all terror, victory, however long and hard the road may be.'[22] With the French Army already in retreat, Churchill authorized the despatch of additional fighter squadrons to France and flew to Paris to investigate the position for himself. When he asked the French Commander-in-Chief, General Gamelin, 'ou est la masse de manoeuvre?' he was appalled when Gamelin replied: 'aucune'. With no realistic prospect of a counter-attack, Churchill's priority was to prevent the encircle-ment of the British Expeditionary Force under Lord Gort. He ordered Gort to retreat towards Dunkirk and the garrison at Calais to fight to the end to delay the German advance.

While the fate of the BEF hung in the balance the War Cabinet discussed an Italian offer to 'mediate' between Germany and the allies, with the implication that Britain and France would enter into negotiations with Germany. Halifax, supported at first by Chamberlain, argued in favour of exploring the Italian proposal. Churchill, while not in principle ruling out the possibility of negotiations, was passionately opposed on the ground that any terms Hitler was likely to offer would be unacceptable. To strengthen his position he summoned a meeting of ministers outside the War Cabinet and was loudly applauded when he declared: 'If this long island story of ours is to end at last, let it end only when each one of us lies choking in his own blood upon the ground.'[23] By the evening of 28 May Churchill had won the crucial debate in the War Cabinet. Within a few days the bulk of the BEF had been successfully evacuated from Dunkirk

In June 1940 Churchill flew twice to France in a fruitless effort to persuade the French government to fight on. In a last-minute bid to revive their morale he even grasped at the idea of a declaration of perpetual union between Britain and France and proposed this to the Reynaud government, which turned it down. Reynaud was succeeded by Marshal Petain, who at once concluded an armistice with Germany. When the French fleet in harbour at Oran refused to surrender to the Royal Navy, Churchill ordered it to be bombarded and sunk (4 July 1940). This brutal act, in which 1,297 Frenchmen were killed, sent an unmistakeable message to the world of Britain's determination to continue the war. Meanwhile, on 17 June, General Charles de Gaulle had arrived in London proclaiming himself the leader of the 'Free French'. Overriding much opposition from within his own government, Churchill gave him official recognition and military support, while keeping open channels of communication with the Vichy regime, which the British continued to regard as the legitimate government of France.

Fearful that the Nazis would be assisted from within by a 'Fifth Column', Churchill ordered a mass round-up of enemy aliens. Between May and July about 22,000 Germans and Austrians were interned, a panic measure which he soon began to regret. As German air attacks intensified in July and August 1940 he toured the country inspecting coastal defences and Fighter Command stations in the eye of the storm. On his instructions the Local Defence Volunteers—for whom a million armbands bearing the letters 'LDV" had already been manufactured—were renamed the Home Guard.[24] But there was little Churchill could do to alter the course of the Battle of Britain. His most important contribution at this point was the bracing effect of his presence, and most of all of his speeches, on the morale of government and people.

The leadership Churchill displayed during the first few months of his premiership extended the revolution in his reputation which had begun in the spring of 1939. It scarcely diminishes Churchill to point out that in some ways luck was on his side in

1940. Having been out of office for most of the 1930s he could not be held responsible for Britain's plight: this time the scapegoats were the 'men of Munich'. With German bombers droning overhead and blood-curdling propaganda issuing from Berlin, the threat of invasion and occupation could not have been more stark. Such were the circumstances of the time that what had previously been perceived as weaknesses or flaws in Churchill's character now came to be seen as strengths. Few now complained that he was a warmonger or a would-be Napoleon: the zeal with which he waged war was a precious asset. Nor was it any longer a black mark against him that he thought of himself as above party. What better recommendation could there be for the head of a government of national unity? His egotism, no longer harnessed to the interests of a party, a department of state, or a controversial cause, was less divisive and almost an expression of the general will. The fact that he was half-American, so often the subject of adverse comment in the past, appeared providential now that British hopes of salvation depended on the assistance of the United States. As for the allegation that he was an impossibilist, an impossibilist was exactly what was called for. Churchill's profound but irrational faith in victory was infectious and exhilarating, and turned out to be right.

This is not to say that Churchill was universally admired. On the contrary there were strong pockets of resistance which not only survived Britain's 'finest hour' but lived on for decades beneath the surface of public life. In the coalfields of south Wales Churchill was never forgiven for Tonypandy. In the Palace of Westminster, as Andrew Roberts has shown, there were Tory MPs who never forgave him for displacing Neville Chamberlain. For at least two months after Churchill's succession to the premiership, they greeted his appearances in the House with a sullen silence, terminated in the end by a demonstration of support orchestrated by the Chief Whip. Despite this they continued to rehearse among themselves the old criticisms of Churchill's character, his judgement, and his associates. They complained of his Olympian detachment from party, his military follies, his partiality for the company of Bracken and Beaverbrook. They grumbled about the concessions he made to the United States and later to the Soviet Union. In the end Churchill obtained such complete control over the levers of power that he was able to marginalize and ignore them.[25] The fundamental explanation of his ability to do so was the depth of the popular support he commanded almost from the start of his premiership.

Among the first to express their faith in Churchill was Mrs Nella Last, a middle-aged housewife living in Barrow-in-Furness, who kept a war diary for Mass-Observation. 'If I had to spend my whole life with a man', she wrote on 11 May 1940, 'I'd choose Mr Chamberlain, but I think I would sooner have Mr Churchill if there was a storm and I was shipwrecked. He has a funny face, like a bulldog living in our street who has done more to drive out unwanted dogs and cats that seemed to come round than all the complaints of householders.'[26]

The newspaper cartoonists quickly established a new iconography of Churchill as the leader and embodiment of a united nation. In the *Daily Mail* (13 May 1940) he was drawn as a sheriff, bursting in through the swing doors of a saloon with revolvers in both hands. David Low, who had often satirized Churchill from a left-wing point of view in the 1920s and 1930s, produced a famous cartoon captioned 'All behind you, Winston' (14 May 1940). With chin thrust forward and sleeves rolled up, Churchill marches at the head of a column with his ministerial colleagues and the whole of the British people falling in behind him. In the *Daily Express* Sidney Strube hit upon the idea of superimposing Churchill's head on the body of a bulldog, with the dog itself standing guard on a map of the British Isles (8 June 1940). The photographers and newsreel cameramen, meanwhile, revelled in Churchill's exhibitionism and spread his image far and wide.

Churchill supplied both imagery and words. His speeches during the summer and autumn of 1940 were the most inspired and inspiring of his long political life. Contrary to folk memory he made few broadcasts at this period, and there is no evidence to support the claim that the BBC employed the actor Norman Shelley to impersonate him. When he declared that he had nothing to offer but 'blood, toil, tears and sweat' (13 May) or vowed that 'we shall fight on the beaches, we shall fight on the landing grounds, we shall fight in the fields and in the streets, we shall fight in the hills, we shall never surrender' (4 June), he was addressing the House of Commons only, though he went on to make recordings of this and other wartime speeches *after* 1945. The same was true of his tribute to the fighter pilots of the Battle of Britain: 'Never in the field of human conflict was so much owed by so many to so few' (20 August).[27] After the fall of France, however, he reluctantly agreed to repeat over the radio a speech made earlier in the day in the House. Families gathered around the wireless on the evening of 18 June 1940 did therefore hear him say: 'Let us therefore brace ourselves to our duty and so bear ourselves that if the British Empire and its Commonwealth lasts for a thousand years, men will still say: "This was their finest hour".'[28]

Mass-Observation, the pioneering social survey founded by Tom Harrisson and Charles Madge, commented on the problems of language involved in bridging the gap between the leaders and the led. Churchill, M-O remarked, achieved this because even though some of his words might occasionally be unintelligible, 'they have a coherence, a force and a rhythm which has an effect of its own, like popular music'.[29] While Churchill's finest phrases roused the emotions, his speeches also commanded attention for another reason. They pierced the fog of rumour and speculation with vivid and authoritative commentaries on the military and strategic situation. Although there was a strong propaganda element in his presentation of the facts, and many secrets lay concealed, they were the speeches of a great parliamentary democrat, leading, informing, and instructing a nation. Not everyone was impressed or won over. There were pockets of society where pre-war mistrust of Churchill lingered, and old wounds festered. By July 1940, however, opinion polls recorded that 88 per cent of the public approved of him as Prime Minister. Another sign of his popularity was the demand for tableware decorated with his portrait. The potteries obliged with mugs, cups, saucers, dishes and plates, and a multitude of toby jugs, some of them garish and hideous, others minor works of art.[30]

In April 1941 Mass-Observation asked a sample of fifty-eight mainly working-class people the question: 'What do you think of Winston Churchill?' Mass-Observation's methods were unscientific but the answers give some idea of the way people thought about Churchill. It was a depressing moment in the history of the war, with the blitz still raging and defeat looming in Greece, but the majority were full of praise for Churchill:

Comments by men

– I think he's marvellous
– He's the best man for the job
– He's the right man in the right job
– Well I think he's a great man

– Fine man—should have been in the government years ago

– Well I think he's our only hope

– There's no finer man

– He's the only man in the country that's got any guts. He's fearless and he hates Hitler. If we got a thundering hiding tomorrow it wouldn't trouble Churchill

– Well he's a great man

– I think he's a brilliant leader

– A great man—nobody like him

Comments by women

– He's the ideal man in the ideal place

– He's good

– Marvellous

– He's a great man, Mr Churchill. He's all right!

– If he'd been in power the year before Munich, we probably wouldn't be fighting this war

– Oh, he's the right man for the job

– I think he's a fine man—the right man in the right place

– He's alright for a war. I wouldn't like him in peacetime though

– He's rather an old fogey but he is quite nice

– A splendid man—the best Prime Minister we've had, within *my* memory

Among those questioned a few expressed hostility. 'Churchill!' exclaimed one man, 'he's monkeyed about since the day he was born.' Another replied: 'I thoroughly dislike him. He is often saying how he despises Conscientious Objectors.' When asked to sum up his character in a word or two, people suggested such descriptions as 'historic', 'great', 'jolly', 'pugnacious', 'British bull-dog', 'British', 'bath-brick', 'warlike', and 'genius'. Dissenting judgements included 'a bugger', 'fat', 'dictatorial', and 'a rotter'.[31]

How representative Mass-Observations respondents were of the public in general is impossible to say. But they do suggest that most people regarded Churchill first as a truly great man,

and secondly as the right man for the job (with the strong implication that he might not be the right man in peacetime). Churchill
breathed a fighting spirit that inspired confidence, but he did
so as an intensely human being who awoke love and respect
rather than fear. Tom Harrisson was present when Churchill,
accompanied by Clementine, visited Plymouth immediately after
the bombing of the city in May 1941:

He brought a breath of real aggression and initiative into an atmosphere
of negative devastation. It was impossible even for the most objective
observer not to be moved by the sight of this great man, fierce faced, with
great tears of angry sorrow in his eyes. He was so visibly moved by the
suffering that he saw, yet so visibly determined to see that it spelt not
defeat, but victory.[32]

One fragment of evidence reminds us that Churchill also
impressed himself on the imagination of the children of wartime
Britain. In their explorations of the lore and language of schoolchildren, Iona and Peter Opie came across a song overheard in a
playground in Stockton-on-Tees:

> When the war is over Hitler will be dead,
> He hopes to go to heaven with a crown upon his head.
> But the Lord said No! You'll have to go below,
> There's only room for Churchill so cheery-cheery-oh.[33]

So long frustrated, the two great ambitions of Churchill's youth—
to be a military hero and a hero of democracy—had come
together in a blaze of glory in his sixty-sixth year.

Baldwin and Chamberlain had been public figures of Victorian
gravitas, always on their dignity in public. Bursting with animal
spirits, and always on the move, Churchill acted with a showmanship that upstaged the shy and stammering King George VI.
His most famous theatrical prop was a large Havana cigar, which
he would light and flourish with much ceremony, but seldom

smoke. His most famous gesture, the V-sign with the palm of the hand turned outwards, was an adaptation of a notoriously rude gesture. Churchill also paid great attention to his wardrobe. He had always been a bit of a dandy, his collection of hats in a variety of styles a gift to the cartoonists of the inter-war years. Now he excelled himself. In addition to his normal Westminster attire of bow tie and striped suit, he appeared at various times in the uniforms of Air Commodore, Elder Brother of Trinity House, and Colonel of Hussars. Early on in the war he gave up wearing a dinner jacket in favour of a zip-up 'siren' suit which he sometimes wore in public, an eccentricity for which he was criticized by Aneurin Bevan. Not the least of his public relations assets were his wife and daughters. He was often accompanied on his travels by Clementine, whose Aid to Russia Fund also made her prominent in her own right, and occasionally by Sarah, who was serving in the WAAF, or Mary, who was in the ATS. Randolph, who became a staff officer in the Middle East, and later parachuted into Yugoslavia with Evelyn Waugh on a special mission to Tito, was a mixed blessing. Though he was courageous, and passionate in his father's defence, his arrogant and outrageous behaviour made many enemies. In October 1939 he married Pamela Digby. In symbolic defiance of Hitler their son, Winston Spencer Churchill, was born at the height of the London blitz (10 October 1940). The marriage, however, was short-lived, and the relationship between Randolph and his father continued to be fraught. 'We have a deep animal love for one another', Churchill reflected, 'but every time we meet we have a bloody row.'[34]

Churchill's popularity was the sheet anchor of his authority as Prime Minister. In Whitehall he was a driving force the like of which had never been seen before, and the response to him was mixed. He imposed on others the restless demands, the workaholic discipline, and the frantic tempo which for decades he had imposed on himself. Within a few days, John Colville recalled, respectable civil servants were to be seen running along the corridors.[35] Churchill was also, at times, a hard taskmaster and a bully. On 27 June Clementine plucked up the courage to warn him, in writing, of the danger that his 'rough sarcastic and overbearing manner' would make him generally disliked by colleagues and subordinates.[36] After two or three hours conversation with him at the Other Club on 5 September, Keynes formed a very different impression:

I found him in absolutely perfect condition, extremely well, serene, full of normal human feelings and completely un-inflated. Perhaps this moment is the height of his power and glory, but I have never seen anyone less infected with dictatorial airs or hubris. There was not the faintest trace of the insolence which LL.G, for example, so quickly acquired.[37]

The fact is that Churchill was a creature of many moods, captivating and infuriating by turns. Brendan Bracken, his most loyal follower, said of him:

Being friendly with him is like being in love with a beautiful woman who drives you mad with her demands until you can bear it not a moment longer and fling out of the house swearing never to see her again. But next day she smiles at you and you know there's nothing you wouldn't do for her and she crooks her little finger and you come running.[38]

It took some time for Churchill to establish his authority. During the first few weeks of the new government the applause for him came from the Labour benches while the majority of Conservatives displayed their loyalty to Chamberlain. As his stature grew during the summer and autumn of 1940, Churchill achieved a personal ascendancy over all parties in the House, but when Chamberlain retired through ill health in September

1940, he prudently arranged for his own succession as leader of the Conservative party. He thereby obtained control of the majority party in the House, an essential power base if he were to weather the storms ahead. The sequel followed in December when the British embassy in Washington fell vacant with the death of Lord Lothian. Churchill despatched a reluctant Lord Halifax to Washington, replacing him as Foreign Secretary with Anthony Eden.

Churchill's authority was great but he never sought or possessed the powers of a despot. As a general rule, he was punctilious in seeking the support of the War Cabinet for major decisions in foreign, imperial, or domestic policy, and there were times when his colleagues overrode his wishes. The War Cabinet, however, soon lost control over the military conduct of the war. On becoming Prime Minister Churchill took the title of Minister of Defence, and the military secretariat of the War Cabinet and the Chiefs of Staff Committee was incorporated into an embryonic department under his personal direction. His Defence Office was headed by Major-General Hastings Ismay and his two deputies, Colonel Leslie Hollis and Colonel Ian Jacob. Working under their direction were the Joint Planning Committee and the Joint Intelligence Committee, whose task it was both to propose operations and to report on the feasibility of plans submitted to them by Churchill and the Chiefs of Staff. Ismay also served as Churchill's representative on the Chiefs of Staff Committee, which continued to meet separately. But as Minister of Defence Churchill had the right both to summon the Chiefs of Staff and to give them instructions on the conduct of the war. Churchill himself followed the progress of the war on all fronts in great detail with the aid of a portable Map Room, organized by Captain Pim. Angela Mack, a Wren serving with the British delegation, observed it at the Yalta conference: 'It had four walls, covered with the maps of the present battle fronts. In the centre was Churchill's chair, which could be swung round to view any of the walls. The maps were kept up to the minute with the progress of the campaigns, every unit marked with a coloured flag.'[39]

The new machinery for the conduct of the war owed much to Churchill's thinking and proved highly successful in preventing the rifts between 'frocks' and 'brasshats' which had occurred in the First World War. At first Churchill called frequent meetings of the Defence Committee of the War Cabinet, which consisted of Attlee, Beaverbrook, and the three service ministers, but as his power grew it was summoned less and less, and the three service ministers were relegated to administrative roles. Thereafter Churchill ran the military side of the war himself in conjunction with the Chiefs of Staff Committee. Though he often summoned the Chiefs of Staff to meet him, the Chiefs of Staff Committee met separately every morning and constituted the most important check on his authority. With his buccaneering spirit, colossal energy, and fertile imagination, he drove his professional advisers hard, and sometimes to distraction. His favourite was the First Sea Lord, Admiral Pound, whose dogged loyalty was, however, tempered by devious methods of resistance. It was much to Churchill's credit that the service chiefs he himself appointed were sturdily independent characters: Sir John Dill in succession to Ironside in May 1940, Sir Charles Portal in succession to Newall in October 1940, and Sir Andrew Cunningham in succession to Pound in September 1943. Dill clashed with Churchill once too often and was removed in December 1941, but in his place Churchill appointed Sir Alan Brooke, of whom he remarked: 'When I thump the table and push my face towards him, what does he do? Thumps the table harder and glares back at me.'[40] Though Churchill often tried to bully Brooke into submission, he never forgot the fatal consequences of Admiral Fisher's resignation in 1915, and seldom overruled the Chiefs of Staff on a strategic issue. 'Remember', he remarked to Anthony Eden in July 1941, 'that on my breast there are the medals of the Dardanelles, Antwerp, Dakar and Greece.'[41]

Within a fortnight of taking over as Prime Minister Churchill acquired 'a source of undreamed-of power; knowledge to use against the unsuspecting enemy, but also a trump card in his negotiations with his Chiefs of Staff and allies'.[42] On 22 May the code-breakers at Bletchley Park broke the main operational key of the Luftwaffe's Enigma enciphering machine. This marked the beginning of Ultra, the daily flow of transcripts of radio messages sent by the German armed forces. Though Ultra was continuously monitored and reported on by the Joint Intelligence Committee, Churchill insisted that he should have direct and independent access to the raw materials. In September 1940 the head of the Secret Intelligence Service, Sir Stewart Menzies, was instructed to send all the original transcripts in a daily box to the Prime Minister. As the volume of transcripts grew, Churchill authorized Menzies to send him a selection only, but he continued to receive a box of what he called his 'golden eggs' almost every day of the war. The wartime expansion of British intelligence services, and the high repute they acquired in Whitehall, owed much to Churchill's support.

When Italy declared war on Britain on 10 July 1940 a new theatre of operations opened up in the Middle East. The following month, at great risk to home defence, Churchill sent 154 tanks to Egypt to reinforce Wavell, the British commander-in-chief. He was now in charge of a promising war against a lesser enemy in a distant theatre. But how was Britain to defeat Germany? As yet he could not tell. In the vain hope of opening up a line of communication with Stalin he sent a prominent left-wing politician, Sir Stafford Cripps, as ambassador to Moscow. Inspired by a vision of the occupied peoples of Europe rising up against their Nazi oppressors he authorized the creation of the Special Operations Executive (SOE) to 'set Europe ablaze'.[43] To harass the enemy he ordered commando raids around the coasts of occupied Europe. Churchill also believed in the importance of strategic bombing, but his main hopes were pinned on the prospect of American intervention.

In October 1939 President Roosevelt had initiated a correspondence with Churchill and the two had exchanged a handful of messages on naval matters. Once Churchill became Prime Minister the correspondence, in which he signed himself 'Former Naval Person', assumed an altogether new significance. Churchill had long possessed a romantic faith in the common destiny of the 'English-speaking peoples': the British Empire and the United States. Perhaps because of this, there was more than a touch of wishful thinking in his view of Roosevelt and he exaggerated the extent of American sympathy for Britain. 'I can still see him at Chequers, one August day', wrote de Gaulle in his memoirs,

raising his fists towards the sky as he cried, 'So they won't come!' 'Are you in such a hurry', I said to him, 'to see your towns smashed to bits?' 'You see,' he replied, 'the bombing of Oxford, Coventry, Canterbury, will cause such a wave of indignation in the United States that they'll come into the war!'[44]

Nevertheless Churchill's view of the United States was grounded in military and strategic reality. As he repeatedly reminded Roosevelt, the defeat of Britain, and the capture or destruction of the Royal Navy, would lay the United States open to attack by

Nazi Germany. Hence the United States must come to the aid of Britain in order to defend itself.

Roosevelt, meanwhile, had been greatly impressed by Churchill during the 'phoney war', but his emissary, Sumner Welles, reported in February 1940 that he had been to see Churchill at the Admiralty and found him drunk at 5 p.m. On learning of his appointment as Prime Minister Roosevelt commented that he 'supposed Churchill was the best man England had, even if he was drunk half of his time'. With the next Presidential election due in November 1940, Roosevelt was also steering a carefully ambiguous course between isolationists demanding a policy of strict neutrality, and interventionists calling for the United States to aid the British.

Churchill's most important achievement in the summer of 1940 was to convince Roosevelt and his advisers that the British had the will to fight on and were therefore worth supporting. Nevertheless he was impatient for more American aid than he received. The 'destroyers-for-bases' deal of September 1940, which gave the United States a 99-year lease on bases in the British West Indies in return for the transfer of fifty old destroyers to the Royal Navy, was of greater military value to the United States than to Britain. In December 1940, prompted by Lothian, the British ambassador in Washington, Churchill sent Roosevelt a long, detailed, and urgent request for military supplies. He warned that unless Britain could secure the imports of food and munitions essential to sustain the war effort, 'we may fall by the way, and the time needed by the United States to complete her defensive preparations many not be forthcoming'. Roosevelt, who was on board a warship cruising in the Caribbean, read and reread the letter as he sat alone in a deckchair.[45] In a rare display of bold leadership, he proclaimed the principle of Lend-Lease, whereby the United States supplied Britain with food, weapons, and other essentials on credit for the duration of the war. Enacted by Congress in March 1941, Lend-Lease was a lifeline for the future, but the US Treasury Secretary, Henry Morgenthau, insisted that the British should pay for orders already placed by selling off British overseas investments and reducing British gold reserves to nil. Morgenthau, fumed Keynes, was treating Britain 'worse than we have ever ourselves thought it proper to treat the humblest and least responsible Balkan country'.[46]

Roosevelt's policy of aid to Britain was facilitated by vigorous pro-British propaganda in the United States. This was partly the work of the British information services but it would have lacked credibility without the support of pro-British American commentators, many of whom were based in London during the Battle of Britain and the Blitz. Within twenty-four hours of his appointment as Prime Minister an Associated Press corre- spondent rushed out a biographical profile declaring that Churchill was already a national hero, admired by the British for his 'bulldog determination'. Already his bricklaying at Chartwell—symbolizing the humane and constructive statesman in exile—featured as prominently in the story as the North-West frontier, the escape from the Boers, and Gallipoli. The following day the paper ran another laudatory profile, accompanied by a cartoon of Churchill as a bricklayer, headed: 'British Turn to Winston Churchill for Dynamic Leadership'.[47] American word- smiths were simply spellbound by his oratory. 'The timorous understatement characteristic of bourgeois decline is swept away in lofty rhetoric', wrote Dorothy Thompson. 'Into his speeches he telescopes the history of a race and makes it present-day history ... Thus he redeems the aristocratic tradition and restores aristocratic leadership.'[48] Unlike their British contemporaries,

American observers came to Churchill free of the bag and baggage of old domestic quarrels. They recognized that in the past he had made mistakes and embraced lost causes, but they were not very interested in them. They were enthralled, however, by Churchill's extrovert style of leadership, in which they saw both eccentricity and aspects of national character. 'His stout, thick-set figure', wrote Hugh Wagnon in the *Washington Post*, 'comes close to being a perfect model of the cartoonist's John Bull, except that he slouches carelessly . . . When he clamps his jaw in determination, he could pass for that other favourite sketch of British character—the bulldog.' The headline of the story summed up Churchill's life as follows: 'Called "Eccentric Dunce" in School, He Rose from Many Political Defeats to world-wide acclaim as Saviour of the Empire.'[49] By the end of 1940 an American love affair with Churchill was bursting into bloom.

Roosevelt and Churchill, however, had yet to meet as war leaders. They had encountered one another once before, at a banquet in Gray's Inn in 1918, but to Roosevelt's chagrin Churchill had forgotten the occasion. The arrival in London of Harry Hopkins in January 1941 marked the beginning of a closer relationship in which Churchill dealt informally with trusted intermediaries of the President like Hopkins himself and Averell Harriman. When he was entertaining important American visitors, Churchill was the most generous and flattering of hosts and one of the most persuasive of propagandists—but he too was susceptible to charm offensives. His first wartime meeting with the President, an event carefully stage-managed for the benefit of a global audience, took place aboard a British battleship, *The Prince of Wales*, at Placentia Bay off Newfoundland, on 9 August 1941. Churchill came away momentarily convinced that Roosevelt was about to bring the United States into the war, but within a few days he realized that he had read too much into the President's warm words. One tangible outcome of the meeting was the Atlantic Charter, a rather nebulous joint declaration of war aims. But from Churchill's point of view a more important consequence was the extension of American activity in the Battle of the Atlantic: for much of 1941 the threat posed by U-boats to Britain's Atlantic lifeline was the greatest of all his anxieties.

When Greece was invaded by Germany in March 1941, Churchill accepted the advice of Eden and Wavell and sent in British and Commonwealth troops, but in April Greece was over-run. In May Crete in turn was invaded and captured and British forces again evacuated. Meanwhile German panzer divisions under the command of Rommel had arrived in North Africa. When a British counter-offensive failed in June 1941 Churchill ran out of patience with Wavell and replaced him as C-in-C Middle East with General Claud Auchinleck. During the autumn of 1941 Churchill bombarded the Chiefs of Staff with projects for landings on the coasts of Norway, Sicily, Italy, and French North Africa. Conversely he paid little attention to the Far East, discounting the idea that Japan would dare to attack the United States or the British Empire. Even if they did attack, he believed, the defences of Singapore would be strong enough to withstand assault for at least six months. Churchill was the driving force of British grand strategy, but his intuitive intelligence, fluttering like a butterfly from one attractive prospect to another, drove Brooke to the verge of despair. 'He cannot grasp the relationship of various theatres of war to each other', he wrote in May 1943. 'He always gets carried away by the one he is examining and in prosecuting it is prepared to sacrifice most of the others.'[50] Brooke was not alone in his view. Ian Jacob, a very great admirer, wrote:

181

One is bound to question whether Churchill could be classed as a strategist at all. He was certainly not the calm, self-contained, calculating personality that is usually brought to mind by the term, nor did he weigh up carefully the resources available to us, the possible courses open to the enemy, and then, husbanding and concentrating his forces, strike at the selected spot. His mind would never be content with such theoretical ideas. He wanted constant action on as wide a scale as possible; the enemy must be made continually to 'bleed and burn', a phrase he often used.[51]

It is scarcely an exaggeration to say that between June 1940 and December 1941, Churchill carried the world on his shoulders. The burdens he bore, and the anxieties he endured, would have crushed many a lesser mortal. When Auchinleck was summoned home to explain why he had not yet taken the offensive, Ismay took him aside and briefed him about the Prime Minister. 'Churchill', he explained,

could not be judged by ordinary standards; he was different from anyone we had ever met before, or would ever meet again. As a war leader, he was head and shoulders above anyone the British or any other nation could produce. He was indispensable and completely irreplaceable . . . He was a child of nature. He venerated tradition, but ridiculed convention. When the occasion demanded, he could be the personification of dignity; when the spirit moved him, he could be a *gamin*. His courage, enthusiasm and industry were boundless, and his loyalty was absolute. No commander who engaged the enemy need ever fear that he would not be supported.[52]

Conversely, Churchill could be ruthless in his treatment of commanders he deemed lacking in offensive spirit. He warmed to the dash and charm of Alexander, and the maverick qualities of Wingate, but the self-effacing and the inarticulate found little favour. Dill he described as 'the dead hand of inanition'. Of Wavell he remarked: 'It may be my own fault, but I always feel as if in the presence of the chairman of a golf club.'[53] Of his dealings with the admirals Captain Roskill wrote: 'Churchill wielded the executioner's axe so indiscriminately, and with so little attempt to ascertain whether his intended victims really were incompetent, that the injustices perpetrated were not few.'[54] 'I wonder', mused Brooke in August 1943,

whether any historian of the future will ever be able to paint Winston in his true colours. It is a wonderful character—the most marvellous qualities and superhuman genius mixed with an astonishing lack of vision at times, and an impetuosity which if not guided must inevitably bring him into trouble again and again.[55]

When Chamberlain was Prime Minister, the business of government was conducted through formal meetings at pre-arranged times. Under Churchill, the formal business was only a small part of the story. As Bridges, the Secretary to the War Cabinet, recalled:

There were no frontiers between home and office, between work hours and the rest of the day: work went on everywhere, in his study, in the dining-room, in his bedroom. A summons would come at almost any hour of the day or night to help with some job. Minutes would be dictated, corrected, redictated. One might find oneself unexpectedly sitting in the family circle or sharing a meal while one took his orders.[56]

Within the intimacy of the inner circle, he was a man of transparent emotions and changeable moods. Another civil servant who observed him at close quarters describes how, when he took the chair at a meeting, 'that child-like face became the reflection of the man—the set bulldog look, the sulky look of a pouting child, the angry violent look of an animal at bay, the tearful look of a compassionate woman, and the sudden spontaneous smiling look of a boy'.[57]

Churchill usually began the day's work in his bedroom, where he would read through the newspapers and begin to deal with the latest boxes of official papers. Visitors would find him sitting up in bed in a dressing gown emblazoned with dragons, top-secret papers strewn over the bedclothes and a favourite cat—'Nelson', or 'Munich Mouser'—curled up at his feet. From time to time he would summon people to see him or dictate minutes for despatch to all corners of Whitehall. The more urgent, which caused great alarm to the recipients, carried a label with the instruction ACTION THIS DAY printed in red. If there were no meetings of the War Cabinet or other appointments he would sometimes stay in bed all morning. Over lunch, at which friends and family rubbed shoulders with politicians and military chiefs, Churchill would discourse on the war, or anything else that came to mind, with a bottle of champagne—he had been a customer of Pol Roger since 1908—followed by brandy. At some point in the afternoon he would undress and retire to bed for an hour's sleep, awakening like a giant refreshed for a bath and more meetings, accompanied by iced whisky and soda. Dinner would follow with more champagne and brandy.

There is, writes Warren Kimball, 'no credible testimony of Churchill's being drunk, in the falling-down slurred-words sense, while he was Prime Minister'.[58] His early training as a soldier had taught him to abhor drunkenness. Yet he was clearly dependent on alcohol, and capable on occasion of absorbing quantities that would have rendered lesser men incapable—a feat that stood him in good stead at Kremlin banquets. He seems to have drunk more heavily in the later stages of the war in order to fight off exhaustion. During the Casablanca conference of January 1943 Harry Hopkins was disturbed to find Churchill in bed enjoying a bottle of wine for breakfast. 'I asked him what he meant by that', Hopkins recorded, 'and he told me that he had a profound distaste on the one hand for skimmed milk, and no deep-rooted prejudice about wine, and that he had reconciled the conflict in favour of the latter.'[59] In February 1945, when Churchill gave a banquet in the desert in honour of King Ibn Saud of Saudi Arabia, he was told that the King could not allow smoking or drinking in his presence. Churchill replied that he was the host, and if it was the King's religion that made him say such things, 'my religion prescribed as an absolute sacred rite smoking cigars and drinking alcohol before, after, and if need be during all meals and the intervals between them'.[60]

If Churchill were spending the weekend at Chequers the guests were often invited to join him in watching a film. On learning in May 1941 that Hitler's deputy, Rudolph Hess, had landed in Scotland, he replied: 'Hess or no Hess, I'm going to watch the Marx Brothers.' Later on in the war he ordered Donald Duck to be interrupted in full flow so that he could give his guests the news that Mussolini had resigned.[61] His favourite movie, produced in Hollywood by his friend Alexander Korda, was *That Hamilton Woman*, with Laurence Olivier as Nelson and Vivien Leigh as Lady Hamilton. The battle scenes were few but Churchill was riveted by the eloquence of Olivier and the beauty of Vivien Leigh. By the time the film show was over it was nearly midnight and Churchill was ready to return to work. Struggling to keep their eyes open, his advisers would be summoned to a meeting at which key strategic or operational issues were discussed and informal decisions reached. Churchill's 'midnight follies', as they were known in Whitehall, caused much resentment among the exhausted officials who were compelled to attend them. Often Churchill would work until 3 or 4 in the morning before taking his sleeping capsules and retiring to bed.[62]

From intelligence sources Churchill was aware in the spring of 1941 that Germany was planning to invade Russia. By the time

Operation Barbarossa was launched on 22 June his own response had been carefully thought out. That same day he broadcast from Chequers declaring that Britain would send all possible aid to Russia, but everything hinged on the meaning of 'possible'. Churchill rejected Stalin's plea for British troops to be sent to fight alongside the Red Army, and likewise his demand for the opening up of a Second Front by the end of 1941. He authorized instead the supply of military equipment. The first of the Arctic convoys to northern Russia set sail from Scapa Flow on 21 August with two squadrons of Hurricane fighters. In September Beaverbrook, now Minister of Supply, accompanied Averell Harriman on an Anglo-American mission to Moscow which pledged the British and American governments to send thousands of aircraft, tanks, and other supplies to Russia. 'As a result', wrote Alanbrooke, 'we kept on supplying tanks and aeroplanes that could ill be spared and in doing so suffered the heaviest losses in shipping . . . We received in return nothing but abuse for handling the convoys inefficiently.'[63] While ensuring that the existence of Ultra was concealed, he also gave instructions for secret intelligence about German activities on the eastern front to be passed on to Stalin. In October 1941 he made the first of many attempts, which tested Alanbrooke's patience to the limit, to persuade the Chiefs of Staff to send a second expedition to Norway. No matter how many times Alanbrooke explained that lack of air cover would make the operation impractical, Churchill had only to catch sight of a map of Norway to set him off again. The most likely explanation was his anxiety to ensure that Russia remained in the war.

Churchill's dealings with the Soviet Union touched on a dilemma at the heart of his war leadership. Between the wars he had been a strong opponent of socialism and communism. But in order to defeat Hitler he was compelled to ally with forces subversive of the world in which he believed. If this were true at home, where the Coalition inaugurated a form of 'war socialism' of which Labour and the trade unions were the main beneficiaries, the contradiction between Churchill the anti-Bolshevik and Churchill the Soviet ally was even more stark. In his broadcast of 22 June Churchill refused, as he put it, 'to unsay one word' he had said against communism in the past. But as he had remarked only the day before: 'If Hitler invaded Hell, he would make at least a favourable reference to the Devil!'[64] When Stalin demanded formal British recognition of the Soviet frontiers of 1941, acquired as Churchill pointed out 'by acts of aggression in shameless collusion with Hitler', he narrowly escaped an embarassing surrender.[65]

Churchill had no advance warning from intelligence services of the Japanese attack on Pearl Harbor on 7 December 1941, the news of which was confirmed for him by the butler, Sawyers, who had heard it on the radio. Churchill was overcome with joy and relief. 'So we had won after all! . . . Once again in our long Island history we should emerge, however mauled or mutilated, safe and victorious. We should not be wiped out. Our history would not come to an end.'[66] Within a week Churchill set sail for the United States with a high-powered delegation on board the *Duke of York*. At a series of meetings in Washington, Churchill and Roosevelt established a Combined Chiefs of Staff representing both countries. On 26 December Churchill received a rapturous reception when he addressed a joint session of both Houses of Congress. 'I cannot help reflecting', he declared, 'that if my father had been American, and my Mother British, instead of the other way round, I might have got here on my own.' From Washington Churchill travelled to Ottawa where put on another brilliant performance in a speech to the Canadian Parliament. In 1940, he recalled, the French generals had told their Prime Minister: '"In three weeks England will have her neck wrung like a chicken". Some chicken!', Churchill declared to thunderous applause, 'some neck!'[67]

Though Churchill was sure of ultimate victory, the immediate prospects were grim. In the hope of deterring Japan from entering the war he had despatched the *Prince of Wales* and the *Repulse* to the Far East. On 10 December 1941 Japanese torpedo bombers sank them both. As he wrote to the Chiefs of Staff a week later, Churchill expected that Singapore would withstand attack for another six months.[68] But on 15 February the fortress and its garrison of 130,000 British and Commonwealth troops surrendered, a body blow from which the Empire in the Far East was never to recover. In January Churchill had been staggered to discover that Singapore had no fixed landward defences. 'I ought to have known', he wrote. 'My advisers ought to have known and I ought to have been told, and I ought to have asked.'[69] In another humiliation, two German battlecruisers, the *Scharnhorst* and the *Gneisenau*, escaped from the Atlantic port of Brest in a night-time passage through the Straits of Dover (16 February).

Though Churchill had won a vote of confidence in the House by a majority of 464 to 1 on 29 January, he was threatened by rumblings of discontent. 'I fear a slump in public opinion which will deprive Winston of his legend', Harold Nicolson confessed to his diary.[70] The most threatening aspect was the canvassing of proposals to lessen Churchill's authority over the Chiefs of Staff by appointing an independent Minister of Defence, or, as *The Times* suggested, a Combined General Staff with an independent chairman. Churchill put his foot down and refused, but he knew that he could not survive many more defeats. 'I am like a bomber pilot', he remarked gloomily. 'I go out night after night and I know that one night I will not return.'[71] Another anxiety was the emergence of a rival in the person of Sir Stafford Cripps, who was hailed by much of the press on his return from Moscow in January 1942 as a potential saviour of the situation. If Cripps had been a more unscrupulous politician he could have made Churchill's life extremely difficult. He returned to Britain with a powerful card to play: the enormous popularity in Britain of the Soviet Union at a time when the Red Army was engaged in a titanic struggle on the eastern front which featured in the headlines every day. In his diplomatic despatches from Moscow Cripps had persistently criticized the British government for failing, as he alleged, to establish a genuine alliance with the Soviet Union in which military and political objectives were jointly decided. It was naive of Cripps to suppose that such an alliance with Stalinist Russia would ever be possible, but his belief that it could be was politically potent. The British public, of course, knew nothing of Cripps's differences with the government, but there was nothing to prevent him from airing them if he wished. There was a vacancy in British politics for a politician ready and able to capitalize on the popularity of Russia, and Cripps had the additional advantage of freedom from party ties. Having been expelled from the Labour Party in 1939 for advocating a Popular Front, he posed no party political risk to the Conservatives, who were inclined to flatter him at Labour's expense. Churchill, however, outmanoeuvered his rival. When Cripps refused the Ministry of Supply, Churchill raised the stakes by offering him a place in the War Cabinet with the posts of Lord Privy Seal and leader of the House. Cripps accepted, and whatever his differences with Churchill gave loyal support to his premiership during the period in which he was most vulnerable to attack.

The role of pro-Soviet demagogue devolved on Beaverbrook, who resigned from the government and allied himself with the Communist Party in the campaign for a Second Front. Beaverbrook, however, was a rogue, unacceptable to most Conservatives and barely distinguishable, through Labour eyes, from Beelzebub. On the Left Churchill's military and strategic judgement were under attack from Aneurin Bevan, a brilliant speaker whose barbed insults got under his skin, and the journalist Frank Owen, who published a series of sensational attacks in the pages of *Tribune* under the pseudonym of 'Thomas Rainsborough'. Churchill was accused of a string of strategic mistakes and an out-of-date mentality:

Churchill, the Modern War Lord, has never yet grasped the elementary fact that an army is just as good (or bad) as the social foundation on which it rests. The shrilling bugles go to his head! He hears the deep drums—and he is drunk! He sees the proud fluttering flags—and he could weep! He often does! About the solid industrial base of modern armies and the inter-relation of those economic forces which comprise it the British War Premier and Minister of Defence knows less than his Minister of Information.

In reply to these diatribes a 'lowly member of the Labour Party' replied:

Mr Churchill has remained:

(1) Because at the greatest crisis this country has ever faced, he had the power to draw us together and hold us fast until we were comparatively safe;

(2) Because he has had the gift of keeping together those of widely differing political views, in the country, the Government and the War Cabinet.

(3) Because in this gargantuan task he has done his utmost (can one man do more?) to weld the peoples of the anti-Axis nations together.

(4) Because he has gained, and held, the affection and respect of a big majority of those who placed him in power—in spite of the mistakes he, and perhaps anybody, has, or would have, made.[72]

The inference was plain enough: whatever mistakes Churchill had made, no one could have done it better.

* * *

With the Japanese in possession of Malaya and Singapore, and advancing into Burma, the defence of India was now an urgent strategic priority. Up to this point Churchill had successfully resisted demands for constitutional change in India, but he was now under strong pressure from Roosevelt and Labour to enlist the cooperation of Congress and the other Indian political parties by introducing a measure of self-government. The War Cabinet despatched Cripps to India on a mission to negotiate a constitutional settlement, but his terms of reference prevented him from offering immediate independence and as Churchill may well have anticipated the mission failed. When the Congress party launched a campaign of civil disobedience in August, the War Cabinet ordered the arrest and internment of Gandhi and thousands of Congress party members. When he appointed Wavell as Viceroy in 1943, it was with the intention of putting the constitutional issue on hold for the rest of the war. Churchill persisted in the illusion that Congress was unrepresentative of the Indian masses, whose welfare it was the mission of the British to protect. When Wavell proposed to renew constitutional discussions with Congress, Churchill imposed a veto, but such concern as he had for the welfare of the masses was vitiated by a streak of contempt evident in some of his more bad-tempered asides.

191

'The P.M.', noted Colville in February 1945, 'said the Hindus were a foul race "protected by their mere pullulation from the doom that is their due" and he wished Bert Harris could send some of his surplus bombers to destroy them.'[73] Churchill hoped that after the war Britain would remain in India as an arbiter holding the balance between Hindus, Muslims, and the Princely States.[74]

In April 1942 Roosevelt sent Marshall and Hopkins to London to persuade the British to agree to a cross-Channel invasion that same year, or possibly in 1943. Churchill appeared to be enthusiastic and full agreement was reached in principle. The British Chiefs of Staff, however, believed that an invasion in 1942 would be premature and disastrous. Gradually, Brooke convinced Churchill that the route to victory lay through Italy via North Africa. Visiting Washington in June, Churchill persuaded Roosevelt to agree to an alternative: Operation Torch, an Anglo-American landing in North Africa.

Churchill was at the White House when the news arrived of another British disaster: the surrender of Tobruk (20 June). On 2 July he defeated a motion of censure in the House by 476 votes to 25, the monthly opinion polls continued to register a phenomenally high approval rating of around 80 per cent, and the national press continued to put on a display of loyalty. But Churchill could read the writing on the wall: Cripps was busy with proposals for the overhaul of the machinery of defence policy and preparing the ground for resignation if more setbacks occurred. In August Churchill flew out to Egypt with Brooke to reorganize the Middle East command. Auchinleck was replaced by Alexander and Montgomery put in command of the Eighth Army. 'The Prime Minister', Brendan Bracken told Churchill's doctor, 'must win his battle in the desert or get out.'[75] From Cairo

Churchill flew on to Moscow for his first meeting with Stalin, who was urgently demanding the opening up of a second front in Europe. Explaining to Stalin that there would be no cross-Channel invasion in 1942, Churchill drew on all his powers of persuasion to impress on him the significance of Anglo-American plans for the strategic bombing of Germany and the invasion of French North Africa. Drawing a sketch of a crocodile, he explained to Stalin that it was Anglo-American strategy 'to attack the soft belly of the crocodile as we attacked the hard snout'.[76] To Churchill's relief, Stalin immediately grasped the strategic importance of 'Torch' and the visit to Moscow ended cordially with a Kremlin banquet lasting seven hours.

Montgomery's decisive victory at El Alamein, followed by the success of the landings in North Africa, transformed both the military prospects and Churchill's own fortunes He ordered the church bells to be rung for the first time since 1940 (15 November 1942), and pugnaciously declared: 'I have not become the King's First Minister in order to preside over the liquidation of the British Empire.'[77] This was almost certainly a reply to American demands for the liquidation of the British Empire which had recently been expressed by Wendell Willkie and others.[78]

Churchill was still not certain how the war would be won. Portal, the Chief of the Air Staff, and Sir Arthur Harris, the Commander-in-Chief of Bomber Command from February 1942, believed that Germany could be defeated by the area bombing of German towns and cities. They were supported by Churchill's scientific adviser, Professor Lindemann, who submitted a paper in March 1942 arguing that bombing would destroy Germany's power of resistance by making one-third of her population homeless. Churchill never wholly accepted this theory. Generally speaking he was a strong supporter of the strategic bombing offensive, and the vast production programme it entailed, but he saw it as an essential precondition for the invasion of the Continent, not as an alternative. 'Even if all the towns of Germany were rendered largely uninhabitable', he wrote to Portal in October 1941, 'it does not follow that the military control would be weakened or even that war industry could not be carried on.'[79]

The British government consistently claimed that the RAF was only bombing military and industrial targets, but reports of the scale of the destruction prompted a dissenting minority to accuse the government of deliberately slaughtering civilians. The bishop of Chichester, George Bell, denounced area bombing as morally wrong in a landmark speech in the House of Lords (4 February 1944) and the Labour MP Richard Stokes repeatedly attacked it in the House of Commons. Churchill himself experienced occasional qualms of conscience. In June 1943 he was watching film of bombing raids on German towns when he suddenly exclaimed: 'Are we beasts? Are we taking this too far?' But the overwhelming desire of most people to beat the Germans as soon as possible, and the smokescreen of disinformation about the nature of the campaign, ensured strong and widespread support for bombing. The Archbishop of Canterbury, William Temple, and the bishops of the Church of England gave the policy their blessing.[80] In spite of his conscience Churchill was always ready to propose ruthless methods where, in his judgement, military necessity required them. Shortly after D-Day, when the Germans launched their V1 or flying bomb attacks on London, he suggested that Britain should retaliate by publishing a list of '100 of the smaller towns in Germany, where the defences were likely to be weak, and announce our intention of destroying them one by one by bombing attack'.[81] His thoughts turned also to the possibility of chemical warfare. On 6 July he demanded from the Chiefs of Staff 'a cold-blooded calculation' of the effectiveness of poison gas, to be used only if it could be shown '(a) that it was life or death for us, or (b) that it would shorten the war by a year'. Churchill argued that since most people recovered from such attacks, they caused less suffering than conventional high explosives. 'It would be absurd to consider morality on this topic', he wrote,

when everybody used it in the last war without a word of complaint from moralists or the Church. On the other hand, in the last war the bombing of open cities was regarded as forbidden. Now everybody does it as a matter of course. It is simply a question of fashion changing as she does between long and short skirts for women.

The Chiefs of Staff responded with a long report arguing that gas would be ineffective. Churchill reluctantly acquiesced.[82]

In February 1945 the RAF and the American Army Air Force launched a series of devastating raids on the city of Dresden, the 'Florence of the Elbe', celebrated in peacetime for its Baroque architecture and artistic treasures. The historic centre of the city was destroyed in a horrific firestorm which claimed the lives of at least 35,000 people (13–14 February 1945). The bombing of Dresden was partly the consequence of an intervention by Churchill. On 25 January 1945 the British Joint Intelligence Committee revived an earlier plan for 'Operation Thunderclap', a devastating raid on Berlin originally intended to complete the destruction of German morale in the final stages of the war. This time, however, the rationale was different. The main objective was to assist the Soviet offensive on the eastern front by wreaking havoc behind the German lines. The focus shifted away from Berlin and 'Bomber' Harris, the Commander in Chief of Bomber

Command, proposed that Chemnitz, Leipzig, and Dresden, all of which were key points in the German transport system, should be added as potential targets. The proposal was enthusiastically received at Supreme Allied Headquarters Europe (SHAEF) and endorsed by the Commander of the United States Air Force, Carl Spaatz. Portal, the Chief of the Air Staff, and Sinclair, the Secretary for Air, would have preferred to concentrate on oil targets, but when they showed signs of hesitation Churchill settled the matter with a forceful demand for the implementation of the revised 'Thunderclap'. He was about to set off for the conference at Yalta, where he would face difficult discussions with Stalin over the future of Poland. 'Thunderclap', we can assume, was welcome to Churchill as a means of strengthening his hand at the negotiating table.[83]

The Dresden raid marked the point at which doubts began to surface in Britain and the United States over the military value, and hence the moral justification, of area bombing. The Nazi propaganda machine had seized the opportunity of presenting it as an allied atrocity: a barbaric assault on a city of no military significance for the sole purpose of terrorizing the civilian population and destroying its cultural treasures. (Dresden was in fact an important centre of war industry and a key junction in the German railway system.) The number of those killed was inflated to 200,000 or more.[84] To make matters worse, a correspondent at SHAEF had reported that the bombing of Dresden was the outcome of an allied decision to embark on the 'deliberate terror bombing of German population centres', and the matter had been raised in the House of Commons by the MP Richard Stokes.[85] On 28 March Churchill himself joined the critics in a memorandum addressed to Ismay. 'It seems to me', he wrote, 'that the moment has come when the question of bombing German cities simply for the sake of increasing the terror, though under other pretexts, should be revised. Otherwise we shall come into control of an utterly ruined land . . . The destruction of Dresden remains a serious query against the conduct of Allied bombing.'[86] Harris was outraged. The Prime Minister seemed to be stigmatizing a policy for which he had been personally responsible, and also perhaps trying to shift the blame. A terrific row ensued in which Harris and Churchill 'resembled lone rhinceroses rampaging around neighbouring parts of Whitehall'.[87] In the end Churchill agreed to withdraw the minute and substitute a milder version, which also made no mention of Dresden.

The reasons for Churchill's spectacular U-turn over Dresden are a matter for speculation: various interpretations are possible. In January 1945 allied counsels were dominated by fears of a resurgent German war effort which might prolong the war into 1946. The priority was to strike hard against the Third Reich. By the end of March, the date of Churchill's controversial minute, the collapse of Germany was inevitable and there no longer seemed to be any justification for bombing it flat. Churchill's anxieties were now focused on Soviet intentions and Stalin's failure to carry out the terms of the Yalta agreement.[88] Perhaps he already foresaw that Britain and the United States might one day need the goodwill and support of the German people. Churchill tried to mend his fences with Harris, and obtained a baronetcy for him after his return to power in 1951, but his victory broadcast of May 1945 was notable for its omission of any direct reference to Bomber Command, and the six volumes of his war memoirs offered only the most oblique and inadequate account of the strategic bombing offensive. The mass killing of German civilians from the air was an embarassing subject during the Cold War, and perhaps a topic that weighed on Churchill's conscience.

Churchill also had very little to say in his war memoirs about the Holocaust. Presumably this was because he was writing a predominantly military history, since he had in fact been deeply concerned about the fate of the Jews. By the autumn of 1941 he was aware from intelligence reports of Nazi atrocities against the Jews on the eastern front. He spoke out against Nazi war crimes and called for the prosecution of the guilty after the war. In a public letter to the Archbishop of Canterbury (29 October 1942) he declared:

The systematic cruelties to which the Jewish people—men, women and children—have been exposed under the Nazi regime are amongst the most terrible events of history. Free men and women denounce these vile crimes, and when this world struggle ends with the enthronement of human rights, racial persecution will be ended.[89]

There were many other proofs of Churchill's pro-Jewish sympathies. During the first eighteen months of the war he was strongly in favour of arming the Jews, a policy which eventually led to the creation of a Jewish Brigade. In July 1944, when Dr Weizmann appealed to him to prevent the deportation of Jews from Hungary by bombing the death camps at Auschwitz and the railway lines leading to them, Churchill welcomed the plan and instructed Eden to 'get anything out of the Air Force you can'. But he failed to pursue the matter and after much procrastination by officials, the project was cancelled on grounds that the Hungarian government had halted the deportations. Deportations from other parts of Europe continued.[90]

Churchill's sympathy for Zionism was much in evidence but sorely tested. Prior to the Second World War he had consistently opposed the partition of Palestine and the creation of a separate Jewish state, but under the influence of Leo Amery, the Secretary for India, he announced a change of mind in July 1943.

Overriding the opposition of Eden and the Foreign Office, he obtained the Cabinet's agreement in January 1944 to a scheme of partition to be imposed, in imperial fashion, on Jew and Arab alike.[91] It was never to see the light of day. On 6 November 1944 Churchill's friend Lord Moyne, the Minister Resident in the Middle East, was murdered in Cairo by Jewish terrorists belonging to the Stern Gang. Incandescent with grief and rage, Churchill denounced them in the House of Commons:

If our dreams of Zionism are to end in the smoke of assassins' pistols and our labours for its future to produce only a new set of gangsters worthy of Nazi Germany, many like myself will have to reconsider the position we have maintained so consistently in the past.

Churchill abandoned the partition plan and began to talk about handing over the 'painful and thankless task' of governing Palestine to the United States.[92]

Churchill and Roosevelt met on nine different occasions and spent about 120 days in one another's company. During the second half of 1942 Churchill was successful in persuading Roosevelt to pursue a Mediterranean strategy in preference to the alternative of an early cross-Channel invasion favoured by the American Chiefs of Staff. At the Casablanca conference in January 1943 Churchill, Roosevelt, and their advisers agreed that once the Germans were defeated in Tunisia, the next step should be the invasion of Sicily: the cross-Channel assault was postponed to 1944. The President and the Prime Minister also proclaimed that there would be no bargaining or negotiation with Germany or Japan: Britain and the United States would continue the war until they had brought about the 'unconditional surrender' of both enemy nations.

Churchill's brain was teeming with ideas for seizing the initiative in the Mediterranean. From Casablanca he flew to Cairo, where he decided to send a British mission to Tito, the leader of the Communist resistance in Yugoslavia. From Cairo he flew to Adana in Turkey for a conference with the Turkish President, Ismet Inonu, who resisted all attempts to persuade him that Turkey should enter the war on the allied side. He was more successful, after the victorious conclusion of the Tunisian campaign in May 1943, in overcoming General Eisenhower's reluctance to invade Sicily. Accompanied by the Chiefs of Staff and a large retinue he crossed the Atlantic on the *Queen Mary* for a series of meetings, code-named TRIDENT, with Roosevelt and his advisers. Here Alanbrooke and Churchill managed to persuade the Americans to confirm the arrangements for 'Operation Husky', a daring amphibious operation launched on 10 July. By the end of the month Sicily had been conquered and Mussolini overthrown.

The Anglo-American alliance, it seemed to Churchill, had become so close and harmonious that destiny was at work, and history moving in the direction of even greater unity. In May 1943 he was the host at a British Embassy lunch attended by a number of top American officials. Discoursing on the post-war settlement Churchill declared that there could be little hope for the world without the 'fraternal association' of Britain and the United States:

I should like the citizens of each, without losing their present nationality, to be able to come and settle and trade with freedom and equal rights in the territories of the other. There might be a common passport, or a special form of passport or visa. There might even be some form of common citizenship, under which citizens of the United States and the British Commonwealth might enjoy voting privileges after residential qualification and be eligible for public office in the territories of the other . . .

Churchill concluded by proposing the continuation of military cooperation after the war, and the extended use by the USA of

British islands in the Pacific as military bases. Having tried out these ideas privately, in May 1943, he gave public expression to them in a speech at Harvard on 6 September in which he spoke of 'ties of blood and history':

Law, language and literature—these are considerable factors. Common conceptions of what is right and decent, a marked regard for fair play, especially to the weak and the poor, a stern sentiment of impartial justice, and above all the love of personal freedom ... these are the common conceptions on both sides of the ocean among the English-speaking peoples.[93]

By the time Churchill spoke Anglo-American tensions were beginning to revive. When the President and the Prime Minister met again at Quebec in August 1943, Churchill's desire to reinforce the Italian campaign caused sharp differences, fuelling American suspicions that he wished to avoid a cross-Channel invasion altogether. Roosevelt, meanwhile insisted on the appointment of an American as Supreme Commander of the forthcoming cross-Channel invasion. Churchill, who had already promised the job to Alanbrooke on three separate occasions, felt obliged to agree because the majority of the troops involved would be American. 'Not for one moment', Alanbrooke recalled, 'did he realize what this meant to me. He offered no sympathy, no regrets at having had to change his mind, and dealt with the matter as if it were of minor importance!'[94]

When the 'Big Three' met at the Teheran conference (27 November to 2 December 1943), Roosevelt made it plain that he intended to deal independently with the Soviet Union and refused to consult with Churchill before meeting Stalin. He also joined Stalin in rejecting Churchill's Mediterranean schemes, which included the seizure of Rhodes, the opening up of supply lines to Tito and the partisans and the persistent pipe dream of

Turkish entry into the war. 'Churchill was gravely disturbed by this development', wrote Ian Jacob. 'It went clean against his concept of the English-speaking peoples as a combined force for good in the future world.'[95] 'When I was at Teheran', Churchill himself remarked, 'I realized for the first time what a very *small* country this is. On one hand the big Russian bear with its paws outstretched—on the other the great American Elephant—& between them the poor little English donkey—who is the only one that knows the right way home.'[96]

Henceforth Britain was the junior partner in the Anglo-American alliance, and Churchill a subordinate whose advice was frequently overridden. Churchill has been criticized for his 'appeasement' of the United States but according to Brooke, he

hated having to give up the position of dominant partner which we had held at the start. As a result he became inclined at times to put up strategic proposals which he knew were unsound merely to spite the Americans . . . There lay in the back of his mind the desire to form a purely British theatre where the laurels would be all ours.[97]

Nevertheless Churchill managed to contain his frustration and stuck to the principle that no dispute with the United States must ever be pushed to the point where it would imperil the alliance: one of his greatest strengths as a war leader was his ability to focus on the main priorities to the exclusion of all else. In January 1944 he established a committee, over which he presided with his customary energy and vigilance, to finalize the technical preparations for 'Overlord', but his doubts and fears about the operation persisted almost to the last minute.

The most vexatious of Churchill's allies was de Gaulle. Churchill admired his haughty demeanour and prickly national-ism whenever disputes arose between the British and the Free French. But the differences between Churchill and de Gaulle were serious. It was British and American policy to detach elements of Vichy France and win them over to the allied side, but they would have to be rewarded with some degree of recognition of their status in a liberated France. De Gaulle, however, would tolerate no rivals for the leadership. Given the fact that he was almost wholly dependent on British support, Churchill found his pretensions extremely tiresome. Since Roosevelt harboured an almost paranoid hostility to de Gaulle, tensions mounted after the United States entered the war. After the allied invasion of North Africa in November 1942, de Gaulle successfully resisted pressure from Roosevelt and Churchill to subordinate him to General Giraud. Compelled to choose between Roosevelt and de Gaulle, Churchill sided with Roosevelt and proposed in May 1943 to break with de Gaulle altogether, a disastrous course from which he was dissuaded by Eden and the Cabinet. Subsequently de Gaulle outmanoeuvered Giraud and established himself, in the months after D-Day, as the unchallenged leader of the French provisional government, which finally received the official recognition of Britain and the United States in October 1944. On 11 November, amidst the cheers of half a million people, Churchill and de Gaulle walked in a triumphant procession down the Champs Elysées. To some extent the two possessed a common goal, the restoration of France as a European power. But in March 1945 Churchill vetoed a proposal by Eden for the sharing of nuclear secrets with the French.[98]

So great was Churchill's desire to be at the scene of the action that he scarcely stopped travelling. With the formation of the 'Grand Alliance' he became a globetrotter undertaking long and hazardous journeys as though they were a matter of routine. In November 1943 Captain Pim, who was in charge of the Prime Minister's map room, calculated that since the outbreak of war he had travelled 110,000 miles by ship or plane. For a man in his late sixties his energy and stamina were astonishing, but the gruelling schedule and constant burden of responsibility took their toll. During his first visit to Washington, in December 1941, he suffered a minor heart attack. At Tunis, in December 1943, he collapsed with a severe bout of pneumonia which put him out of action for nearly a month. Though he rallied and returned to work he was a leader on the brink of exhaustion for the rest of the war.

Only the last-minute intervention of King George VI prevented Churchill from observing the first wave of the D-Day landings on 6 June from on board a cruiser. A few days later, accompanied by Brooke and Smuts, and enormously relieved by the successful establishment of a beachhead in Normandy, he crossed the Channel in high spirits to visit Montgomery's headquarters. As the campaign in north-west Europe unfolded, however, and American forces began to predominate over those of Great Britain, Churchill became more and more of a spectator. After the capture of Rome on 4 June, both he and the British Chiefs of Staff were eager to press on with the Italian campaign, and he was captivated by the idea of a rapid advance on Vienna. Firmly rebuffed by Eisenhower and Roosevelt, he was incensed when four French and three American divisions were diverted from Italy for landings in the Riviera (Operation Anvil) in August 1944. Churchill also blamed the Americans for the frustration of his strategic ambitions in the Far East, where British and Commonwealth forces were tied up in Burma at the expense of operations to recapture Singapore. 'Thus two-thirds of our forces are being mis-employed for American convenience', Churchill wrote to his wife in August 1944.[99]

In September, after a therapeutic visit to Alexander's army in Italy, Churchill crossed the Atlantic for another meeting with Roosevelt at Quebec, the 'Octagon' conference of 13–16 September 1944. There he was presented by the US Treasury Secretary, Henry Morgenthau, with a plan for the de-industrialization or 'pastoralization' of Germany. Churchill's immediate response was a 'verbal lashing' in which he denounced the idea as 'unChristian', but he changed his mind the following day when Cherwell persuaded him that it would benefit British exports after the war. Churchill then composed a draft of the plan which he and Roosevelt both signed, but he soon changed his mind again—realizing, perhaps, that the destruction of German industry would make it easier for the Soviet Union to dominate Europe.[100] He was much relieved when the plan was rejected by officials on both sides of the Atlantic.

It is easy to exaggerate the consistency of Churchill's views about Soviet expansionism. In the case of Yugoslavia it was his decision to support the Communist partisans, led by Tito, at the expense of the right-wing Chetniks, led by Mihailovic. When Fitzroy Maclean, the head of the British mission to Tito, warned Churchill in December 1943 that the outcome would be a Communist Yugoslavia, Churchill asked him whether he intended to make Yugoslavia his home after the war. When Maclean replied that he did not Churchill said: 'Neither do I. And, that being so, the less you and I worry about the form of government they set up, the better.'[101]

He oscillated between phases of deep foreboding about Soviet intentions, and moments of optimism when he believed that he could establish a good working relationship with Stalin. At the heart of his dilemma lay the problems of a nation which suffered a more tragic fate than any other in the Second World War: Poland. The exiled Polish government in London, led from July 1943 by Stanislas Mikolajczyk, was deeply anti-Soviet and determined to recover the territories occupied by the Soviet Union in 1939. Stalin, who reciprocated their hostility to the full, had broken off diplomatic relations with the London Poles after the Katyn Forest affair. They nevertheless expected the British, who had gone to war in 1939 in defence of the independence of Poland, to support them.

The British, however, could not afford to alienate a major ally for the sake of a minor one. At the Teheran conference Churchill had told Stalin that the Poles would be made to accept a loss of territory to the Soviet Union in the east, with the Curzon Line as the new frontier, in return for which they would receive compensation in the form of German territory in the west. In January 1944, as the Red Army fought its way into Poland, Stalin set up the Lublin Committee, a body of Soviet puppets, to administer the 'liberated' territories. It was clear that he would be in a position to impose whatever settlement he wished on Poland. Churchill therefore urged Mikolajczyk to accept the revised frontiers and enter into discussions with the Lublin Committee, but the London Poles had other ideas. They were planning an uprising by the Polish underground army to seize control of Warsaw in advance of the entry of Soviet troops. By the end of July Soviet troops were on the outskirts of Warsaw and the rising began on 1 August. Over the next three months the Polish Home Army fought a desperate battle in which they were brutally and remorselessly destroyed while Soviet troops failed to intervene. Stalin condemned them as criminal adventurers and refused to drop arms supplies by air. He also refused American aircraft permission to make use of airfields in the Soviet Union for the same purpose.

Churchill and the War Cabinet were alarmed by Stalin's attitude, and distressed by the fate of the rising, but powerless to intervene militarily. Churchill contemplated the drastic step of cutting off of the arctic convoys to Russia, but decided not to risk a breach with Stalin. 'Terrible and humbling submissions must at times be made to the general aim', he wrote in his war memoirs.[102] Such was the power and prestige of Britain's Soviet ally that few in Britain protested against Stalin's behaviour, and Churchill found himself once more in curious complicity with the Left. The British intelligentsia, observed George Orwell, 'cannot raise between them one single voice to question what they believe to be Russian policy, no matter what turn it takes . . . Their attitude towards Russian foreign policy is not "Is this policy right or wrong?" but "This is Russian policy: how can we make it appear right?"'[103]

Churchill soon reverted to the idea of a settlement with Stalin. On his second visit to Moscow in October 1944 he wrote out on a single sheet of paper a proposal for the division of the Balkan countries into spheres of influence expressed in percentages. Rumania, for example, was to be 90 per cent in the Russian sphere and 10 per cent in the British; Greece 90 per cent British and 10 per cent Russian. Stalin read the paper, put a large tick on it, and handed it back. For Churchill the most important feature of the agreement was the promise that Greece would be saved from Communism. 'I have had very nice talks with the Old Bear [Stalin]', Churchill wrote to his wife. 'I like him the more I see of him. *Now* they respect us here & I am sure they wish to work with us.'[104]

In December 1944, Churchill's optimism about Stalin was confirmed by events in Greece. When German forces withdrew from the country in October 1944 Churchill sent in a British occupying force under General Ronald Scobie with orders to support the provisional government of Papandreou. Greece, however, was on the brink of a civil war between monarchist forces loyal to the exiled King George II, and the communist controlled EAM ('National Liberation Front') and its guerilla wing ELAS ('People's National Army of Liberation'). Both monarchists and communists were represented in the Papandreou government, but each side was manoeuvring against the other. Convinced that a communist-led government was imminent, the British authorities ordered ELAS to disband. On 3 December fighting broke out between ELAS and the police in Athens and ELAS retaliated by seizing control of the city.

In the knowledge that he had Stalin's permission to act, Churchill gave full rein to his anti-communist convictions. At 4.50 a.m. on 5 December he despatched a telegram to General Scobie instructing him to suppress EAM–ELAS. 'It would be well of course if your authority were reinforced by the authority of some Greek government', Churchill wrote. 'Do not however hesitate to act as if you were in a conquered city where a local rebellion is in progress ... We have to hold and dominate Athens. It would be a great thing for you to succeed in this without bloodshed if possible, but also with bloodshed if necessary.'[105] To Churchill's embarassment, the telegram leaked and publication in the American press produced a wave of protest, in which the State Department joined, against the machinations of British imperialism.

Fighting between British troops and ELAS was still in progress when Churchill suddenly decided, on Christmas Eve, to fly with Eden to Athens to arrange a settlement. On Boxing Day he presided at a conference of all the Greek parties, including delegates from ELAS, which eventually resulted in the appointment of Archbishop Damaskinos as Regent and the conclusion of a ceasefire and a peace agreement that rapidly collapsed.

Churchill believed that he had saved Greece from a Communist take-over, but 'the communists' motive in launching the December insurgency still remain unclear'.[106]

Churchill's intervention provoked a harsh rebuke from his old adversary H. G. Wells:

His ideology, picked up in the garrison life of India, on the reefs of South Africa, the maternal home and the conversation of wealthy Conservative households, is a pitiful jumble of incoherent nonsense. A boy scout is better equipped. He has served his purpose and it is high time he retired upon his laurels before we forget the debt we owe him. His last associations with the various European Royalties who share his belief in the invincible snobbishness of mankind and are now sneaking back to claim the credit and express their condescending approval of the underground resistance movements that have sustained human freedom through its days of supreme danger, are his final farewell to human confidence.[107]

Churchill was sharply criticized by the *Guardian*, and much to his indignation by *The Times*. Barrington Ward, the editor, and his deputy E. H. Carr, had once been appeasers of Nazi Germany. During the war they had become appeasers of the Soviet Union and enthusiasts for the Left both at home and abroad. 'There is no ground for pride or satisfaction', wrote Carr in one of his leaders, 'in the knowledge that British troops have been engaged in house-to-house fighting in a working-class suburb of Athens.' There were cheers from the Tory benches when Churchill rounded on *The Times* in the House of Commons.[108] Outrage over Greece was expressed mainly by the intellectual Left. Churchill had the support of his Labour colleagues, notably Ernest Bevin, and the Labour Party, whose annual conference took place during the crisis, proved to be remarkably manageable.

Churchill was deeply impressed by the fact that Stalin had carried out his promise and refrained from intervention. When the 'Big Three' assembled for a conference at Yalta conference in the Crimea (4–11 February 1945) the most awkward problem on the agenda was the future of Poland. With the Red Army in occupation of the country, and a Provisional Polish 'Government of National Unity' established under Soviet control, Stalin was clearly in a position to determine the realities on the ground. It was agreed that Poland was to lose territory to the Soviet Union in the east, where the Curzon Line would be the new frontier, while obtaining territory in the west from Germany. Stalin promised to allow free elections in Poland and Churchill, encouraged by his behaviour over Greece, tried his best to believe him. 'Poor Neville believed he could trust Hitler', Churchill told his ministers. 'He was wrong. But I don't think I'm wrong about Stalin.'[109]

When the House of Commons debated the Yalta agreement, on 28 February, Churchill declared: 'I know of no Government which stands to its obligation, even to its own despite, more solidly than the Russian Soviet Government.'[110] But he was faced with an ominous development. Throughout the war a small band of right-wing Conservative MPs had remained faithful to appeasement and the memory of Neville Chamberlain. They had endured as best they could the triumph of the Churchillian regime and the taunts of those who condemned the appeasers as 'guilty men'. Yalta gave them an opportunity of turning the tables. 'The conscience of the gentlemen of England and of the Conservative Party', wrote Chips Channon, 'has been stricken by our failure to support our pledged word to Poland.'[111] Alec Dunglass, who had been Chamberlain's Parliamentary Private Secretary at the time of Munich, and was later to be Prime Minister as Sir Alec Douglas Home, emerged from obscurity to speak and vote against Yalta. In the division on 1 March, twenty-five Conservative MPs voted against the government.

As in the debate over Greece, Churchill's speech on Yalta demonstrated that he still possessed the power to dominate the House of Commons, but the critics had found a point on which he was vulnerable. The arguments on which he relied bore an uncanny resemblance to the arguments of Chamberlain and his allies in support of the Munich agreement. 'Winston is as amused as I am', wrote Harold Nicolson, 'that the warmongers of the Munich period have now become appeasers, while the appeasers have become the warmongers.'[112]

In Poland, Stalin's agents and puppets were busy destroying all potential opposition. As reports began to arrive of the arrest or liquidation of non-Communists Churchill became alarmed and appealed to Roosevelt for a joint Anglo-American protest. Fears of Soviet ambitions also led him to plead with Roosevelt and Eisenhower to give priority to an advance on Berlin with the aim of capturing it before the Russians could get there. 'I deem it highly important', he wrote to Eisenhower, 'that we should shake hands with the Russians as far to the East as possible.'[113] But Eisenhower refused to alter his plans, and Roosevelt was a dying man whose officials maintained his policy of cooperation with the Soviet Union. When Roosevelt died at Warm Springs (12 April 1945) Churchill decided not to attend the funeral—a sign perhaps of some coolness towards an ally with whom he had become disenchanted. Eisenhower's armies halted on the Elbe, leaving the Red Army to capture Berlin and Prague.

In August 1941 Churchill had authorized a top-secret programme of research, code-named 'Tube Alloys', into the production of a British atom bomb. Meanwhile parallel research was in progress in the United States. In June 1942 Churchill and Roosevelt reached an unwritten agreement to make nuclear research a joint enterprise with free exchange of information and the sharing of results. Disputes then arose when the Americans cut off the supply of information, but these were resolved by Churchill and Roosevelt at Quebec in the secret agreement of 19 August 1943. The free exchange of scientific data was resumed and it was agreed that no information should be given to any other power. With his usual concentration on the military issues at the expense of post-war questions, Churchill formally disclaimed all British interest in the industrial and commercial applications of the project. It was also agreed that neither Britain nor the United States would use the bomb without obtaining the other's approval.[114] The agreement was subsequently overridden when Congress (which had never been informed of it) passed the McMahon Act of 1946 forbidding the sharing of nuclear secrets with any other power.

Churchill's consent to the use of nuclear weapons against Japan was sought and received (4 July 1945) before the bombing of Hiroshima (6 August) and Nagasaki (9 August). Though the bombs were dropped after he left office, and the decision to use them was ultimately Truman's, Churchill was conscious of his own responsibility. He expected, he told Mackenzie King in May 1946,

that he would have to account to God as he had to his own conscience for the decision made which involved killing women and children and in such numbers . . . War might go on for another year or so with cities destroyed and numbers so much greater than could possibly be foreseen and with a breaking down of civilisation bit by bit. He had had to decide what in the end would be the best for mankind and felt that he, regardless of what the consequences might be, had done what was right.

Churchill also confided his belief that 'this was a universe governed by moral laws of justice and right'.[115]

Owing to his intense concentration on the conduct of the war, and frequent absences from Britain, Churchill's contacts with home affairs were intermittent. For the most part he was content to delegate. The management of the war economy was largely in the hands of the Lord President's Committee, chaired successively by Chamberlain, Anderson, and Attlee, while Bevin, the Minister of Labour, dealt with industrial relations and the Reconstruction Committee under Woolton took charge of post-war problems. But no Prime Minister can afford to ignore domestic political currents for long. The price Churchill paid for doing so was defeat in the general election of 1945.

The publication in December 1942 of the Beveridge Report opened up a host of peacetime questions. In place of the 'safety net' arrangements for the lower-income groups, which Churchill and Lloyd George had initiated, Beveridge proposed a new 'social service state' embracing all classes in a comprehensive system of social security, coupled with family allowances and policies to prevent mass unemployment. The Report also foreshadowed major reforms in health, housing, and education. Appearing just after the psychological turning point of the victory at Alamein, the Report was popular partly because of its promise of social security for all, and partly because it conjured up visions of the peacetime life for which millions were longing. Churchill was incensed with Beveridge—'an awful windbag and a dreamer'[116]—for raising issues which distracted attention from the war and threatened to produce controversy between the parties. Like the Chancellor of the Exchequer, Kingsley Wood, he also disapproved on the grounds that no government could commit itself in advance to the peacetime expenditure involved.

The immediate consequence was a crisis in the Coalition as a division of opinion arose between Labour MPs clamouring for the immediate implementation of the Report, and Conservatives whose aim was to postpone and emasculate it. The War Cabinet attempted to paper over the cracks and Churchill himself, in a broadcast in March 1943, sought a middle way between acceptance and rejection of the report. But his determination to postpone any legislation until after the war left the Conservatives wide open to attack from Labour on post-war questions. In May 1944 he was startled when the government lost a vote in the House of Commons on the question of equal pay for women teachers. Determined to teach his critics a lesson, Churchill turned the question into a vote of confidence which he won by a crushing majority. This merely served to confirm the widespread popular impression that Churchill was the right man in the right place in wartime, but unlikely to make a good peacetime leader. Clementine agreed and urged him to give up the leadership of the Conservative party: ' "You shouldn't use your great prestige to get them in again. They don't deserve it." '[117]

As the end of the war in Europe approached, Churchill wavered between fighting a general election and seeking to maintain the Coalition for a further period. In May 1945 he invited the Labour and the Liberal parties to continue in office until the defeat of Japan, which was not expected to occur for another eighteen months. When both parties refused, Churchill resigned and returned at the head of an interim or 'Caretaker' administration: a Conservative government with a sprinkling of 'non-party' figures. During the opening broadcast of the election campaign Churchill astonished many of his admirers by warning that a Labour government would introduce into Britain of 'some form of Gestapo, no doubt humanely administered in the first instance'. Churchill had been genuinely worried during the war by the inroads of state bureaucracy into civil liberty, and was clearly influenced by F. A. Hayek's anti-totalitarian tract, *The Road to Serfdom* (1944), which included a chapter on the socialist origins of Nazism. He may also have been alarmed by the war-time expansion of MI5, who were in effect the British political police.[118] The claim that his own deputy Prime Minister would resort to Nazi methods was nevertheless patently absurd. 'By far the commonest reaction', reported Mass-Observation, 'was one of real distress and concern that a figure so admired, even by his opponents, should lose his prestige.' But a week or so later, when M-O asked people which speeches on the radio they had liked best, Churchill was the name most frequently mentioned. 'This type of reply', M-O commented, 'indicates a simple loyalty that transcends criticism.'[119] The Gestapo speech was to rankle for years with Labour supporters, in whose collective memory of Churchill it ranked with Tonypandy and the General Strike. But it was irrelevant to his reputation as a war leader, and probably made no difference to the outcome of the general election. The new generation which voted for the first time in 1945 was pre-dominantly Labour, shaped by the egalitarianism and left-wing propaganda of the war years.

Unusually, there was an interlude between polling day (5 July) and the declaration of the results (26 July), during which Churchill attended the Potsdam conference. Stalin—whom he was never to meet again—seems again to have persuaded him, for the moment, that his intentions were benign. After a brief holiday Churchill was back in Britain for the result of the general election, which proved to be a landslide Labour victory. 'It may well be a blessing in disguise', Clementine remarked. 'At the moment it seems quite effectively disguised', Churchill replied.[120] At 7 p.m. on 26 July he drove to Buckingham Palace and resigned, declining the King's offer of the Order of the Garter.

SEVEN

Climbing Olympus, 1945–1965

In one sense Clemmie was right about Churchill's defeat in 1945. From the point of view of his reputation, it *was* a blessing. Lloyd George, the conquering hero of 1918, had rapidly fallen into disrepute at the head of a peacetime government beset by troubles at home and abroad. Churchill would probably have suffered a similar fate as Prime Minister after 1945. Given the economic plight in which the British found themselves, any post-war administration would have had to enforce a further period of rationing and austerity, with appeals to the public to work hard and tighten their belts. Churchill, with his unashamed enjoyment of luxury and privilege, would have been the easiest of targets for a Labour opposition exploiting the frustration caused by post-war shortages, or cutbacks in housing and the social services.

It is also unlikely that any post-war government could have avoided the Cold War, rearmament, peacetime conscription, or British participation in the Korean War of 1950. Haunted by his reputation as a warmonger and anti-Communist, Churchill would have found it particularly hard to convince the Labour Opposition that all these policies were essential. The odds are that, whatever his intentions, he would have become a deeply divisive figure, bundled out of office at the next general election, and retiring under a cloud. There were times when Churchill himself appreciated his good fortune. At a meeting of the shadow cabinet at the time out the outbreak of the Korean War, in June 1950, he remarked: 'The old man is very good to me. I could not have managed this situation had I been in Attlee's place. I would have been called a warmonger.' When Sir David Maxwell Fyfe, whom Churchill invariably addressed as 'Sir Donald', enquired which old man he was referring to, Churchill replied: 'God, Sir Donald.'[1] The six years Churchill spent in opposition between 1945 and 1951 enabled him to adopt an Olympian role as an elder statesman, semi-detached from party politics, which he was to maintain with some success after his return to office in 1951.

*   *   *

Shortly after Churchill's defeat in the general election of 1945 David Low published a cartoon in the *Evening Standard* entitled 'Two Churchills'. Seated on top a giant plinth inscribed 'The Leader of Humanity', a buoyant Churchill with a huge cigar looks down on a grumpy Churchill, 'The Party Leader', standing by. 'Cheer up!' says Winston on high to Winston below. 'They will forget *you* but they will remember *me* always.'[2] The 'Leader of Humanity' refused to accept in 1945 that his work was done. Not that was he willing to dispense with the services of his lesser self, the party leader, without whom he could not hope to climb back into power. When the Conservative Chief Whip, James Stuart, went to see him to convey the message that a number of leading Conservatives believed he should resign, he burst into a rage, stamped his foot on the ground, and squashed the critics flat. But with the next general election a distant prospect he paid little attention to party politics and absented himself for long periods from the House of Commons.

Churchill did lash out at times against socialist policies, which as ever he regarded as fallacious. In October 1945 he and Clemmie entertained the Canadian Prime Minister, Mackenzie King, to lunch at Hyde Park Gate. Churchill, recorded King in his diary, feared that 'conditions were going to be pretty serious in England as a consequence of the policy of destroying the rich to equalize incomes of all . . . he himself would have been prepared to take three quarters of the income of wealthy men but he would have left them enough to have an incentive to work'.[3] In December 1945 he coined the phrase 'set the people free', of which he was to make frequent use in the Attlee years. Convinced that socialist politicians were bureaucratic bunglers, and socialist policies bad for the economy, he roundly accused Labour of responsibility for the hardships and crises of the late 1940s: the housing shortage, the continuation of food rationing—including the rationing of bread for the first time in 1946—and the perpetuation of a host of controls over economic life in which he claimed to detect the seeds of a communist state.

In the immediate aftermath of the war his views were out of key with the times. The Labour party was carrying through Parliament a series of bills taking into public ownership the Bank of England, coal, gas, electricity, and the railways. It looked as though a historic and irreversible shift was taking place and a new kind of economic order emerging. Nor was it only Labour politicians who proclaimed their faith in state intervention: collectivism was intellectually respectable, and economic liberalism of the classical variety the creed of eccentrics. Even the Conservatives felt the need to adapt their policies to the New Look. In the spring of 1947 a committee under the chairmanship

of R. A. Butler produced the 'Industrial Charter', a policy statement in which pledges to restore free enterprise were carefully
balanced with the acceptance of a more positive role for the state
in the management of the the economy. When it was endorsed
by the party's annual conference in October 1947 Churchill
realized that he would have to refer to it in his speech, and
summoned Reginald Maudling, one of Butler's young men in
the Conservative Research Department, to advise him:

'Give me five lines, Maudling', he said, 'explaining what the Industrial
Charter says.' This I did. He read it with care and then said: 'But I do not
agree with a word of this.' 'Well, sir', I said, 'that is what the conference
adopted.' 'Oh well', he said, 'leave it in', and he duly read it out in the
course of his speech, with the calculated coolness which he always
accorded to paragraphs in speeches, rare as they were, which had been
drafted by other people . . .'[4]

In the context of peacetime problems Churchill, as Aneurin
Bevan remarked, 'looked like a dinosaur at a light engineering
exhibition'.[5]

Perhaps in the end the dinosaur was Bevan. For all his nega-
tivism, Churchill was prescient in his attacks on some aspects
of the socialist state. In 1945 the political initiative lay with the
supporters of nationalization and economic planning. By 1951 it
was in the hands of liberalizing economists and Tory politicians.
The fuel crisis of the winter of 1946–7, in which much of British
industry had to be closed down and three million people were
thrown out of work, did much to undermine the credibility of
economic planning. Nationalization proved to be such an anti-
climax that the Labour Party's enthusiasm began to wane. The
persistence of rationing and austerity led to growing popular discontent and the protests of the British Housewives' League. As
the Cold War intensified and turned into an ideological struggle

219

against Stalinism, Churchill's emphasis on the freedom of the individual from state control acquired a new relevance. William Beveridge, the 'founder of the welfare state', wrote a letter to the *Daily Telegraph* in praise of Churchill: 'The fundamental issue is that between freedom and totalitarianism, between the view which makes the State the servant of the individual and that which makes the individual the servant of the State.'[6] When George Orwell gave the hero of *1984* the name 'Winston Smith' he was surely paying a tribute to Churchill. In 1950 the political philosopher Karl Popper published *The Open Society and its Enemies*, a powerful assault on utopian political theory from Plato to Marx. On Churchill's eightieth birthday Popper sent him a copy inscribed on the flyleaf: 'To the defender of the Open Society as a token of the author's gratitude'.[7]

Churchill was no more in harmony with the age of austerity than he was with the age of planning. He had always spent lavishly. Now at last he could afford to do so. In 1946 a consortium of wealthy benefactors, led by Lord Camrose, purchased Chartwell and presented it to the National Trust, on condition that he and Clementine would have the right to live there for the rest of their lives. Meanwhile the Chartwell Trust was established to manage the prodigious sums Churchill could now command as an author. The *Daily Telegraph* paid £555,000 for his war memoirs, while the American book and serial rights were sold for $1,400,000. The Chartwell Trust ensured Churchill an income sufficient to keep him in the style to which he was accustomed, while protecting his estate from death duties and providing for his family after his death. A wealthy man for the first time, Churchill began to buy up agricultural land around Chartwell, and set himself up as a gentleman farmer.

Churchill's marriage to Clemmie remained the cornerstone of

his private life, but his oldest friend and companion, his younger brother Jack, died in February 1947. 'I feel lonely now that he is not here', wrote Churchill to Hugh Cecil, 'after 67 years of brotherly love.'[8] Churchill was fortunate to discover a new friend and ally in his son-in-law Captain Christopher Soames, whose marriage to Mary Churchill took place that same month. When ill health compelled him to leave the Army, he and Mary moved into Chartwell Farm, next door to her parents, and he took on at Churchill's request the role of farm manager for the estate. Unlike his father Lord Randolph, or his grandfather Leonard Jerome, Churchill had never shown much interest in the Turf. But in 1949 Soames persuaded him to buy a French stallion, Colonist II. At a stroke he converted his father-in-law into an ardent race-goer who invested in thirty-seven racehorses over the next few years.[9] Colonist II, sporting Lord Randolph's colours, won thirteen races before he was finally put to stud. When he flopped in his last race Churchill reproached himself: 'I said to Colonist, "This is your last race. From now on you will spend your life in agreeable female company." I fear that his mind was not on the race.'[10] Soames, meanwhile, embarked on a career in politics. Elected as Conservative MP for Bedford in 1950, he was to serve as Churchill's Parliamentary Private Secretary for the duration of his peacetime premiership.

Towards the end of 1945 Churchill received an invitation to give one in a series of annual lectures at Fulton College in Missouri. There, on 5 March 1946, in the presence of President Truman, he gave the first public warning by a leading British or American statesman of the dangers of Soviet expansionism. 'From Stettin in the Baltic to Trieste in the Adriatic', he declared, 'an iron curtain has descended across the Continent.'[11] By comparison with the warnings he had once given about Nazi Germany his remarks about Russia were comparatively restrained. But delivered at a time when popular goodwill towards a wartime ally, and optimism about the prospects for the United Nations, still prevailed, they aroused much hostility in the United States and western Europe.

The passage about the 'Iron Curtain', which occurred about two-thirds of the way through the speech, was controversial chiefly because of the proposal with which Churchill led up to it. He floated once more his vision of a 'fraternal association of the English-speaking peoples'. But this time he went beyond rhetoric and called for a military arrangement between the United States and the British Empire in which weapons and strategy would be coordinated and joint use made of air and naval bases in the possession of either country throughout the world. Churchill attempted to sugar the pill with the argument that his plan would strengthen the authority of the United Nations, but it was clearly a prescription for the restoration of balance-of-power politics. For many politicians and commentators, his words summoned up the spectre of a renewed struggle for world power leading ultimately to World War Three. In Britain the pro-Labour press condemned the speech and 105 Labour MPs signed a motion deploring it. As Churchill knew, however, his anxieties about Soviet intentions were shared by many insiders in Washington and Whitehall. Truman himself, though claiming that he had no prior knowledge of the speech's contents, had read and endorsed it in advance. Neither Attlee nor Bevin had known what Churchill would say, but he assured them that he had spoken with the President's support, and they made no comment.[12]

Though convinced of the Soviet threat, Churchill was deploying it in support of his long cherished project of Anglo-American unity. This was a project on which the American political nation was divided. The response of the *New York Times*, which paid tribute to Churchill as 'the towering leader who guided the British Empire and indeed our whole civilization through their darkest hours', was broadly supportive:

Whether all of Mr Churchill's proposals are acceptable to the United States is not the main point now. The American people have long realized that the United States and Great Britain are governed by a common destiny which brought them together in two world wars and would inevitably do so in any future war. Sharing Mr. Churchill's anxieties about the future, they will give a sympathetic hearing to his proposal for averting a new catastrophe.[13]

In the *Washington Post*, however, Walter Lippmann argued that Churchill had failed to understand the enormous problems his proposal would cause for Americans. There could be no alliance between the United States and a colonial empire that stretched from Malta to Hong Kong: 'That is not a workable argument to propose to a people as deeply imbued as the Americans with the tradition and the conviction that empires are at best a necessary evil, to be liquidated as soon as possible.' Three weeks later an opinion poll of residents of Washington DC revealed that 52 per cent were against an Anglo-American alliance, 33 per cent in favour. Lippmann was right.[14] Though the Cold War did subsequently reduce American hostility towards British imperialism, no United States government was prepared to contemplate a military alliance with the entire British Empire.

Churchill's Fulton speech proved to be a landmark: the first public declaration of the Cold War in the western world. As tensions between the West and the Soviet Union rose in 1947 and 1948, his warnings about the Soviet Union ceased to be controversial. Indeed they began to be hailed as prophetic and the inevitable parallel drawn with the warnings he had issued in the 1930s. Among the dwindling band of Churchill's critics the suspicion that he was a 'warmonger' lingered on, with some justification. Precious few people knew at the time that in the late 1940s Churchill was urging a showdown with the Soviet Union. Britain and the United States, he argued, should exploit their temporary nuclear monopoly to deliver an ultimatum: if it was rejected, the atom bomb would be dropped on Russia. At lunch with Mackenzie King on 25 November 1947 he rehearsed the case he would put to the Russians:

We fought for liberty and are determined to maintain it. We will give you what you want and is reasonable in the matter of boundaries. We will give you ports in the North. We will meet you in regard to conditions generally. What we will not allow you to do is to destroy Western Europe; to extend your regime further there. If you do not agree to that here and now, within so many days, we will attack Moscow and your other cities and destroy them with atomic bombs from the air.[15]

Churchill was convinced that if they were addressed in this fashion, the Russians would back down.

It was of course Truman and Bevin and their officials who organized the containment of the Soviet Union and the subsequent establishment of the North Atlantic Treaty Organization (NATO) in 1949. But it was Churchill who became the American hero of the Cold War. Naming him in January 1950 as Man of the Year, *Time* magazine explained: 'His chief contribution was to warn of rocks ahead, and to lead the rescue parties. He was not the man who designed the ship; what he did was to launch the lifeboats. That a free world survived in 1950, with a hope of more progress and less calamity, was due in large measure to his exertions.'[16] 'To the world at large', wrote the *New York Times* in 1953, 'Sir Winston is the statesman incarnate; to the West a symbol of implacable resistance to tyranny.'[17] But the

American response to Churchill was never all he hoped it would be. American leaders welcomed the support which he and other British politicians gave to the United States. They were not prepared in return to underwrite the British Empire.

In pre-war days Mackenzie King had been a strong appeaser who regarded Churchill as a menace. Now he shared Churchill's fears and watched and listened with awe as the great man held forth. 'His eyes seemed to be bulging out of his head', he recorded,

so much so that one could see the greater part of the whites of his eyes as well as the pupils, which looked as though they would come out of his head altogether . . . The gleam in his eyes was like fire. There was something in his whole appearance and delivery which gave me the impression of a volcano at work in his brain . . . I confess that as I looked at him at the table, I felt that perhaps in more respects than one, he was the greatest man of our times. Not by any means the greatest in any one field but rather in a combination of fields—in the aggregate.[18]

The news of a successful Soviet atomic test in August 1949 seems to have been put an end to Churchill's vision of an ultimatum that would make or break the world.

Shortly after his return from Fulton in March 1946 Churchill had begun to assemble a research team, led by the Oxford historian William Deakin, to assist him in the writing of his war memoirs. In addition to his own papers, including the long series of wartime minutes and telegrams of which he had retained copies, Churchill obtained inside information from many sources both at home and abroad. His method was to have all the relevant documents set up in galley proof so that he could then dictate passages linking the documents. Gradually, with much redrafting, Churchill imposed his own structure, style, and interpretation. Appearing in six volumes between 1948 and 1954,

The Second World War was published in hardback in fifty countries and eighteen languages.

It was not history, Churchill insisted, but a contribution to history. Nevertheless he imprinted his version of events on the minds of a generation. Churchill's six volumes included a prodigious quantity of original documents, printed either as appendices or in the main body of the text. As a body of primary source materials they were unrivalled and even today they retain much of their value as works of reference. But they were so well documented as to create the illusion that they represented a definitive account of events. They were, however, the work of a politician and historian seeking to define his place in history. The documents, therefore, were carefully selected to support Churchill's interpretation of events. The moment Churchill entered the government in September 1939 he began to write long letters to Chamberlain about the conduct of the war. 'As we meet every single day at the War Cabinet', wrote Chamberlain to his sister Hilda,

this would seem unnecessary, but of course I realise that these letters are for the purpose of quotation in the Book that he will write hereafter. Hitherto I haven't answered them, but the one I got yesterday was so obviously recording his foresight and embodied warnings so plainly for purposes of future allusion that I thought I must get something in the record too which would have to be quoted in the Book.[19]

In the fullness of time Chamberlain's prophecy came true. Churchill did publish his letter to Chamberlain, together with Chamberlain's reply. For the most part, however, Churchill published only the letters and minutes he sent to others, omitting the replies. His account therefore gave the impression of a war directed by a solitary thinker committing his thoughts to paper in logical fashion. As one historian has put it: 'What had in actuality been an incessant dialogue between Churchill and his military advisers, and with his political advisers too, was in his book transformed into a monologue only occasionally interrupted by what were no more than distant voices and echoes.'[20]

Historians today are more interested in what Churchill left out than in what he put in. There was no mention of Ultra, of course, which remained top secret until some years after Churchill's death. Nor did Churchill make any reference to the War Cabinet's discussion of a compromise peace at the time of Dunkirk: indeed he specifically denied that the issue had ever been raised. As already indicated, his treatment of the strategic bombing offensive was so sketchy as to suggest that he had come to regard it as an embarassment, and there was no mention of the bombing of Dresden. In harmony with the spirit of the Cold War, he played down the extent of the differences between the British and Americans while seeking to establish his own prescience about the dangers of Soviet expansion. The most misleading of the volumes, however, was the first. *The Gathering Storm* distorted both his own record and that of the National Government. He exaggerated the extent of the differences between himself on the one hand, and Baldwin and Chamberlain on the other, over rearmament and foreign policy. He neglected to explain one of the fundamental causes of appeasement, the threat posed to the British Empire by the potential conjunction of three aggressor nations: Germany, Italy, and Japan. Nor would any reader have guessed how much the Churchill Coalition owed to the preparations made between 1934, when Germany was identified by the Defence Requirements Committee as Britain's main potential enemy, and 1939, by which time Britain was already in possession of radar, and already producing the Hurricanes and Spitfires that won the Battle of Britain.[21]

In Churchill, the historian and the politician were always closely allied, and the six volumes of *The Second World War* were an important part of the platform he constructed for himself after 1945 as a global statesman, speaking with the insight of a prophet and the wisdom of a philosopher king. If the 'Iron Curtain' speech was the first of his great contributions to the ordering of the post-war world, the other was the speech he delivered at the University of Zurich in September 1946.

As at Fulton, he was attempting to detach his audience from wartime emotions and prepare them for a new post-war reality. He called for the reconciliation of France and Germany and the establishment of a United Europe in which the sovereignty of nation states was pooled for the common good. Evidently his call for the unification of Europe owed something to the Cold War context, but it was a concept he had first formulated in 1930, and reverted to between 1940 and 1945. So great was Churchill's stature that his speeches gave a powerful impetus to the movement for a united Europe and he came to be regarded as one of its founding fathers. This is where the true significance of Churchill's initiative lay: outside rather than inside Britain, and most of all in assisting the reconciliation of France and Germany. But he also flirted with the idea of British participation in Europe. He accepted the leadership of the British European movement, an all-party pressure group organized by his son-in-law Duncan Sandys, and attacked the Labour government for failing to play a more constructive role in the construction of European unity. The Attlee government took no part in the Hague conference of May 1948, but Churchill attended as honorary president. In June 1950 he criticized the government for refusing to participate in the conference called to implement the Schuman Plan for a European Iron and Steel Community. In

August, at the opening session of the Consultative Assembly of the Council of Europe at Strasburg, he successfully moved a resolution in favour of the creation of a European Army and appeared to suggest that Britain would play a part in it.

One of his aims was party political—to embarass the government by creating the impression that the Conservatives were more eager than Labour to participate in the Schuman Plan and other moves towards European unity. But this led some observers to the mistaken conclusion that Churchill was a committed 'European'. In fact he never wavered from views he had expressed long before the Second World War. In 1930 he had welcomed the idea, floated by the French statesman Aristide Briand, of a united Europe, but stressed that the destinies of the British were separate from those of the Continental powers:

We see nothing but good and hope in a richer, freer, more contented European commonalty. But we have our own dream and our own task. We are with Europe, but not of it. We are linked, but not comprised. We are interested and associated, but not absorbed.[22]

As he explained in a speech to the Conservative party conference in October 1948, Churchill believed that Britain had a unique role to play as the link between 'the three great circles among the free nations and democracies'—Britain and the Empire, the United States, and a United Europe.[23]

The Empire, however, never fully recovered from the Second World War. In India British authority was on the brink of collapse by 1945 and withdrawal was inevitable, but Churchill was dismayed by the government's preparations for the transfer of power, which he regarded as hasty and irresponsible. 'In handing over the Government of India to these so-called political classes', he warned in March 1947, 'we are handing over to men of straw, of whom, in a few years, no trace will remain . . . It is with deep grief I watch the clattering down of the British Empire with all its glories and all the services it has rendered to mankind.'[24] Churchill nonetheless had to accept that it was too late to put the clock back, and finally gave his support to the Independence of India Bill.

By 1949 a general election was imminent. Determined as far as possible to return to office with his hands free, Churchill had resisted for as long as he could the clamour from the party for a detailed party programme. But in April 1949 the Conservative shadow Cabinet decided that a comprehensive statement should be issued and a manifesto entitled *The Right Road for Britain* was drafted by Quintin Hogg. This brought together proposals already published in a number of party documents, including the *Industrial Charter* of 1947, in which Churchill had played very little part. Now he threw himself into the drafting of the manifesto. He was deeply interested in the substance and presentation of the 'big picture' and in agreement with the party's general approach, which struck a careful balance between the restoration of market forces on the one hand, and the maintenance on the other of the key nationalized industries, full employment, and the social services. Though Churchill had no faith in socialist economics, he was still proud of his record as an Edwardian social reformer, and liked to claim that the Attlee government's welfare reforms were the offspring of his own wartime administration— as, to some extent, they were.[25]

In January 1950 Attlee called a general election. Churchill took a less prominent part in the campaign than in 1945, and his attacks on socialism were balanced by a more conciliatory tone in home affairs. He also called, in a speech in Edinburgh, for a 'summit' meeting between the leaders of the great powers—the first indication of a new approach to the Soviet Union. The government, however, was returned to power with a precarious majority of six, and managed to struggle on until the autumn of 1951. Churchill strongly supported the government over the Korean war, which broke out in June 1950, but attacked them vigorously for their alleged weakness in Iran, where a revolutionary regime under Dr Mussadiq nationalized the Anglo-Iranian oil company. (As Prime Minister Churchill was later to be a party to the Anglo-American inspired coup which led to the overthrow of Mussadiq in 1953.)

When another general election was called in October 1951, Churchill again floated the idea of a 'conference at the summit'. He was strongly attacked from the Labour side as a 'warmonger' and on polling day the *Daily Mirror* carried on its front page a large picture of a revolver and the question: 'Whose finger? Today YOUR finger is on the trigger.' This time, however, Labour were defeated and the Conservatives returned to power with a majority of seventeen.

Returning to 10 Downing Street at 77, Churchill formed a government with many echoes of his wartime premiership. He even resumed the title of Minister of Defence, though after a few months he persuaded a reluctant Field-Marshal Alexander to accept the post. Eden returned in the role of Foreign Secretary, Crown Prince, and long-suffering subordinate. Ismay and Cherwell were both given Cabinet posts, and Colville recalled as his Private Secretary. Churchill attempted to create a Coalition by inviting the Liberal leader, Clement Davies, to be Minister of Education, but the offer was declined. In home affairs the appointments of R. A. Butler as Chancellor of the Exchequer, Walter Monckton as Minister of Labour, and Harold Macmillan as Minister of Housing signalled a relatively moderate approach.

In a curious experiment, Churchill began by appointing a number of peers, including Leathers and Woolton, as 'overlords' to coordinate the policies of groups of departments. The 'overlords', however, having no departments to sustain them in the battles of Whitehall, soon faded away.

At the death of King George VI on 6 February 1952, Churchill broadcast a graceful tribute over the radio. He was deeply moved by the king's death and the succession of Elizabeth II, from whom he accepted the Order of the Garter in April 1953. The Coronation (2 June 1953) was the last great pageant of an Empire whose decline was masked, for the time being, by the charismatic conjunction of the aged statesman and the beautiful young Queen.

The great man was no longer a dynamic force. A supply of 'action this day' labels, carefully preserved from the war years, was placed before him at the Cabinet table, but this time he left them unused. As he was going deaf, he had to be supplied with a hearing aid for Cabinet meetings. With much guidance from the Cabinet Secretary, Norman Brook, he chaired the Cabinet in his usual discursive style, but shortly after the Coronation he suffered a stroke which paralysed his left leg and arm and the left-hand side of his face. The nature of his illness was concealed by a secret circle of conspirators, led by R. A. Butler and Lord Salisbury, who doctored the medical bulletin and persuaded the press to collude in the fiction that Churchill was merely taking a rest. His son-in-law, Christopher Soames, took over the running of 10 Downing Street in the interim. At first Churchill thought he was finished but within a few days he began to recover and by the autumn he was well enough to return to work. On great occasions, like his speech to the Conservative party conference at Margate (10 October 1953) he could still put on a dazzling performance, but the remainder of his political life hung by a thread.

On the home front the first few months of his peacetime government had been overshadowed by economic crisis, a fresh round of austerity, and a great debate in Whitehall over whether or not to adopt the radical course of floating the pound (Operation 'Robot'). These were matters in which Churchill was out of his depth, though not without a politician's instinct for survival. The programme of the Tory party, he explained late one night at Chequers, must be 'houses and meat and not being scuppered'.[26] Largely on the advice of Cherwell, who warned that 'Robot' would result in mass unemployment and the loss of the next general election, he decided against it. Generally speaking Churchill was bored by domestic affairs, but he rejoiced in the abolition of food rationing, and welcomed the decision to end the BBC's monopoly of television. Simultaneously he gave strong support to Harold Macmillan's housing programme against opposition from the Treasury. Determined to avoid industrial strife he instructed his Minister of Labour, Walter Monckton, to pursue a policy of appeasing the trade unions at the cost, if necessary, of inflationary wage settlements. On racial questions, Churchill was still a late Victorian. When Violet Bonham-Carter asked for his views about a Labour party visit to China in May 1954 he replied: 'I hate people with slit eyes and pigtails. I don't like the look of them or the smell of them—but I suppose it does no great harm to have a look at them.'[27] He tried in vain to manoeuvre the Cabinet into restricting West Indian immigration. 'Keep England White' was a good slogan , he told the Cabinet in January 1955.[28]

Churchill sought a quiet life at home in order to concentrate on his main objective, the restoration of Britain as a great power.

From the moment he returned to office in 1951, he threw himself into a passionate last-ditch defence of Britain's military base in the Suez Canal Zone against the demands of Egyptian leaders for a British withdrawal. 'He never wavered', writes Roger Louis, 'from his Victorian opinion that the Egyptians were an inferior and essentially cowardly people.'[29] This was an issue on which Churchill was frequently at odds with his Foreign Secretary, Anthony Eden, whose attempts to reach a settlement with Egypt he stigmatized as appeasement. By 1954, however, Churchill was compelled to recognize that his views commanded little support. Consoling himself with the thought that the Suez base was strategically obsolete in a nuclear age, he accepted the inevitable.

Closer to home, Churchill displayed no more enthusiasm than the Labour government for British involvement in the Schuman Plan and his support for the creation of a European Army (which he privately referred to as a 'sludgy amalgam') stopped well short of full British participation. In vain did the French remind him of his Strasburg speech and the spacious visions of European unity he had sketched out in opposition. 'The Prime Minister concealed his retreat in a smokescreen', reported the French ambassador in London. 'He nevertheless made one point quite clear: however much England wished to collaborate as fully and effectively as possible with the European army, she would not see herself diluted in this denationalised amalgam.'[30] Eventually this tiresome problem went away: in 1954 the French National Assembly rejected the plan.

In Churchill's view the most urgent task awaiting him on his return to Number Ten was the restoration of the Anglo-American 'special relationship'. In January 1952 he crossed the Atlantic in the *Queen Mary* for discussions with President

Truman. Outwardly relations were full of bonhomie, but the President and his advisers did not share Churchill's conception of an Anglo-American global alliance. They rejected his pleas for American military support in the Suez Canal Zone and made few concessions to his request for the restoration of the Quebec agreement on the use of nuclear weapons. When Eisenhower was elected President in November 1952, Churchill hastened to Washington for consultations with his former wartime comrade-in-arms. But greatly though Eisenhower liked and admired Churchill, he thought his view of Anglo-American relations sentimental and privately concluded that he was living in the wartime past. Churchill's pleas for diplomatic support over Egypt were rejected. Nor did 'Ike' warm to Churchill's idea of a summit conference with the Russians. Even more discouraging was the new Secretary of State, John Foster Dulles, a doctrinaire anti-communist for whom Churchill developed a strong antipathy.

Although Churchill pressed repeatedly for discussions with the Kremlin, he never defined the terms of the settlement he was seeking, and his motives appear to have been mixed. Surrounded by whispers that he was unfit for office, and under constant pressure to make way for Eden, he badly needed a justification for clinging to power, and also, perhaps, relished the prospect of outmanoeuvring the Labour Party. Whatever his motives, there is no doubt that his last great ambition was to play the role of peacemaker. With the death of Stalin, on 5 March 1953, his hopes of détente rose, but his attempts to seize the initiative were interrupted by illness. In December 1953 Eisenhower attended a conference in Bermuda at Churchill's invitation, but again rejected his proposals for a common approach to Russia. When Churchill flew to Washington in June 1954 he was surprised

235

and elated when Eisenhower withdrew his objections and even agreed that Churchill should go alone to Moscow. During the return voyage on the *Queen Elizabeth* Churchill in cavalier fashion despatched a telegram to Molotov without consulting the Cabinet. The consequence, when he got home, was a Cabinet crisis in which he was strongly opposed by Eden and other senior ministers. From this impasse the Russians, quite unwittingly, extricated him by clumsy diplomacy.

Churchill was, of course, no unilateral disarmer. It was under his chairmanship that the Defence Committee of the Cabinet decided in June 1954 to recommend that Britain must build its hydrogen bomb as a deterrent against Soviet attack. But Churchill also grasped the fact that with both the United States and the Soviet Union in possession of nuclear weapons, the world now stood on the brink of self-destruction. His last major speech in the House of Commons (1 March 1955) was devoted to the dangers of nuclear holocaust but ended on a note of hope: 'It may well be that we shall, by a process of sublime irony, have reached a stage where safety will be the sturdy shield of terror, and survival the twin brother of annihilation.'[31] Until late in the day Churchill had intended to include in the speech a passage throwing doubt on the viability of any disarmament plan, due to the ease with which plutonium could be concealed from arms inspectors. Fortunately for Churchill's reputation as a prophet of world peace, Macmillan persuaded him to delete it.[32] Churchill now had finally to accept that he would be too old to lead the Conservatives into another general election. In April 1955, after entertaining the Queen and the Duke of Edinburgh to dinner at 10 Downing Street, he tendered his resignation. The Queen offered him a dukedom but he declined.

Given the precarious state of his health, Churchill was fortunate to have got through his peacetime premiership with dignity and without major embarrassment. At the end there was no great achievement he could point to, but he did succeed in softening the rougher edges of his reputation. His quest for an end to the nuclear arms race belied his image as a warmonger, and the conciliatory policies of his government at home demonstrated that he was no longer the class warrior of Labour legend. As he aged he mellowed visibly, allowing old enmities to fade away. Among the former adversaries he welcomed to Downing Street were Nehru, the Prime Minister of India, and De Valera, the President of the Irish Republic. Honours continued to rain upon him, most notably the Nobel Prize for Literature, awarded by the Swedish Academy in 1953. Owing to his absence at the Bermuda conference, Churchill was unable to get to Stockholm to receive the award, but Clemmie accepted it on his behalf. As John Ramsden observes, there grew up around him a genuine warmth of regard which found expression on the occasion of his eightieth birthday in 1954. 30,000 birthday cards arrived and '2000 of Britain's most prominent citizens stood and cheered Churchill to the echo as he entered Westminster Hall to the strains of Elgar'.[33] For Churchill, however, the occasion was marred by the presentation to him of Graham Sutherland's portrait. Although he declared with apparent good humour that it was 'a remarkable example of modern art', he was deeply wounded by the artist's presentation of him as an old man battling against physical decay. His private comment was: 'I look like a down-and-out drunk who has been picked out of the gutter in the Strand.'[34] The painting was later cut up and burnt by Clementine.

The Sutherland portrait was not the only example of the protection of Churchill from unflattering comments or unwelcome

237

truths. In post-war Britain authors, publishers, and the press hesitated to disturb the legend. In a review of *The Gathering Storm* published on both sides of the Atlantic in 1949 the philosopher Isaiah Berlin composed a perceptive and eloquent tribute in which he described Churchill as 'a man larger than life, composed of bigger and simpler elements than ordinary men, a gigantic historical figure during his own lifetime, superhumanly bold, strong and imaginative, one of the two greatest men of action this nation has produced, an orator of prodigious powers, the saviour of his country, a mythical hero who belongs to legend as much as to reality, the largest human being of our time'.[35] For Berlin, the review was an act of homage to a man who 'saved us all'. But, as he explained some forty years later, 'I never liked him. He was too brutal.'[36]

If Berlin had expressed such a view in print in 1949 it would have caused a sensation. But such was Churchill's stature that many reservations lay concealed and here and there the historical record was discreetly doctored in his favour. In his biography of Neville Chamberlain (1946) Keith Feiling omitted Chamberlain's more waspish criticisms of Churchill. G. M. Young's *Stanley Baldwin* (1952) was equally tactful. In the first draft of the book Young described Baldwin's view of the leading figures in the Lloyd George Coalition as follows: 'The Inner Ring, the Camarilla, Lloyd George, Churchill, Birkenhead and Beaverbrook, bent on nothing but the pursuit of power, were degrading public life and bringing Parliament into public contempt.' After negotiations with the Cabinet Secretary, Norman Brook, the passage was rewritten: 'The Inner Ring were at odds with the official and prescribed policy, and irrepressibly vocal at awkward moments.'[37]

In 1961 the military historian J. F. C. Fuller published a sharp critique of Churchill's strategy in his book *The Conduct of War, 1789–1961*. What readers did not know was that his publishers had refused, on the grounds that it might be libellous, to include this profile of Churchill's character:

A man of unlimited courage, he was possessed of a brilliant but unstable intellect, and was erratically imaginative and profoundly emotional. A militarist to his fingertips, he loved war for its own sake, and yet, when soft emotion stirred him, tears would well up in his eyes. As a statesman he was out of his depth, because so often he confused means and ends, and failed to realize that a statesman's first task is to prevent war, and his second, should this be impossible, to bring war to a profitable and speedy end. As a strategist he was a calamity, and because of his pugnacious temperament and love of fighting, tactics fitted him better. But, unfortunately, the glamour of battle—most of which is apocryphal—so completely intoxicated him that killing Germans became his irresistible aim. Had he been a corporal, this would have been in keeping, but it had nothing whatever to do with the duties of a Minister of Defence. The truth would appear to be that throughout his turbulent life he never quite grew up, and, like a boy, loved big bangs and playing at soldiers.[38]

Churchill remained an MP until 1964, sometimes voting in parliamentary divisions, but never again speaking in the House. At the height of the Suez crisis in October 1956 the Prime Minister, Anthony Eden, contacted Churchill's Private Secretary to ask whether Churchill would accept a seat in the Cabinet. Montague Browne took it upon himself to refuse on his master's behalf. Churchill's private verdict on the Suez fiasco was telling: 'I would never have done it without squaring the Americans, and once I'd started I'd never have dared stop.'[39] When Eden resigned, Churchill was among those advising the Queen to choose Harold Macmillan as his successor.

In his retirement Churchill set one new project in motion. Impressed by Cherwell's warnings about the lack of scientific and technological manpower in Britain, he led a financial appeal for the establishment of a British equivalent of the Massachusetts Institute of Technology. The outcome, though less ambitious than Churchill intended, was a new Cambridge college named after him and devoted to science and technology. Churchill also returned to the task of revising his *History of the English-Speaking Peoples*. Published in four volumes in 1956 and 1957, it was outwardly impressive but inwardly the least successful of his histories. That it should take the form of a narrative of kings, battles, and constitutional landmarks, with social and economic history relegated to the margins, was only to be expected. The real problem was that it lacked the true Churchillian fire of passionate engagement with the subject. Much of the book read like a carefully polished synthesis of the drafts prepared for him by academic historians. Churchill had originally intended that it would demonstrate the common heritage and destiny of Britain and the United States, but this was a theme he failed to analyse or develop. In spite of this all four volumes were warmly received and American reviewers went into raptures. 'As dramatic, as noble and as moving as anything he has ever written', wrote the *Baltimore Sun* of the fourth volume, which included Churchill's account of the American Civil War. The *New York Times* called it 'the legacy of a man of superhuman energy, great intellectual powers and the utmost simplicity of soul'. The *San Francisco Examiner* thought it should be 'in the home of every English-reading family interested in its historical and spiritual heritage'.[40] The greatest American tribute of all came in 1963, when both Houses of Congress passed a resolution to confer on Churchill Honorary Citizenship of the United States. By this stage Churchill had withdrawn deep into himself and was almost past caring. At the presentation in Washington, which

Randolph attended on his father's behalf, President John F. Kennedy declared that Churchill had 'mobilised the English language and sent it into battle', a phrase borrowed from the English journalist Beverley Nichols.[41]

While Churchill's legend grew in the United States, it was put to the test in Britain with the publication in 1957–9 of the Alanbrooke diaries, edited in two volumes by Arthur Bryant.[42] Alanbrooke had been offended by the fact that Churchill had given so little credit to him in his war memoirs. Bryant, who had been an ardent appeaser in the 1930s, was a manipulative editor who steered a devious course between homage to Churchill and the subversion of his reputation. He toned down or omitted some of Alanbrooke's more damning judgements, which in the circumstances of the time would probably have damaged Alanbrooke more than Churchill. But the passages he did publish were sufficiently critical to produce shock and dismay among Churchillian loyalists. To add insult to injury, he argued that it was Alanbrooke, not Churchill, who had been the mastermind of British strategy and the architect of victory. Reviewing the second volume in the *Evening Standard*, Milton Shulman protested that it presented a picture of a 'dedicated, all-seeing field marshal doing his best to win the war almost single-handed at the conference table while constantly being hampered and harassed by the childish petulance of Winston Churchill and the strategic ignorance of his American colleagues, Marshall and Eisenhower'.[43] In the circumstances Alanbrooke's sense of grievance was understandable: Churchill had certainly been grudging in his recognition of the CIGS's role. Bryant, on the other hand, greatly exaggerated it. Churchill was the visionary and the driving force behind British grand strategy: Alanbrooke's most important contribution was to ensure that Churchill's more dangerous projects were never implemented.[44]

'No single book', wrote Martin Gilbert in the official biography, 'gave a more distorted picture of Churchill's war leadership, or would provide for many years to come so much material for critical, hostile and ill-informed portrayals of Churchill in the war years.'[45] Perhaps Gilbert is referring here to Bryant's interpretation of the diairies. The real shock of the Alanbrooke diaries, however, was the tearing away of the façade of Victorian statesmanship erected by Churchill. In the diaries he stood revealed in all his moods as a creature of flesh and blood. The Churchill myth was never the same again, but in revealing Churchill close up, with all his faults and foibles on view, the diaries also brought to life his strengths and virtues: his courage in adversity, the brilliant flow of his conversation, the patent sincerity of his loves and hates. It was at this point that a divergence began to appear within the ranks of Churchill's admirers between two different schools of thought. The Churchillian loyalists, spearheaded by the members of his wartime inner circle, strove to maintain as far as possible the image Churchill had created of himself, and the historical claims associated with it. Ismay's memoirs, published in 1960, can be read as a temperately argued rebuttal of Alanbrooke. The liberal Churchillians welcomed Alanbrooke's portrait of Churchill as far more lifelike and revealing than previous accounts, and very much to his credit. Reviewing the second volume of the diaries, A. J. P. Tayor concluded that Churchill 'emerges from the record greater than ever—impossibly difficult to deal with in private, but always rising to the challenge of events when it came to the point'.[46] Churchill himself was deeply hurt by the publication of the diaries but Clemmie was philosophical. 'You know my dear Charles', she remarked to Moran, 'I am not really angry with Alanbrooke. We must get used to criticism of Winston. I realise the poor darling cannot be a demi-god forever.'[47]

The Churchillian loyalists and the liberal Churchillians were at one in opposing a third school of thought: the anti-Churchillians. Of these the pioneer was J. F. C. Fuller, already referred to above. Writing in 1961, he anticipated the arguments 'revisionists' were to put many years later by condemning the British decision to enter the Second World War as a mistake:

Because Bolshevism and National Socialism were equally repugnant to the Democracies, and because Hitler's aim was to establish a *Lebensraum* in Eastern Europe, which would inevitably entangle him with Russia, there can be no doubt whatsoever that in 1939 the best policy for France and Great Britain would have been to keep out of the war, let the two great dictatorial powers cripple each other, and in the meantime have re-armed at top speed.

Fuller did not argue that Churchill should have made peace with Hitler. He did assert that Churchill should have made every effort to stimulate the anti-Hitler Opposition instead of adopting the policy of 'unconditional surrender', or trying to break the morale of the German people through strategic bombing. Basing himself on the report of the United States Strategic Bombing Survey, published in 1945, he claimed that in spite of all the attacks on German towns and cities, German war production increased between 1940 and 1944. Fuller, however, gave Churchill some credit for attempting in the latter stages of the war to forestall the Soviet advance into eastern Europe.[48]

Churchill himself, who was always mindful of the transience of fame, doubted whether his place in history was secure. 'Historians', he remarked to Lord Boothby, 'are apt to judge war ministers less by the victories achieved under their direction than by the political results which flowed from them. Judged by that standard, I am not sure that I shall be held to have done very well.'[49] As his mental and physical faculties decayed Churchill was losing the battle he had fought for so long against the 'Black Dog' of depression. Searching for solace in the light and colours of the Mediterranean, he took long holidays with his literary adviser Emery Reves and his wife Wendy Russell at La Pausa, their villa on the French Riviera. Clementine, who was often in poor health herself, did not approve of Winston's growing affection for Wendy and seldom joined him on these excursions. Churchill also took eight cruises aboard the yacht *Christina* as the guest of the Greek shipowner Aristotle Onassis. Once, when the *Christina* had to pass through the Dardanelles, Onassis gave instructions that it was to do so during the night, so as not to disturb his guest with unhappy memories.

Churchill's final years were melancholy. He approved the appointment of Randolph as his official biographer, but the love–hate relationship between father and son was never resolved. Sarah was descending into alcoholism and Diana committed suicide in the autumn of 1964. Churchill himself suffered a number of minor strokes. It was a figure ravaged by age and sorrow who appeared at the window of his London home at Hyde Park Gate to greet the photographers on his ninetieth birthday in November 1964. On 10 December he dined for the last time at the Other Club, sitting in silence but apparently knowing where he was. During the night of 9–10 January he suffered a major stroke and never regained consciousness. After lingering for a fortnight he died shortly after 8 o'clock on the morning of Sunday 24 January, sixty years to the day after the death of Lord Randolph.

At his death, obituarists throughout the western world paid

homage to Churchill in a chorus of praise more prolonged than any other democratic statesman has ever received. But the greatest tribute of all was the state funeral which, on the instructions of the Queen, had long been planned by officials under the code-name 'Operation Hope-Not'. After lying in state for three days in Westminster Hall the coffin, covered in a Union Jack, was taken in procession to St Paul's Cathedral for the funeral service, then embarked at Tower Pier on a Port of London launch. As the launch passed up river, the quayside cranes were dipped in salute. From Waterloo station the coffin travelled slowly by train to Bladon. In the fields along the route, and at the stations through which the train passed, thousands stood in silence to pay their last respects. In the village churchyard at Bladon, where his mother and father and his brother Jack were buried, his body was interred in a private family ceremony. During the season of mourning the sceptics maintained a decent silence, but Evelyn Waugh confided his candid opinion of Churchill to his friend Ann Fleming: 'Always in the wrong, always surrounded by crooks, a most unsuccessful father—simply a "Radio Personality" who outlived his time.'[50]

In September 1965 the Queen unveiled a memorial stone in the floor of Westminster Abbey inscribed: 'Remember Winston Churchill'. It seemed unlikely that anyone who had lived through the Second World War could possibly forget him. Whether he would still be remembered and admired by a generation growing up in the cultural revolution of the 1960s, let alone by generations yet unborn, had yet to be seen.

EIGHT

Churchill Past and Present

How did a man who for decades had been written off as erratic and untrustworthy come to be acclaimed as the 'saviour of his country'? Had he been the victim of a conspiracy of the second-rate to frustrate and belittle a statesman who stood head and shoulders above them? Or was his wartime reputation a myth which concealed the flaws and mistakes of a notoriously accident-prone politician? Such questions have always been close to the heart of the debate over Churchill that began soon after his death and continues to this day. The differences of opinion have been due in part to the variegated character of a long and eventful life that usually veered between triumph and disaster, and never settled down to a steady middle course. Churchill was at all times a high-risk politician who frequently paid the penalty, and eventually reaped a stupendous reward, for sublime and persistent egotism.

Unlike his friend Sir Oswald Mosley, the founder of the British Union of Fascists, Churchill never succumbed to the illusion that he was bigger than the political system. Though he was not afraid in 1911 to contemplate the abolition of the House of Lords, his respect for the House of Commons was profound and he was perfectly serious in describing himself, during the Second World War, as a servant of Parliament.

The House of Commons had compelled his predecessor to resign and he knew that the same fate awaited him if the war continued to go wrong. Churchill revered the constitution and did not mean to rebel, but he was an *enfant terrible* who stretched the unwritten rules of political conduct to breaking point. As he freely admitted, the driving force of his life was an all-consuming political ambition, but it was never merely an ambition to get to the top. His goal was play a heroic part on the stage of history. 'If there was one thing that marked him off from the comparable figures in history', wrote Attlee, 'it was his characteristic way of standing back and looking at himself—and his country—as he believed history would. He was always, in effect, asking himself, "How will I look if I do this or that?" and "What must Britain do now so that the verdict of history will be favourable?"'[1] This was the creed of an egotist whose loyalty to party was transient and conditional. He changed parties twice and treated parties and other political groupings as vehicles to advance his career. Moreover his political style was combative and he relished the prospect of smashing his opponents up in debate. Most politicians shrank instinctively from the overtones of class war in British politics. Rhetorically speaking, Churchill was a class warrior who fought the upper classes before 1914 and the labour movement for much of the period between the wars.

If the style of his politics caused friction, so did his record in office. As a Cabinet minister he was a difficult colleague with a disconcerting habit of abandoning agreements carefully worked out a day or two before. In a sense which almost everyone recognized he was brilliant. But his mind worked through a process of rapid intuition nourished by a fertile imagination. Admiration mingled with alarm in the minds of politicians and civil servants as ideas poured from his lips in a cascade of priceless phrases.

This was the wellspring from which Churchill drew the sparkling prose of his speeches and writings, but whether it made for good government was another matter. To a great extent the role of his advisers, whether civil servants or military chiefs, was to act as gatekeepers, facilitating the more practical of his ideas and excluding the impractical. As Sir Edward Troup, his Permanent Secretary at the Home Office, recalled: 'Once a week or oftener Mr Churchill came to the office bringing with him some adventurous or impossible projects; but after half an hour's discussion something was evolved which was still adventurous but not impossible.'[2] The pace at which Churchill worked, and his constant demands for action, placed an enormous strain on his advisers. In social and economic affairs, however, he was restrained to some extent by an awareness of his own limitations. In military affairs, he was sure of his own judgement and confident that he knew better than most of the admirals or generals. Alanbrooke, during the Second World War, had to fight much harder than Troup to divert Churchill from his favourite projects.

Between 1900 and 1939 there was a more or less continuous tension between Churchill's style and the rules of the political game. It was aggravated after 1918 by the decline of the Liberal party, whose free-thinking ethos and adventurous politics had provided Churchill with something like a political home, and the hegemony of two parties which both preached high-minded doctrines of social purpose. The inter-war years, however, merely served to consolidate prejudices against him that were already in circulation by 1915. The consequence, inevitably, was a negative mythology in which Tonypandy and Gallipoli always featured prominently, and Churchill was persistenty accused of lack of judgement and lack of principle. It would be hard to decide which of the two charges was more damaging or more exaggerated.

Churchill's judgement was uneven but compared favourably with that of any of the three main political parties. He was generally consistent in his political beliefs and his apparent shifts were mainly a consequence of a fixed world-view applied to changing circumstances. In normal times, however, British politics had no need of a Man of Destiny.

The German occupation of Prague in March 1939 compelled a genuine reassessment of Churchill's judgement, assisted by the pro-Churchill propaganda of anti-appeasers who adopted him as a stick with which to beat Neville Chamberlain. What no one anticipated was the transformation that occurred at the time of Dunkirk and the fall of France. The politics of class and party, the barbed wire on which he had entangled himself so often in the past, were quickly cleared out of the way. In their place a vacancy arose for which sublime egotism, magnificent oratory, and a passion for warfare were outstanding qualifications. Seizing an opportunity for which he had been rehearsing all his life, Churchill put on a matchless performance which lifted him on to an exalted plane, where he remained in the estimate of the press and the public for the rest of the war. While his reputation soared, Baldwin, Chamberlain, and their associates were subjected to a relentless campaign of vilification which began with the publication of *Guilty Men*, the work of three Beaverbrook journalists, in July 1940. Churchill refused to carry out a purge of the government, but he and his Labour allies in the Coalition both had a vested interest in the devaluation of the 'Men of Munich'.

Churchill's defeat in the general election of 1945 gave the opportunity, and the incentive, to carry the revolution in his reputation a stage further. He resolved to give his place in history a more enduring form by writing his war memoirs. Published in six volumes with a wealth of documentation, they were the work of a great popular historian whose revelations about the conduct of the war also served his political purposes. They were intended to prove that Churchill had taken all the important decisions in the military and strategic conduct of the war, and got them all right, or as right as possible given the neglect from which the armed forces had suffered before he came to power. As John Ramsden has shown, he also succeeded brilliantly in turning the history of the Second World War into a platform for his return to the international stage.[3] Capitalizing upon his reputation as a pre-war Cassandra he relaunched himself at Fulton in 1946 as the leading prophet and statesman of the Cold War. His war memoirs could therefore be read on two levels. On one level they were an account of the past. On the other, they were a prescription for the West in its dealings with the Soviet Union: collective security, rearmament, and Anglo-American unity were repeatedly signposted as the lessons to be learned.

There was much truth in the Churchillian myth. Churchill *was* prophetic in his warnings of the dangers posed by the rise of Hitler. He *was* the founder and leader of a Coalition government that mobilized Britain for war. At the critical moment his leadership *was* decisive in ensuring that a compromise peace with Hitler was avoided. As a popular leader his inspirational powers were beyond dispute. As Prime Minister and Minister of Defence he successfully resolved the problem of civil–military relations which had bedevilled the politics of the First World War. It is hard to imagine that any British Prime Minister could have done more to bind together the alliance of Britain, the United States, and the Soviet Union.

By all these measures Churchill was a great war leader. Where then is the myth? It lies in the notion that he was always (or almost always) right, and more deeply in a denial of his true personality and the true character of his genius. Churchill was a great war leader but far from infallible. During the 1930s he was perceptive about Germany but confused about Italy and complacent about Japan. The Norwegian campaign of 1940 was a Churchillian disaster. Dakar, Greece, Crete, Singapore, the Italian campaign, and the strategic bombing offensive all raised question marks about his strategic judgement. His faith in the benevolence of Roosevelt and the United States was exaggerated and his attitude to Stalin inconsistent. There were moments when he was rash and impetuous, moments when he was exhausted and depressed, moments when he behaved badly to colleagues or subordinates. The Churchillian myth turned a man of flesh and blood into a statue and a symbol of the Cold War. Much of the so-called revisionism that began after his death, and offended the loyalists who guarded the statue, was not in the least anti-Churchillian. On the contrary it was an attempt to recover the full humanity, and the uneven, intuitive genius, of a character fore-shadowed in Dryden's lines on Achitophel: 'a man so various that he seemed to be, not one, but all mankind's epitome'.

Since Churchill's death, Churchill's own interpretation of history has been modified or superseded by research, a process in which the official biography has played an important part. This phenomenal work, begun by Randolph Churchill with two volumes taking the story up to 1914, and completed in a further six volumes by Sir Martin Gilbert, has been accompanied by a series of companion volumes of documents, of which fourteen have appeared so far. The official biography is sometimes said to perpetuate the Churchill myth and it is true that Randolph Churchill's volumes were partisan. But in Gilbert's hands the biography is essentially a chronicle which makes the evidence from the Churchill papers, and a multitude of other sources, available to readers and researchers alike. It is clear from Gilbert's occasional writings that his admiration for Churchill is profound, but in the biography itself he makes little attempt to mould the materials into a thesis or a set of judgements. Inherently revisionist in the sense that it replaces Churchill's own account of the events in which he was involved, it is a resource quarried by historians and biographers writing from many different points of view.

Among them are the iconoclasts—Clive Ponting, David Irving, John Charmley,[4] and others, who argue that Churchill was everything his harshest critics claimed before 1939, and worse. Ponting's book is a sustained attempt at character assassination that fails to convince because it gets the character wrong. To claim that Churchill was opposed to democracy and social progress is to distort the record of a politician whose faith in parliamentary democracy and compassion for the underdog were deeply rooted. To claim that he was a racist is misleading for the simple reason that it abstracts him from a context in which most educated people, and the most advanced social reformers, believed in racial distinctions. Churchill, moreover, abhorred the racial doctrines of the Nazis and the persecution of the Jews.

In the case of Irving and Charmley the principal charge against Churchill is that he committed Britain in 1940 to a war that destroyed the British Empire, reduced Britain to dependence on the United States, and gave the Soviet Union control of eastern Europe. The argument rests on the assumption that Hitler would have been prepared in 1940 or 1941 to guarantee the future of the British Empire in return for a free hand in Europe. But as David Reynolds has pointed out, whenever Hitler had a free hand in Europe his thoughts turned towards naval expansion and the control of the Atlantic.[5] The assumption that his ambitions were limited to Europe is reminiscent of Neville Chamberlain's belief that they were limited to the incorporation of ethnic Germans in the Reich.

Iconoclasm has failed to convince, and there are places where the Churchill myth still flourishes. His life in the 1930s has been dramatized for television in two successful series: Southern Television's *The Wilderness Years* (1981), with Robert Hardy as Churchill and Sian Phillips as Clementine, and the BBC's *The Gathering Storm* (2002), with Albert Finney and Vanessa Redgrave in the lead roles. The high quality of the acting in both series compensated for the dubious character of the history, which appeared to be stuck in the 1950s. In the United States, meanwhile, Churchill has long been regarded as a political philosopher whose writings and speeches contain lessons for the present and future, and a role model for leadership in public life. There is, however, no such thing as the 'American view of Churchill'. Iconoclasts are also to be found in the United States, where Ralph Raico, a professor of history associated with the Von Mises Institute of free market economics, can write:

There is a way of looking at Winston Churchill that is very tempting: that he was a deeply flawed creature, who was summoned at a critical moment to do battle with a uniquely appalling evil, and whose very flaws contributed to a glorious victory in a way, like Merlin, in C. S. Lewis's great Christian novel, *That Hideous Strength*. Such a judgment would, I believe, be superficial. A candid examination of his career, I suggest, yields a different conclusion: that, when all is said and done, Winston Churchill was a Man of Blood and a politico without principle, whose apotheosis serves to corrupt every standard of honesty and morality in politics and history.[6]

The Churchill Centre, founded by his American admirers to perpetuate his memory, has done much to encourage debate. In

Britain the hagiography of the post-war period has been superseded in recent years by a generally more critical approach. The
loyalists, who used to protest angrily against any critical comment on the great man, have been supplanted by liberals like Roy
Jenkins, who concludes his biography with the following tribute:

I now put Churchill, with all his idiosyncrasies, his indulgences, his
occasional childishness, but also his genius, his tenacity and his persistent
ability, right or wrong, successful or unsuccessful, to be larger than life, as
the greatest human being ever to occupy 10 Downing Street.[7]

Churchill, then, is no longer the hero that he used to be, but in
the end the recognition of his frailties and flaws has worked in his
favour. It has brought him up to date by making him into the kind
of hero our disenchanted culture can accept and admire: a hero
with feet of clay.

Notes

PROLOGUE

1. Cadogan, *The Diaries*, 280, 719, diary entries for 9 May 1940 and 22 Feb. 1945.
2. Bonham-Carter, *Winston Churchill as I Knew Him*, 16, 18.
3. Germains, *The Tragedy of Winston Churchill*, 278, cited in Gardner, *Churchill in his Time*, 1.
4. Rowse, *The Spirit of English History*, title page.
5. Berlin, *Mr Churchill in 1940*, 39.
6. Ramsden, '"That Will Depend on Who Writes the History"', 4 n. 1.

1. THE YOUNGEST MAN IN EUROPE, 1874–1901

1. RSC, *WSC* i. 16; Leslie, *The Fabulous Leonard Jerome*, 34. Leslie gives the name as Mehitabel.
2. Gilbert, *Never Despair*, 1297.
3. Foster, *Lord Randolph Churchill*, 17. Cannadine, 'The Pitfalls of Family Piety', 11.
4. RSC, *WSC* i. 19, Duke of Marlborough to Lord Randolph, 31 Aug. 1873.
5. Ibid. 53.
6. Churchill, *My Early Life*, 19.
7. Bingham, 'School Days', 20–2.
8. RSC, *WSC* i. 197.
9. Gilbert, *Churchill's Political Philosophy*, 1.

255

10. P. Churchill and Mitchell, *Jennie*, 161.

11. Lord Rosebery, *Lord Randolph Churchill*, 72.

12. Mather, 'Lord Randolph Churchill'.

13. Gilbert, *Churchill: A Life*, 49.

14. RSC, *WSC* i. 318, Winston to Lady Randolph, 6 Apr. 1897.

15. Churchill, *The River War* (1899), ii. 248–9.

16. *WSC Companion*, ii, pt. 1, p. xxvii, Churchill to Ivor Guest, 19 Jan. 1899.

17. *WSC Companion*, i, pt. 2, 676.

18. Woods (ed.), *Young Winston's Wars*, 51–2, *Daily Telegraph*, 9 Oct. 1897.

19. Morris, *Pax Britannica*, 151 n. 2.

20. Churchill, *The River War* (1960 edn.), 22–3.

21. Langworth, 'Churchill and Polo'; Harvey (ed.), *Encyclopaedia of Sport*, 233.

22. *Finest Hour*, 93 (Winter 1996–7), 20, speech of 1 June 1899.

23. Churchill, *My Early Life*, 58.

24. Woods (ed.), *Young Winston's Wars*, 70, *Daily Telegraph*, 2 Nov. 1897.

25. Ibid. 277, *Morning Post*, 17 Feb. 1900.

26. Blunt, *My Diaries*, ii. 417, entry for 20 Oct. 1912.

27. Churchill, *Complete Speeches*, i. 35, speech of 26 June 1899.

28. RSC, *WSC* i. 449.

29. Atkins, *Incidents and Reflections*, 122.

30. *Morning Post*, 27 Jan. 1900, repr. in Woods (ed.), *Young Winston's Wars*, 250. Churchill later reproduced much of this report in *My Early Life*.

31. Sandys, *Churchill Wanted Dead or Alive*, 129–30.

32. Hall, *The Book of Churchilliana*, 48. The author notes that Churchill featured on more than thirty cigarette cards between 1901 and 1939.

33. Menpes, 'Young Winston', 33.

34. Addison, *Churchill on the Home Front*, 10–14.

35. For an excellent and thoroughly entertaining account of Churchill's North American tour, see Pilpel, *Churchill in America*, 34–56.

36. Ibid. 39.

37. RSC, *WSC* i. 434.

38. Ensor, *England, 1870–1914*, 268.

39. RSC, *WSC* i. 545.

40. Churchill, *My Early Life*, 9–10.

2. THE RENEGADE, 1901–1911

1. Gilbert, *Churchill: A Life*, 139.

2. Churchill to Harcourt, 14 Mar. 1901. Bodleian Library, MS Harcourt dep 43.

3. Churchill, *Complete Speeches*, i. 78, speech of 13 May 1901.

4. Havighurst, *Radical Journalist*, 124.

5. RSC, *WSC* ii. 35, Cecil to Churchill, 28 Dec. 1901.

6. Addison, *Churchill on the Home Front*, 26, Churchill to Rosebery, 10 Oct. 1902.

7. Webb, *The Diary of Beatrice Webb*, ii. 287, entry for 8 July 1903.

8. Magnus, *King Edward VII*, 432.

9. Foster, *Lord Randolph Churchill*, 400. Foster's concluding chapter, entitled 'Epilogue: The Politics of Piety', supplies a detailed and brilliant exposition of Churchill's methods of historical composition.

10. *The National Review*, no. 275 (Jan. 1906), 775.

11. *The National Review*, no. 287 (Jan. 1907), 758.

12. Hyam, *Elgin and Churchill at the Colonial Office*, 502, 497.

13. Ibid. 503–4.

14. Mungeam, *British Rule in Kenya*, 173.

15. Hyam, *Elgin and Churchill*, 208.

16. Churchill, *My African Journey*, 70–1.

17. Churchill, *Complete Speeches*, i. 676, speech of 11 Oct. 1906.

18. Masterman, *C. F. G. Masterman*, 97.

19. Bonham-Carter, *Winston Churchill as I Knew Him*, 161.

20. Churchill, *Complete Speeches*, i. 1028–30, speech of 4 May 1908.

21. Paterson, *Churchill*, 71–2.

22. Masterman, 'Winston Churchill: The Liberal Phase Part One', 743.

23. Lucy Masterman Diary, 8 Dec. 1910, Masterman Papers 29/2/2/3/5, University of Birmingham Library.

24. RSC, *WSC* ii. 517, quoting from Knollys to Esher, 10 Feb. 1909.

25. Ibid. 334–5.

26. *The Crawford Papers*, ed. Vincent, 153, entry for 9 May 1910.

27. Stafford, *Churchill and Secret Service*, 30, citing Ewart's diary for 17 Dec. 1909.

28. *Washington Post*, 19 Dec. 1909.

29. Gardiner, *Prophets, Priests and Kings*, 234.

30. Masterman, 'Winston Churchill: The Liberal Phase Part One', 747.

31. Clarke, *Lancashire and the New Liberalism*, 195–6.

32. Masterman, 'Winston Churchill: The Liberal Phase Part One', 746.

33. Beatrice Webb, *Our Partnership*, 465–6.

34. MacCallum Scott Diary, vol. 8, 30 July 1917.

35. Addison, *Churchill on the Home Front*, 49.

36. Mendelssohn, *The Age of Churchill*, 437.

37. Addison, *Churchill on the Home Front*, 161.

38. Churchill, *My Early Life*, 273.

39. Radzinowicz and Hood, *The Emergence of Penal Policy*, 770–4; for a detailed analysis of Churchill's penal policy see Baxendale, *Penal Thought and Practice*.

40. Baxendale, *Penal Thought and Practice*, 134.

41. Masterman, 'Winston Churchill: The Liberal Phase Part Two', 822.

42. Radzinowicz and Hood, *The Emergence of Penal Policy*, 332–4.

43. Morgan, *Conflict and Order*, 44–8.

44. Wrigley, *Churchill*, 305–6.

45. Stafford, *Churchill and Secret Service*, 34–6.

3. THE LILLIPUT NAPOLEON, 1911–1915

1. W. S. and Clementine Churchill, *Speaking for Themselves*, 23, 31, Winston to Clementine, 30 May 1909, 19 Sept. 1909.

2. Gilbert, *In Search of Churchill*, 175.

3. Wrigley, 'Churchill and the Trade Unions', 282.

4. Ben-Moshe, *Churchill*, 17.

5. Marder, *From the Dreadnought to Scapa Flow*, i. 255.

6. Gretton, *Former Naval Person*, 117.

7. The British government retained its stake until the 1970s, when it began to reduce its holding. The final 1.8% of the shares were sold for £520m in Dec. 1995.

8. RSC, *WSC* ii. 687–91; Roskill, *Churchill and the Admirals*, 25–6.

9. In his history of the Second World War, Churchill claimed that it was he who initiated the proposals which finally resolved the dispute in 1937. This claim, however, is disputed by Roskill. See Churchill, *The Second World War*, i. 124, 534–6 and Roskill, *Churchill and the Admirals*, 86–7. Churchill was broadly in favour of the Admiralty's position.

10. Lambert, 'British Naval Policy, 1913–1914', 625.

11. Massingham, 'Mr Churchill's Career', 617.

12. Gardiner, *The Pillars of Society*. This was a republication with minor changes of the book as originally published before the outbreak of war in 1914.

13. Riddell, *More Pages from my Diary*, 78, entry for 6 July 1912.

14. Grigg, *Lloyd George*, 368.

15. Riddell, *More Pages*, 194, entry for 6 Jan. 1914.

16. Rhodes James, *Churchill: A Study in Failure*, 62.

17. Jalland, *The Liberals and Ireland*, 222.

18. Wood, *Churchill*, 144.

19. RSC, *WSC* i. 501.

20. *The Crawford Papers*, ed. Vincent, 330; 333, diary entry for 2 May 1914.

21. Gertrude Bell Diary for 1 May 1914, The Gertrude Bell Archive, http://www.gerty.ncl.ac.uk/diaries/d2104.htm; accessed 19 Dec. 2003.

22. Beaverbrook, *Men and Power*, 126.

23. Wood, *Churchill*, 145.

24. W. S. and Clementine Churchill, *Speaking for Themselves*, 96, Winston to Clementine, 28 July 1914.

25. Gardiner, 'Certain People of Importance', 49.

26. Stafford, *Churchill and Secret Service*, 71–5.

27. Gretton, *Former Naval Person*, 147.

28. Stafford, *Churchill and Secret Service*, 66, and see 59–81.

29. Gilbert, *Churchill*, 281.

30. Prior, *Churchill's World Crisis as History*, 34–5.

31. MacCallum Scott, *Winston Churchill in Peace and War*, 95–7, quoting the *Morning Post* of 23 Oct. 1914.

32. Asquith, *Letters to Venetia Stanley*, 284.

33. Best, *Churchill: A Study in Greatness*, 57.

34. Gilbert, *Winston S. Churchill*, iii. 101–15.

35. Marder, *From the Dreadnought to Scapa Flow*, ii. 85.

36. Asquith, *Letters to Venetia Stanley*, 266, Asquith to Venetia Stanley, 7 Oct. 1914.

37. *The Riddell Diaries*, 91–2, entry for 10 Oct. 1914.

38. Beaverbrook, *Men and Power*, 125.

39. Prior, *Churchill's World Crisis*, 231–4; Cruttwell, *A History of the Great War*, 271; Churchill, *The World Crisis*, ii. 78–9.

40. Prior, *Churchill's World Crisis*, 245.

41. Williams, 'Winston S. Churchill', in *Dictionary of National Biography, 1961–1970*, ed. Williams and Nicholls, 199.

42. *Morning Post*, 27 Apr. 1915, quoted in the *Washington Post*, 28 Apr. 1915.

43. Churchill, *The World Crisis*, iv, pt. 1, 244.

44. Beaverbrook, *Men and Power*, 125, quoting Wilson to Bonar Law, 16 May 1915.

45. Marder, *From the Dreadnought to Scapa Flow*, ii. 288.

46. *Lloyd George: A Diary by Frances Stevenson*, 50.

47. Sheffield, *Forgotten Victory*, 96.

48. Gilbert, 'Winston Churchill and the Strain of Office', 30.

4. THE WINSTONBURG LINE, 1915–1924

1. Churchill, *Thoughts and Adventures*, 307.

2. Longford, *Pilgrimage of Passion*, 409.

3. *WSC* iii. 628–8; Captain X, *With Winston Churchill at the Front, 72–8; Sunday Post*, 25 Feb. 1990.

4. Lloyd George, *War Memoirs*, iii. 1071–2, 1067.

5. MacCallum Scott, *Winston Churchill in Peace and War*, 153. His diaries in the Library at the University of Glasgow describe Churchill's briefings.

6. Marder, *Dreadnought to Scapa Flow*, ii. 288.

7. Beaverbrook, *Men and Power*, 132–3, Younger to Lloyd George, 8 June 1917.

8. Ibid. 139.

9. Ponting, *Churchill*, 212.

10. Churchill, *The World Crisis*, iv, pt. 2, 481.

11. Sassoon, *Siegfried's Journey*, 78.

12. Federal Bureau of Investigation Memorandum.

13. Kersaudy, *Churchill and De Gaulle*, 26.

14. De Groot, *Liberal Crusader*, 46.

15. Winter, *A Seat for Life*, 173.

16. TNA PRO CAB 23/10, WC 575, 3 June 1919. Churchill was opposing the removal of wartime powers of censorship.

17. *Lloyd George: A Diary by Frances Stevenson*, 196–7, diary for 17 Jan. 1920.

18. Rose, *Churchill*, 146.

19. Gilbert, *Churchill*, 412.

20. Addison, *Churchill on the Home Front*, 214.

21. Churchill, *The World Crisis*, v. 348.

22. Rose, *Churchill*, 154.

23. Balfour-Paul, 'Britain's Informal Empire in the Middle East', 495.

24. Letter of 25 Mar. 1921, Gertrude Bell Archive, http://www.gerty.ncl.ac.uk/letters/11414.htm; accessed 18 Dec. 2003.

25. Churchill, 'Zionism versus Bolshevism', *Illustrated Sunday Herald*, 8 Feb. 1920, repr. in *The Collected Essays of Sir Winston Churchill*, iv: *Churchill at Large*, ed. Michael Wolff (1976), 29.

26. *WSC Companion*, iv, pt. 2, 1420, remarks by Churchill to a Palestinian delegation, 30 Mar. 1921.

27. Rose, *Chaim Weizmann*, 217.

28. *WSC Companion*, v, pt. 3, 601–2; ibid. 847–8. I am grateful to Sir Martin Gilbert for drawing my attention to the importance of Churchill's evidence to the Peel Commission.

29. *WSC Companion*, iv, pt. 3, 1561, Churchill to Trenchard, 22 July 1921.

30. Ponting, *Churchill*, 257–8.

31. For example, the BBC's world affairs correspondent wrote: 'Foreign powers have always found Iraq ungovernable. Britain discovered that in the 1920s. With Winston Churchill's approval, it even used gas bombs against Kurdish tribesmen who would not pay their taxes.' See Reynolds, 'Iraq the Ungovernable'; Simpson, 'Saddam or not, they just don't want us here'; Cox, 'Falsely Accused'.

32. *WSC Companion*, iv, pt. 3, 1648, Wilson to General Congreve, 11 Oct. 1921.

33. 'A Gentleman with a Duster' (Harold Begbie), *The Mirrors of Downing Street*, 103.

34. Roskill, *Hankey: Man of Secrets*, ii. 232; Sylvester, *Life with Lloyd George*, 77.

35. Charles Carrington to the author, 12 Oct. 1982.

36. Addison, *Churchill on the Home Front*, 212.

37. Pearson, *Facades: Edith, Osbert and Sacheverell Sitwell*, 137.

38. Sitwell, *Laughter in the Next Room*, 27; Pearson, *Facades*, 342.

39. *The Star*, 10 May 1922. Low's cartoons are held at the Centre for the Study of Cartoons and Caricature at the University of Canterbury, and can be viewed online at http://library.kent.ac.uk/cartoons/.

40. Churchill, *Thoughts and Adventures*, 213.

41. W. S. and Clementine Churchill, *Speaking for Themselves*, 203.

42. Churchill, *The World Crisis*, v. 454.

43. Churchill, *Shall We Commit Suicide?*, 7–8. This is a reprint by the International Churchill Society of a pamphlet published by the Eilert Printing Company in New York in late 1924. The article was first published in *Nash's Pall Mall Magazine*, 24 Sept. 1924.

44. Bacon et al., *'The World Crisis' by Winston Churchill*.

45. Quoted in Berlin, *Mr Churchill in 1940*, 9. Berlin does not identify Read, who was writing in 1928, by name.

46. Wells, *The Shape of Things to Come*, 67.

47. Pelling, *Winston Churchill*, 287.

48. Gilbert, *Winston S. Churchill*, v. 59.

5. RESPECTABILITY WON AND LOST, 1924–1939

1. Colvin, 'The Great Mr Churchill'.

2. Skidelsky, *Keynes: Economist as Saviour*, 198; Addison, *Churchill on the Home Front*, 247–8, Churchill to Niemeyer 22 Feb. 1925.

3. Grigg, *Prejudice and Judgment*, 182–4.

4. Skidelsky, *Keynes: The Economist as Saviour*, 203.

5. *WSC Companion*, v, pt. 1, 306.

6. Wilson, *A Study in the History and Policies of the Morning Post*, 264.

7. Davidson, *Memoirs of a Conservative*, 242.

8. Ibid. 243.

9. *The Reith Diaries*, 96, diary entry for 9 May 1926.

10. http://king.archives.ca (accessed 9 Dec. 2003), Diary for 3 May 1926.

11. Gilbert, *Winston S. Churchill*, v. 173.

12. Cole, *A History of the Labour Party*, 185.

13. Wells, *Meanwhile*, 106.

14. Ephesian, *Winston Churchill*, 267.

15. Feiling, *Neville Chamberlain*, 129.

16. *WSC Companion*, v, pt. 1, 1328–9, NC to Irwin 12 Aug. 1928.

17. Johnson, 'Churchill and France', 53.

18. Beloff, 'The Special Relationship', 154.

19. *WSC Companion*, i, pt. 2, 937, Churchill to Lady Randolph, 22 May 1898.

20. Churchill, Preface to McVeagh, *Home Rule in a Nutshell*.

21. Churchill, *Complete Speeches*, iii. 2614–15, speech of 4 July 1918.

22. Churchill, *The Second World War*, i. 19–20.

23. O'Brien, 'Churchill and the US Navy 1919–1929', 34, quoting from Churchill's Cabinet memorandum of 29 June 1927.

24. *WSC Companion*, v, pt. 1, 1033, Cabinet memorandum of 20 July 1927.

25. *WSC Companion*, v, pt. 1, 342.

26. Ibid. 308.

27. RSC, *Twenty-One Years*, 74. Randolph, however, was unteachable. Many years later he was involved in an argument at a dinner party when a fellow guest, an executive with British Petroleum, attempted to put in a word. 'You have nothing to contribute to this', Randolph shouted. 'You are only a clerk in an oil store.' The story is told by John Colville in *The Churchillians*, 24.

28. *Appleton Post-Crescent*, 11 Sept. 1929.

29. *New York Times*, 26 Oct. 1929.

30. For Churchill's North American tour see Pilpel, *Churchill in America*, 78–85, a witty and sparkling account, and Gilbert, *Churchill*, 492–4.

31. Churchill, *Complete Speeches*, v. 5205, speech of 23 Nov. 1932.

32. Pilpel, *Churchill in America*, 111.

33. Churchill, 'Parliamentary Government and the Economic Problem'.

34. *WSC Companion*, v, pt. 2, 163, Fisher to Irwin, 20 June 1930.

35. Gilbert, *Churchill*, 499.

36. Howard, *RAB: The Life of R. A. Butler*, 46, quoting a letter from Butler to his parents, 4 Mar. 1931.

37. Davidson, *Memoirs of a Conservative*, 355.

38. Ball, 'Baldwin and the Conservative Party', 124.

39. Davidson, *Memoirs of a Conservative*, 384.

40. J. H. Morgan to A. C. Murray, 4 Dec. 1949, Arthur C. Murray Papers 8811, National Library of Scotland.

41. Gilbert, *Churchill: A Photographic Portrait*, fig. 200.

42. *WSC Companion*, v, pt. 2, 567, Hoare to Willingdon, 6 Apr. 1933.

43. Campbell, 'The Development of RDF and the Heavy Bomber', 92, Neville to Hilda Chamberlain, 9 Mar. 1935. I am grateful to Mr Campbell for this reference from his D.Phil. thesis.

44. Ibid. 389, Beaverbrook to Garvin, 2 Jan. 1932.

45. *Lloyd George: A Diary*, 253, diary for 13 Feb. 1934.

46. TNA PRO CAB 23/29, Minutes of a conference of ministers at 10 Downing Street, 5 Feb. 1922.

47. Campbell, *F. E. Smith*, 733, 762.

48. Ibid. 823–5.

49. Ponting, *Churchill*, 254 (quoting *WSC Companion*, v, pt. 3, 616).

50. Rose, *Churchill*, 193.

51. W. S. and Clementine Churchill, *Speaking for Themselves*, 412, Winston to Clementine, 21 Feb. 1936.

52. Churchill, *The Second World War*, i. 65–6; Gilbert, *Winston S. Churchill*, v. 447–8.

53. Attlee, 'The Churchill I Knew', 23.

54. Gilbert, *Winston S. Churchill*, v. 457.

55. Churchill, *Complete Speeches*, v. 5262, speech of 13 Apr. 1933.

56. Overy, 'German Air Strength 1933 to 1939', 469.

57. *WSC Companion*, v, pt. 3, 1594.

58. Liddell Hart, 'Churchill in War', 16.

59. Churchill, *Complete Speeches*, vi. 5720, speech of 26 Mar. 1936.

60. Interview with Isaiah Berlin, 30 Jan. 1991.

61. Diary of William Lyon Mackenzie King, 21 Oct. 1936, Canadian National Archives, www.http//king.archives.ca.

62. Churchill, *Complete Speeches*, v. 4990–1, speech of 6 Mar. 1931; Conquest, *The Great Terror*, 43–7, 454.

63. Hobsbawm, *Age of Extremes*, 391; Lowe, 'Armed Forces', 1230.

64. In Apr. 1936 Hankey reported to Inskip after a conversation with Churchill that he was apparently 'a bosom friend of M Maisky'. See *WSC Companion*, v, pt. 3, 108, Hankey to Inskip, 19 Apr. 1936.

65. Rose, *Churchill*, 239; see also Carlton, *Churchill and the Soviet Union*, 50–8.

66. Churchill, *Step by Step*, article of 30 Dec. 1938.

67. *The Crawford Papers*, 575, diary for 12 Dec. 1936.

68. McKenzie, *British Political Parties*, 47 n. 1.

69. Nicolson, *Diaries and Letters, 1930–1939*, 332, diary for 16 Mar. 1938.

70. Ibid. 328, diary for 2 Mar. 1938.

71. Churchill, *Complete Speeches*, vi. 5962, speech of 9 May 1938.

72. Mowat, *Britain between the Wars*, 619.

73. Feiling, *Neville Chamberlain*, 381.

74. Churchill, *Complete Speeches*, vi. 6004, 6005, 6003, speech of 5 Oct. 1938.

75. Amery, *The Empire at Bay*, 527, diary for 5 Oct. 1938; Channon, *Chips: The Diaries of Sir Henry Channon*, 173, diary for 5 Oct. 1938.

76. Koss, *The Rise and Fall of the Political Press in Britain*, ii. 583, quoting Fraser to Dalton, 20 Oct. 1938.

77. *The Record*, Dec. 1938, 128.

6. THE MAKING OF A HERO, 1939–1945

1. Diary of Mackenzie King, 10 June 1939, Canadian National Archives.

2. Cantril, *Public Opinion, 1935–1946*, 106.

3. *Picture Post 1938–1950*, ed. Tom Hopkinson, 63.

4. *Washington Post*, 6 July 1939.

5. *Daily Telegraph*, 3 July 1939.

6. *Observer*, 9 July 1939; *Daily Mirror*, 13 July 1939.

7. Neville to Hilda Chamberlain, 15 Apr. 1939, Chamberlain Papers.

8. Vincent, John, 'Chamberlain', 382.

9. Nicolson, *Diaries and Letters, 1939–1945*, 33, entry for 26 Sept. 1939.

10. Fyfe, *Britain's War-Time Revolution*, 15, 17; *Daily Herald*, 4 Oct. 1939; *Daily Mirror*, 3 Oct. 1939. Connor wrote under the pseudonym 'Cassandra'.

11. *New York Times*, 8 Oct. 1939. The article appeared beneath a cartoon of Churchill as a bricklayer.

12. *Manchester Guardian*, 21 Feb. 1940.

13. Cantril, *Public Opinion 1939–1946*, 97; *News Chronicle*, 1 Jan. 1940.

14. *The Crawford Papers*, 614, diary for 18 Feb. 1940. This was the last entry in a diary begun in May 1892.

15. Roskill, *Churchill and the Admirals*, 94; *Sunday Times*, 13 July 1980.

16. Marder, 'Winston is Back', 54.

17. Liddell Hart, 'The Military Strategist', 187.

18. Churchill, *The Second World War*, i. 527.

19. Amery, *The Empire at Bay*, 595.

20. Howard, *RAB: The Life of R. A. Butler*, 94.

21. Churchill, *The Second World War*, iii. 556.

22. Gilbert, *Finest Hour*, 333.

23. Dalton, *Second World War Diary*, 28, entry for 28 May 1940.

24. Mackenzie, *The Home Guard*, 47–9.

25. Roberts, *Eminent Churchillians*, 209 and ch. 3, 'The Tories versus Churchill during the "Finest Hour"'.

26. Last, *Nella Last's War*, 55, diary for 11 May 1940.

27. Churchill, *Complete Speeches*, vi. 6220 (13 May), 6231 (4 June), 6266 (20 Aug.).

28. Ibid. 6238 (18 June).

29. *Change No. 2: Home Propaganda*, Mass-Observation file 910, Mass-Observation Archive, p. 18.

30. Hall, *The Book of Churchilliana*, 33–7, 146–9.

31. Mass-Observation file report No. 654, 10 Apr. 1941, 'Answers to Questions about Churchill'.

32. Mass-Observation file report No. 683, 4 May 1941, 'Plymouth'.

33. Opie, *The Lore and Language of Schoolchildren*, 104.

34. Gilbert, *Never Despair*, 308.

35. Colville in Wheeler-Bennett (ed.), *Action This Day*, 50.

36. W. S. and Clementine Churchill, *Speaking for Themselves* 454, Clementine to Winston, 27 June 1940.

37. Skidelsky, *Keynes: Fighting for Britain*, 80, quoting Keynes to Florence Keynes, 6 Sept. 1940.

38. Williams, *Nothing so Strange*.

39. Mack, 'Yalta: Memories of a Wren', 31.

40. Alanbrooke, *War Diaries*, p. xvi.

41. Keegan, *The Second World War*, 259. Keegan does not give the original source.

42. Stafford, *Churchill and Secret Service*, 189.

43. Dalton, *Diary*, 62, entry for 22 July 1940.

44. De Gaulle, *Complete War Memoirs*, 104.

45. Churchill, *The Second World War*, ii. 495, 503.

46. Skidelsky, *Keynes: Fighting for Britain*, 103.

47. *Washington Post*, 11–12 May 1940. The articles were by Jack Culmer and Medley Donovan respectively.

48. *Washington Post*, 23 Sept. 1940.

49. *Washington Post*, 31 Dec. 1940.

50. Alanbrooke, *War Diaries*, 401, entry for 10 May 1943.

51. Jacob, in Wheeler-Bennett (ed.), *Action This Day*, 198.

52. Ismay, *The Memoirs of Lord Ismay*, 269–70.

53. Alanbrooke, *War Diaries*, p. xv; Lewin, *Churchill as Warlord*, 57.

54. Roskill, *Churchill and the Admirals*, 278.

55. Alanbrooke, *War Diaries*, 451.

56. *Winston Churchill: Memoirs and Tributes Broadcast by the BBC*, 95.

57. Mallaby, *From My Level*, 29–30.

58. Kimball, *Forged in War*, 22.

59. Hopkins, *The White House Papers*, ii. 685.

60. Gilbert, *Road to Victory*, 1225.

61. Maclean, *Eastern Approaches*, 280.

62. For Churchill's day see Sir Ian Jacob in Wheeler-Bennett, *Action This Day*, 180–1, 183.

63. Alanbrooke, *War Diaries*, 233.

64. Colville, *The Fringes of Power*.

65. Carlton, *Churchill and the Soviet Union*, 96–8.

66. Churchill, *The Second World War*, iii. 539.

67. Gilbert, *Road to Victory*, 29, 34.

68. Churchill, *The Churchill War Papers*, iii. 1639, Churchill to the Chiefs of Staff, 17 Dec. 1941.

69. Churchill, *The Second World War*, iv. 43.

70. Nicolson, *Diaries and Letters, 1939–1945,* 209, diary for 16 Feb. 1942.

71. Ibid. 221, diary for 22 Apr. 1942.

72. Gardner, *Churchill in his Time,* 175–80.

73. Colville, *The Fringes of Power,* 563, diary for 23 Feb. 1945.

74. Moore, *Churchill, Cripps and India, 1939–1945,* 136–8.

75. Moran, *Winston Churchill: The Struggle for Survival, 1940–1965,* 72.

76. Churchill, *The Second World War,* iv. 433.

77. Gilbert, *Road to Victory,* 254.

78. Thorne, *Allies of a Kind,* 209–11.

79. Churchill, *The Churchill War Papers,* iii. 1313, Churchill to Portal, 7 Oct. 1941.

80. Chandler, 'The Church of England and the Obliteration Bombing'.

81. Gilbert, *Road to Victory,* 437.

82. Ibid. 840–1, 864–5.

83. This outline is based on a thorough analysis of the question in an unpublished paper, 'The Origins of the Raid' by Sebastian Cox, the head of the Air Historical Branch of the Ministry of Defence. I am grateful to Mr Cox for allowing me to read and cite this paper. For another excellent treatment of the subject see Taylor, *Dresden,* 179–92.

84. Taylor, *Dresden,* 368–72.

85. Ibid. 361–5.

86. For the original and revised versions of Churchill's minute see Webster and Frankland, *Strategic Air Offensive,* iii. 112, 117.

87. Taylor, *Dresden,* 378.

88. Gilbert, *Road to Victory,* 1242–3.

89. Ibid. 245.

90. M. Cohen, *Churchill and the Jews,* 294–305.

91. Ibid. 254–6.

92. Ibid. 258, 260.

93. Churchill, *The Second World War*, iv. 720; v. 110.

94. Alanbrooke, *War Diaries*, 442.

95. Jacob, in Wheeler-Bennett, *Action This Day*, 209.

96. Bonham-Carter, *Champion Redoubtable*, 312–13, diary for 1 Aug. 1944.

97. Alanbrooke, *War Diaries*, 473.

98. *Finest Hour*, 104 (Autumn 1999), 104, dateline London, 21 Oct. 1999, release of records at the PRO.

99. W. S. and Clementine Churchill, *Speaking for Themselves*, 501, Winston to Clementine, 17 Aug. 1944.

100. Skidelsky, *Keynes: Fighting for Britain*, 363.

101. Maclean, *Eastern Approaches*, 402–3.

102. Churchill, *The Second World War*, vi. 124.

103. Orwell, *The Collected Essays, Journalism and Letters*, iii. 262, *Tribune* article of 1 Sept. 1944.

104. W. S. and Clementine Churchill, *Speaking for Themselves*, 506, Winston to Clementine, 13 Oct. 1944.

105. Gilbert, *Road to Victory*, 1085–6.

106. Clogg, 'Greece', 507.

107. Gardner, *Churchill in his Time*, 266.

108. MacDonald, *The History of The Times*, v. 121. The article appeared on 1 Jan. 1945.

109. Dalton, *Diary*, 836, entry for 23 Feb. 1945.

110. Gilbert, *Road to Victory*, 1234, speech of 27 Feb. 1945.

111. Channon, *Chips*, 398, diary for 28 Feb. 1945.

112. Nicolson, *Diaries and Letters, 1939–1945*, 440–1, diary for 27 Feb. 1945.

113. Gilbert, *Road to Victory*, 1276, citing Churchill to Eisenhower, 2 Apr. 1945.

114. Ibid. 470–1.

115. Pickersgill and Forster, *The Mackenzie King Record*, iii. 236. Mackenzie King dined with Churchill on the evening of 22 May 1946.

116. Harvie Watt, *Most of My Life*, 117.

117. Bonham-Carter, *Champion Redoubtable*, 314, entry for 1 Aug. 1944.

118. Stafford, *Churchill and Secret Service*, 315.

119. Mass-Observation file report No. 2268, 'General Election 1945', 13, 15, Mass-Observation archive.

120. Churchill, *The Second World War*, vi. 583.

7. CLIMBING OLYMPUS, 1945–1965

1. *The Diaries of Harold Nicolson*, iii. 178, diary for 28 June 1950.

2. *Evening Standard*, 31 July 1945, accessed online at http://library.kent.ac.uk/cartoons/.

3. Pickersgill and Forster, *The Mackenzie King Record*, iii. 85. The lunch took place on 26 Oct.

4. Ramsden, *The Making of Conservative Party Policy*, 114.

5. Bevan, 'History's Impresario', 57.

6. *Daily Telegraph*, 21 Apr. 1947.

7. The inscription is noted in a catalogue of books for sale in 1976 from a Lincolnshire bookseller, Anthony W. Laywood. All the books listed bore the bookplates of Winston Churchill or his son Randolph. I am grateful to Mr Alan Bell for sending me a copy of the catalogue.

8. Gilbert, *Never Despair*, 317.

9. Thomson, 'All The Racehorses Churchill ever Owned'; see also Thomson, 'Churchill and the Lure of the Turf'; Colville, *The Churchillians*, 26–7.

10. Montague Browne, *Long Sunset*, 151.

11. Gilbert, *Never Despair*, 200.

12. Bullock, *Ernest Bevin: Foreign Secretary 1945–1951*, 224–7.

13. *New York Times*, 6 Mar. 1946.

14. *Washington Post*, 7 Mar. 1946; 25 Mar. 1946.

15. Pickersgill and Forster, *The Mackenzie King Record*, iv. 112.

16. *Time* Person of the Year Archive: Winston Churchill 1950, http://www.time.com/time/poy2000/archive/1949.html (accessed 8 Dec. 2001).

17. Ramsden, 'How Winston Churchill Became "The Greatest Living Englishman"', 2.

18. Pickersgill and Forster, *The Mackenzie King Record*, iv. 112, 117–18.

19. Chamberlain Papers, Neville to Hilda Chamberlain , 17 Sept. 1939. For Churchill's publication of the exchange of letters see Churchill, *The Second World War*, i. 359–60.

20. Ben-Moshe, *Churchill: Strategy and History*, 333.

21. For a detailed examination and critique of Churchill's composition of *The Gathering Storm*, see Reynolds, 'Churchill's Writing of History'.

22. Churchill, 'The United States of Europe', in *Collected Essays*, ii. 184.

23. Gilbert, 'Churchill and the European Idea', 201, citing Churchill's speech of 9 Oct. 1948.

24. Churchill, *Europe Unite*, 21, 25, speech of 6 Mar. 1947.

25. Addison, *Churchill on the Home Front*, 386–402.

26. Colville, *The Fringes of Power*, 644, diary for 22–3 Mar. 1952.

27. Bonham-Carter, *Daring to Hope*, 137, diary for 29–30 May 1954.

28. Hennessy, *The Prime Minister*, 205.

29. Louis, 'Churchill and Egypt, 1946–1956', 473.

30. Vaisse, 'Churchill and France, 1951–1955', 166.

31. Gilbert, *Never Despair*, 1100.

32. *The Macmillan Diaries*, 397–8, diary for 26 Feb. to 1 Mar. 1955.

33. Ramsden, 'How Churchill Became "The Greatest Living Englishman"', 7.

34. Montague Browne, *Long Sunset*, 171.

35. Berlin, *Mr Churchill in 1940*, 39. The reference is to a reprint of the review in book form.

36. Interview with Sir Isaiah Berlin, 30 Jan. 1991.

37. TNA PRO PREM 11/239 Norman Brook to Churchill, 29 Sept. 1952; Young, *Baldwin*, 30.

38. J. F. C. Fuller to Jay Luvaas, 28 July 1963, enclosing a copy of the original draft. I am grateful to Professor Luvaas for providing me with a copy of this letter. For the published version, in which Fuller quoted the critical opinions of others, see Fuller, *The Conduct of War, 1789–1961*, 253–4.

39. Montague Browne, *Long Sunset*, 213.

40. I have taken these quotations from the 'Churchill's People' edition of Churchill, *A History of the English-Speaking Peoples*, iv: *The Great Democracies*.

41. Montague Browne, *Long Sunset*, 319.

42. Bryant, *The Turn of the Tide, 1939–1943*; *Triumph in the West*.

43. Quoted in Bond, 'Alanbrooke and Britain's Strategy', 177.

44. This is the case argued by Bond in 'Alanbrooke and Britain's Strategy'.

45. Gilbert, *Never Despair*, 1232.

46. Ramsden, *Man of the Century*, 215.

47. Moran, *Winston Churchill*, 722, diary for 10 Apr. 1957.

48. Fuller, *The Conduct of War*, 264, 282, 287–9.

49. Quoted in Ben-Moshe, *Churchill: Strategy and History*, 329.

50. *The Letters of Evelyn Waugh*, 630, Waugh to Ann Fleming 27 Jan. 1965.

8. CHURCHILL PAST AND PRESENT

1. *Churchill by his Contemporaries*, 22.

2. Bonham Carter, *Churchill*, 220–1.

3. Ramsden, *Man of the Century*, 154–222.

4. Ponting, *Churchill*; Irving, *Churchill's War*; Charmley, *Churchill: The End of Glory*.

5. Reynolds, 'Churchill the Appeaser?', 197–220.

6. Raico, *Rethinking Churchill*, pt. 5.

7. Jenkins, *Churchill*, 912.

Bibliography

Unless otherwise stated, the place of publication is London.

ADDISON, PAUL, *Churchill on the Home Front, 1900–1955* (1992).

ALANBROOKE, FIELD MARSHAL LORD, *War Diaries, 1939–1945*, ed. Alex Danchev and Daniel Todman (2001).

AMERY, LEO, *The Empire at Bay: The Leo Amery Diaries, 1929–1945*, ed. John Barnes and David Nicholson (1988).

ASQUITH, H. H., *H. H. Asquith: Letters to Venetia Stanley*, ed. Michael and Eleanor Brock (Oxford, 1982).

ATKINS, J. B., *Incidents and Reflections* (1947).

ATTLEE, LORD, 'The Churchill I Knew', in *Churchill by his Contemporaries: An Observer Appreciation* (1965).

BACON, REGINALD S., et al., *'The World Crisis' by Winston Churchill: A Criticism* (1927).

BALFOUR-PAUL, GLEN, 'Britain's Informal Empire in the Middle East', in Judith M. Brown and William Roger Louis (eds.), *The Oxford History of the British Empire: The Twentieth Century* (1999).

BARNETT, ANTHONY, *Iron Britannia: Why Parliament Waged its Falklands War* (1982).

BAXENDALE, A. S., 'The Penal Thought and Practice of Winston Leonard Spencer Churchill' (M.Phil. thesis, Queen Mary College, University of London, 2004).

BEAVERBROOK, LORD, *Men and Power, 1917–1918* (1956).

BELL, GERTRUDE: Gertrude Bell Archive, http://www.gerty.ncl.ac.uk.

BELOFF, MICHAEL, 'The Special Relationship: An Anglo-American Myth', in Martin Gilbert (ed.), *Essays for A. J. P. Taylor* (1966).

BEN-MOSHE, TUVIA, *Churchill: Strategy and History* (1992).

BERLIN, ISAIAH, *Mr Churchill in 1940* [1949].

BEST, GEOFFREY, *Churchill: A Study in Greatness* (2001).

BEVAN, ANEURIN, 'History's Impresario', in *Churchill by his Contemporaries: An 'Observer' Appreciation* (1965).

BINGHAM, ERIC and HILDA, 'School Days: Young Winston's Mr Somervell', *Finest Hour*, 86 (Spring 1995), 20–2.

BLUNT, WILFRED SCAWEN, *My Diaries*, ii: *1900–1914* (1920).

BOND, BRIAN, 'Alanbrooke and Britain's Strategy', in Lawrence Freedman, Paul Hayes, and Robert O'Neill (eds.), *War, Strategy and International Politics: Essays in Honour of Sir Michael Howard* (Oxford, 1992).

BONHAM-CARTER, VIOLET, *Champion Redoubtable: The Diaries and Letters of Violet Bonham-Carter, 1914–1945*, ed. Mark Pottle (1998).

—— *Daring to Hope: The Diaries and Letters of Violet Bonham-Carter, 1946–1969*, ed. Mark Pottle (2000).

—— *Winston Churchill as I Knew Him* (1965).

BRYANT, ARTHUR, *Triumph in the West* (1959).

—— *The Turn of the Tide, 1939–1943* (1957).

BULLOCK, ALAN, *Ernest Bevin: Foreign Secretary, 1945–1951* (1983).

CADOGAN, SIR ALEXANDER, *The Diaries of Sir Alexander Cadogan, 1938–1945*, ed. David Dilks (1971).

CAMPBELL, IAIN, 'The Development of RDF and the Heavy Bomber: Case Studies in the Rearmament of the Royal Air Force' (unpublished, 1980).

CAMPBELL, JOHN, *F. E. Smith: First Earl of Birkenhead* (1983).

—— *Margaret Thatcher*, ii: *The Iron Lady* (2003).

CANNADINE, DAVID, 'The Pitfalls of Family Piety', in Robert Blake and William Roger Louis (eds.), *Churchill* (Oxford, 1993).

CAPTAIN X [Andrew Dewar Gibb], *With Winston Churchill at the Front* (1924).

CANTRIL, HADLEY, *Public Opinion, 1935–1946* (Princeton, 1951).

CHAMBERLAIN, NEVILLE, Papers in the Library of the University of Birmingham.

CHANDLER, ANDREW, 'The Church of England and the Obliteration Bombing of Germany in the Second World War', *English Historical Review*, 108, no. 429 (Oct. 1993), 920–46.

CHANNON, SIR HENRY, *Chips: The Diaries of Sir Henry Channon*, ed. Robert Rhodes James (1967).

BIBLIOGRAPHY

CHARMLEY, JOHN, *Churchill: The End of Glory* (1992).

CHURCHILL, PEREGRINE, and MITCHELL, JULIAN, *Jennie* (1976).

CHURCHILL, RANDOLPH S., *Twenty-One Years* (1964).

CHURCHILL, WINSTON S., *The Churchill War Papers*, iii: *The Ever-Widening War 1941*, ed. Martin Gilbert (2000).

—— *The Collected Essays of Sir Winston Churchill*, ii: *Churchill and Politics*, ed. Michael Wolff (1976)

—— *Europe Unite: Speeches, 1947 and 1948*, ed. Randolph S. Churchill (1950).

—— *His Complete Speeches, 1897–1963*, ed. Robert Rhodes James (New York, 1974), i: *1897–1908*; iii: *1914–1922*; v: *1928–1935*; vi: *1935–1942*.

—— *A History of the English-Speaking Peoples*, iv: *The Great Democracies* (1974 edn.).

—— *My African Journey* (1972 edn.).

—— *My Early Life* (1944 edn.).

—— 'Parliamentary Government and the Economic Problem', in *Thoughts and Adventures* (1932), 229–41.

—— Preface to Jeremiah McVeagh, *Home Rule in a Nutshell: A Pocket Book for Speakers and Electors*, 3rd edn. (n.d. but preface dated Dec. 1911).

—— *The River War* (1899 edn.).

—— *The River War* (1960 edn.).

—— *The Second World War*, i: *The Gathering Storm* (1948); ii: *Their Finest Hour* (1949); iii: *The Grand Alliance* (1950); iv: *The Hinge of Fate* (1951); v: *Closing the Ring* (1952); vi: *Triumph and Tragedy* (1954).

—— *Secret Session Speeches* (1946).

—— *Shall We Commit Suicide?* (1994).

—— *Step by Step, 1936–1939* (1939).

—— *Thoughts and Adventures* (1932).

—— *The World Crisis*, i: *1911–1914* (1923); ii: *1915* (1923); iv: *1916–1918*, pts. 1 and 2 (1927); v: *The Aftermath* (1929).

—— and Churchill, Clementine, *Speaking for Themselves: The Personal Letters of Winston and Clementine Churchill*, ed. Mary Soames (1998).

CLARKE, PETER, *Lancashire and the New Liberalism* (Cambridge, 1971).

CLOGG, RICHARD, 'Greece', in I. C. B. Dear (ed.), *The Oxford Companion to the Second World War* (Oxford, 1995).

COHEN, MICHAEL, *Churchill and the Jews* (1985).

COLE, G. D. H., *A History of the Labour Party from 1914* (1948).

COLVILLE, JOHN, in John Wheeler-Bennet (ed.), *Action This Day: Working with Churchill* (1968).

—— *The Churchillians* (1981).

—— *The Fringes of Power: Downing Street Diaries, 1939–1955* (1985).

COLVIN, IAN, 'The Great Mr Churchill', *Atlantic Monthly*, Feb. 1925.

CONQUEST, ROBERT, *The Great Terror* (Harmondsworth, 1971).

COX, SEBASTIAN, 'Falsely Accused', *Sunday Telegraph*, 7 Dec. 2003.

The Crawford Papers: The Journals of David Lindsay Twenty-seventh Earl of Crawford and Tenth Earl of Balcarres 1871–1940 during the Years 1892 to 1940, ed. John Vincent (Manchester, 1984).

CRUTTWELL, C. R. M. F., *A History of the Great War, 1914–1918* (1936 edn.).

DALTON, HUGH, *The Second World War Diary of Hugh Dalton, 1940–1945*, ed. Ben Pimlott (1986).

DAVIDSON, J. C. C., *Memoirs of a Conservative: J. C. C. Davidson's Memoirs and Papers, 1910–1937*, ed. Robert Rhodes James (1969).

DE GAULLE, CHARLES, *The Complete War Memoirs of Charles de Gaulle, 1940–1946* (New York, 1964).

DE GROOT, GERARD, *Liberal Crusader: The Life of Sir Archibald Sinclair* (1993).

ENSOR, R. C. K., *England, 1870–1914* (1936).

EPHESIAN [Carl Bechhofer Roberts], *Winston Churchill* (1927).

Federal Bureau of Investigation, Freedom of Information and Privacy Acts, Winston Churchill Part 1b, Memorandum of 27 July 1943, accessed online at http://foia.fbi.gov/churchill1b.pdf.

FEILING, KEITH, *Neville Chamberlain* (1946).

FOSTER, R. F., *Lord Randolph Churchill: A Political Life* (Oxford, 1981).

FULLER, MAJOR-GENERAL J. F. C., *The Conduct of War, 1789–1961* (1961, 1972 edn.).

FYFE, HAMILTON, *Britain's War-Time Revolution* (1944).

GARDINER, A. G., *The Pillars of Society* (1916 edn.).

—— *Prophets, Priests and Kings* (1914 edn.).

GARDNER, BRIAN, *Churchill in his Time: A Study in a Reputation, 1939–1945* (1968).

'A Gentleman with a Duster' [Harold Begbie], *The Mirrors of Downing Street: Some Political Reflections* (1920).

GERMAINS, VICTOR WALLACE, *The Tragedy of Winston Churchill* (1931).

GILBERT, MARTIN, *Churchill: A Life* (1991).

—— 'Churchill and the European Idea', in R. A. C. Parker (ed.), *Winston Churchill: Studies in Statesmanship* (1995).

—— 'Churchill for Today', *Finest Hour*, 113 (Winter 2001–2).

—— *Churchill's Political Philosophy* (1981).

—— *Finest Hour: Winston S. Churchill, 1939–1941* (1983).

—— *In Search of Churchill: A Historian's Journey* (1994).

—— *Never Despair: Winston S. Churchill, 1945–1965* (1988).

—— *Road to Victory: Winston S. Churchill, 1941–1945* (1986).

—— *Winston S. Churchill*, iii: *1914–1916* (1971); v: *1922–1939* (1976).

—— 'Winston Churchill and the Strain of Office, 1914–1915', in *Facing Armageddon: The First World War Experienced* (1996), 27–36.

GRETTON, SIR PETER, *Former Naval Person: Winston Churchill and the Royal Navy* (1968).

GRIGG, JOHN, *Lloyd George: The People's Champion, 1902–1911* (1978).

GRIGG, P. J., *Prejudice and Judgment* (1948).

HALL, DOUGLAS, *The Book of Churchilliana* (2002).

HARVEY, CHARLES (ed.), *Encyclopaedia of Sport* (1959).

HARVIE WATT, G. S., *Most of My Life* (1980).

HAVIGHURST, ALFRED, *Radical Journalist: H. W. Massingham, 1860–1924* (1974).

HENNESSY, PETER, *The Prime Minister: The Office and its Holders since 1945* (2001).

HOBSBAWM, ERIC, *Age of Extremes: The Short Twentieth Century, 1914–1991* (1995).

HOPKINS, HARRY L., *The White House Papers of Harry L. Hopkins*, ii: *January 1942 to July 1945*, ed. Robert E. Sherwood (1949).

HOWARD, ANTHONY, *RAB: The Life of R. A. Butler* (1987).

HYAM, RONALD, *Elgin and Churchill at the Colonial Office, 1905–1908* (1968).

IRVING, DAVID, *Churchill's War: The Struggle for Power* (1989 edn.).

ISMAY, H. L., *The Memoirs of Lord Ismay* (1960).

BIBLIOGRAPHY

JACOB, SIR IAN, in Sir John Wheeler-Bennett (ed.), *Action This Day: Working with Churchill* (1968).

JALLAND, PAT, *The Liberals and Ireland: The Ulster Question and British Politics to 1914* (1980).

JENKINS, ROY, *Churchill* (2000).

JOHNSON, DOUGLAS, 'Churchill and France', in Robert Blake and William Roger Louis (eds.), *Churchill* (1993).

KEEGAN, JOHN, *The Second World War* (1989).

KERSAUDY, FRANÇOIS, *Churchill and De Gaulle* (1981).

KIMBALL, WARREN, *Forged in War: Churchill, Roosevelt and the Second World War* (1997).

KOSS, STEPHEN, *The Rise and Fall of the Political Press in Britain*, ii (1984).

LAMBERT, ANDREW, 'British Naval Policy, 1913–1914: Financial Limitation and Strategic Revolution', *Journal of Modern History*, 67 (Sept. 1995), 595–626.

LANGWORTH, BARBARA, 'Churchill and Polo', *Finest Hour*, 72 (3rd quarter, 1991).

LAST, NELLA, *Nella Last's War: A Mother's Diary, 1939–1945*, ed. Richard Broad and Suzie Fleming (Bristol, 1981).

LESLIE, ANITA, *The Fabulous Leonard Jerome* (1954).

LEWIN, RONALD, *Churchill as Warlord* (1973).

LIDDELL HART, BASIL, 'Churchill in War', *Encounter*, Apr. 1966.

—— 'The Military Strategist', in A. J. P. Taylor et al., *Churchill: Four Faces and the Man* (Harmondsworth, 1973), 153–202.

LLOYD GEORGE, DAVID, *War Memoirs*, iii (1934).

Lloyd George: A Diary by Frances Stevenson, ed. A. J. P. Taylor (1971).

LONGFORD, ELIZABETH, *A Pilgrimage of Passion: The Life of Wilfred Scawen Blunt* (1979).

LOUIS, WILLIAM ROGER, 'Churchill and Egypt, 1946–1956', in Blake and Louis (eds.), *Churchill*.

LOWE, HEINZ-DIETRICH, 'USSR: Armed Forces', in I. C. B. Dear and M. R. D. Foot (eds.), *The Oxford Companion to the Second World War* (Oxford, 1995).

MACCALLUM SCOTT, A., Diary, University of Glasgow Library, MS General 1465.

—— *Winston Churchill in Peace and War* (1916).

MacDonald, Iverach, *The History of The Times*, v: *Struggles in War and Peace, 1939–1966* (1984).

Mack, Angela, 'Yalta: Memories of a Wren', *Everyone's War*, no. 5 (Spring/Summer 2002).

McKenzie, Robert, *British Political Parties* (2nd edn., 1964).

MacKenzie, S. P., *The Home Guard* (1995).

MacKenzie King, William Lyon, Diary, Canadian National Archives, http//www.king.archives.ca.

MacLean, Fitzroy, *Eastern Approaches* (1949).

MacMillan, Harold, *The Macmillan Diaries: The Cabinet Years, 1950–1957*, ed. Peter Catterall (2003).

Magnus, Philip, *King Edward VII* (Harmondsworth, 1967).

Mallaby, George, *From My Level* (1965).

Marder, Arthur J., *From the Dreadnought to Scapa Flow*, i: *Road to War* (1961); ii: *The War Years: To the Eve of Jutland* (1965).

—— 'Winston is Back: Churchill at the Admiralty, 1939–1940', *English Historical Review Supplement*, 5 (1972).

Massingham, H. W., 'Mr Churchill's Career', *The Nation*, 13 Jan. 1912, pp. 616–17.

Masterman, Lucy, *C. F. G. Masterman: A Biography* (1939).

—— 'Winston Churchill: The Liberal Phase Part One', *History Today* (Nov. 1964).

—— 'Winston Churchill: The Liberal Phase Part Two', *History Today* (Dec. 1964).

Masterman Papers: papers of Charles Masterman at the University of Birmingham Library.

Mather, John H., 'Lord Randolph Churchill: Maladies et Mort', *Finest Hour*, 93 (1996–7), 23–8.

Mendelssohn, Peter de, *The Age of Churchill: Heritage and Adventure, 1874–1911* (1961).

Menpes, Mortimer, 'Young Winston in South Africa', *Finest Hour*, 105 (1999–2000), 33.

Montague Browne, Anthony, *Long Sunset* (1995).

Moore, R. J., *Churchill, Cripps and India, 1939–1945* (Oxford, 1979).

Moran, Lord, *Winston Churchill: The Struggle for Survival, 1940–1965* (1966).

MORGAN, JANET, *Conflict and Order: The Police and Labour Disputes in England and Wales, 1900–1939* (Oxford, 1987).

MORRIS, JAMES, *Pax Britannica: The Climax of an Empire* (1975 edn.).

MOWAT, CHARLES LOCH, *Britain between the Wars* (1955).

MUNGEAM, G. H., *British Rule in Kenya, 1895–1912* (1966).

NICOLSON, HAROLD, *Diaries and Letters, 1930–1939*, ed. Nigel Nicolson (1966).

—— *Diaries and Letters, 1939–1945*, ed. Nigel Nicolson (1970 edn.).

—— *Diaries and Letters, 1945–1962*, ed. Nigel Nicolson (1971 edn.).

O'BRIEN, PHILLIPS, 'Churchill and the US Navy, 1919–1929', in R. A. C. Parker (ed.), *Winston Churchill: Studies in Statesmanship* (1995).

OPIE, IONA, and OPIE, PETER, *The Lore and Language of Schoolchildren* (Oxford, 1967).

ORWELL, GEORGE, *The Collected Essays, Journalism and Letters of George Orwell*, iii: *As I Please, 1943–1945*, ed. Sonia Orwell and Ian Angus (Harmondsworth, 1970).

OVERY, RICHARD, 'German Air Strength, 1933 to 1939: A Note', *Historical Journal*, 27 (1984).

PATERSON, TONY, *Churchill: A Seat for Life* (Dundee, 1980).

PEARSON, JOHN, *Facades: Edith, Osbert and Sacheverell Sitwell* (1978).

PELLING, HENRY, *Winston Churchill* (1974).

PICKERSGILL, J. W., and FORSTER, D. W., *The Mackenzie King Record*, iii: *1945–1946* (Toronto, 1970); iv: *1947–1948* (1970).

Picture Post 1938–1950, ed. Tom Hopkinson (Harmondsworth, 1970).

PILPEL, ROBERT H., *Churchill in America, 1895–1961: An Affectionate Portrait* (1977).

POMBINI, PAOLO, 'Churchill and Italy, 1922–1940', in R. A. C. Parker (ed.), *Winston Churchill: Studies in Statesmanship* (Oxford, 1995).

PONTING, CLIVE, *Churchill* (1994).

PRIOR, ROBIN, *Churchill's World Crisis as History* (1983).

RADZINOWICZ, LEON, and HOOD, ROGER, *The Emergence of Penal Policy in Victorian and Edwardian England* (Oxford, 1990).

RAICO, RALPH, *Rethinking Churchill*, pt. 5, http://www.lerockwell.com/orig/raico-churchill5html, accessed 20 Sept. 2004. Originally published in *The Costs of War: America's Pyrrhic Victories*, ed. John V. Denson (New Brunswick, NJ, 1997).

RAMSDEN, JOHN, *Churchill: Man of the Century* (2002).

—— 'How Churchill Became "The Greatest Living Englishman"', *Contemporary British History*, 12/3 (Autumn 1998).

—— *The Making of Conservative Party Policy* (1980).

—— *Man of the Century: Winston Churchill and his Legend since 1945* (2003).

—— ' "That Will Depend on Who Writes the History": Winston Churchill as his Own Historian', an inaugural lecture at Queen Mary and Westfield College, University of London, 1966.

REITH, JOHN, *The Reith Diaries*, ed. Charles Stuart (1975).

REYNOLDS, DAVID, 'Churchill the Appeaser? Between Hitler, Roosevelt and Stalin in World War Two', in Michael Dockrill and Brian McKercher (eds.), *Diplomacy and World Power: Studies in British Foreign Policy, 1890–1950* (Cambridge, 1996), 197–220.

—— 'Churchill's Writing of History', in *Transactions of the Royal Historical Society*, 6th ser. 11 (2001), 221–47.

REYNOLDS, PAUL, 'Iraq the Ungovernable', http://news.bbc.co.uk/1/hi/world/middle east/3166797.stm, 20 Aug. 2003.

RHODES JAMES, ROBERT, *Churchill: A Study in Failure, 1900–1939* (1970).

RIDDELL, LORD, *The Riddell Diaries, 1908–1923*, ed. John M. McEwen (1986).

—— *More Pages from my Diary, 1908–1914* (1934).

ROBERTS, ANDREW, *Eminent Churchillians* (1994).

ROSE, NORMAN, *Chaim Weizmann* (1989 edn.).

—— *Churchill: An Unruly Life* (1994).

ROSEBERY, LORD, *Lord Randolph Churchill* (1906).

ROSKILL, STEPHEN, *Churchill and the Admirals* (1977).

—— *Hankey: Man of Secrets*, ii: *1919–1931* (1972).

ROWSE, A. L., *The Spirit of English History* (1943).

SANDYS, CELIA, *Churchill Wanted Dead or Alive* (1999).

SASSOON, SIEGFRIED, *Siegfried's Journey* (1982 edn.).

SHEFFIELD, GARY, *Forgotten Victory: The First World War: Myths and Realities* (2002 edn.).

SIMPSON, JOHN, 'Saddam or not, they just don't want us here', *Daily Telegraph*, 16 Nov. 2003.

SITWELL, OSBERT, *Laughter in the Next Room* (1949).

SKIDELSKY, ROBERT, *John Maynard Keynes: The Economist as Saviour, 1920–1937* (1992).

—— *John Maynard Keynes: Fighting for Britain, 1937–1946* (2001 edn.).

STAFFORD, DAVID, *Churchill and Secret Service* (1997).

Sunday Post, 25 Feb. 1990: 'The War Hero of Johnstone Will Never Forget that Day'.

SYLVESTER, A. J., *Life with Lloyd George* (1975).

TAYLOR, A. J. P., *English History* (1965).

THOMSON, KATHARINE, 'All The Racehorses Churchill ever Owned', http://www.winstonchurchill.org/faqprsonal.htm.

—— 'Churchill and the Lure of the Turf', *Finest Hour*, 102 (Spring 1999), 26–30.

THORNE, CHRISTOPHER, *Allies of a Kind: The United States, Britain and the War against Japan, 1941–1945* (1978).

VAISSE, MAURICE, 'Churchill and France, 1951–1955', in R. A. C. Parker (ed.), *Winston Churchill: Studies in Statesmanship* (Oxford, 1995).

VINCENT, JOHN, 'Chamberlain, the Liberals and the Outbreak of War, 1939', in *English Historical Review*, 113, no. 451 (1998), 367–83.

WAUGH, EVELYN, *The Letters of Evelyn Waugh*, ed. Mark Amory (New York, 1980).

WEBB, BEATRICE, *The Diary of Beatrice Webb*, ii: *1892–1905*, ed. Norman and Jeanne MacKenzie (1986 edn.).

—— *Our Partnership* (1948).

WELLS, H. G., *Meanwhile* (1933 edn.).

—— *The Shape of Things to Come* (1933, 1967 edn.).

WHEELER-BENNET, JOHN (ed.), *Action This Day: Working with Churchill* (1968).

WILLIAMS, E. T., 'Winston S. Churchill', in *Dictionary of National Biography, 1961 to 1970*, ed. E. T. Williams and C. S. Nicholls (Oxford, 1981).

WILLIAMS, FRANCIS, *Nothing so Strange: An Autobiography* (1970).

WILSON, KEITH M., *A Study in the History and Policies of the Morning Post, 1905–1926* (1990).

Winston Churchill: Memoirs and Tributes Broadcast by the BBC (1965).

WOOD, IAN S., *Churchill* (2000).

WOODS, FREDERICK (ed.), *Young Winston's Wars* (1972).

WRIGLEY, CHRIS, 'Churchill and the Trade Unions', *Transactions of the Royal Historical Society* 6th ser. 11 (Cambridge, 2001), 273–94.

BIBLIOGRAPHY

WRIGLEY, CHRIS, *Winston Churchill: A Biographical Companion* (2002).
YOUNG, G. M., *Stanley Baldwin* (1952).

Index

Abdication crisis (1936) 146–7
Abdullah, Emir 100
Abyssinia, Italy's attack on 143
Africa, and Churchill at Colonial Office 38–9
Agadir crisis (1911) 59
Aid to Russia Fund 172
Air Defence Committee, Churchill joins 142
air power, inter-war use within Empire 101–2
Aitken, Max, *see* Beaverbrook, Lord
Alanbrooke, F M, *see* Brooke, General Sir Alan
alcohol, and Churchill's consumption of 184–5
Alexander, General Sir Harold 192, 231
Altmark 158
Amalgamated Union of Building Trade Workers, Churchill refused membership 117
Amery, L S 115, 151, 198
Anderson, Sir John 162, 213
Anglo-American relations:
  and Churchill 26–7
  1951–5 administration 234–5
  brief anti-Americanism 127
  calls for military alliance (1946) 222–3
  English-speaking peoples' concept 124–5
  hopes for post-war 200–1

opposes naval parity 126–7
pro-Americanism 129
welcomes American naval expansion 129
and First World War 125
and Second World War 177–81, 187, 199, 200
tensions within 201–2, 204, 211
Anglo-French naval agreement (1912) 62
Anglo-German naval agreement (1935) 141
Anglo-Iranian oil company 61, 231
Anglo-Irish Treaty (1921) 96–7
Anglo-Soviet Trade Treaty (1920) 95
Anne, Queen 8
anti-Semitism, Churchill repelled by 140
Antwerp, defence of (1914) 71–3
Anvil, Operation 204
Arab revolt (1916) 97–8
Arctic convoys 186
Ashley, Maurice 138
Asquith, H H 3, 59
  and Churchill:
    brings into Cabinet (1908) 29, 41
    on his 1909–10 speeches 45
    and his request for field command (1914) 74
    vetoes promotion to Brigadier-General 83
  forms Coalition 79
  replaced by Lloyd George (1916) 84

287

Asquith, Margot 69
Asquith, Violet:
    on Churchill and Lloyd George 41
    and Churchill as genius 3
Atkins, J B, on Churchill 22–3
Atlantic, Battle of the 181
Atlantic Charter (1941) 181
atom bomb:
    Churchill and use of 212
    development programme 211–12
Attlee, Clement 2, 213, 230
    on Churchill 5, 140
        his regard for history 247
    in Churchill's War Cabinet 162,
        175
    and Fulton speech (1946) 222
    Labour would not accept Churchill
        as PM 161–2
Auchinleck, General Claud 181, 182,
    192
Auschwitz death camp 198
austerity, post-war 218, 219
Austria:
    declares war on Serbia 69
    German occupation 148
Aylesford, Lady 10

Baldwin, Stanley:
    and Abdication crisis (1936) 146
    and Beaverbrook 131
    becomes Prime Minister 110
    on Churchill 133
    endorses Irwin Declaration on India
        132
    invites Churchill onto Air Defence
        Committee 142
    and National government 133
    offers Churchill Treasury 111
    and rearmament 143
Balfour, Arthur 8
    becomes Prime Minister 33
    on Churchill 22
    resignation 36
    and tariff reform campaign 34

Balfour Declaration (1917) 98, 100
Balkans, Churchill-Stalin division of
    207
Baltimore Sun 240
Barbarossa, Operation 185–6
Baring, Sir Evelyn 17
Barnes, Reggie 14
Barrymore, Ethel 47
Baruch, Bernard 129
Battenberg, Prince Louis of 59, 76
Battle of Britain 165, 168
Beatty, David 59, 74
Beaverbrook, Lord:
    and Abdication crisis (1936) 146
    on Churchill 135
    Clementine's disapproval of 48
    and 'Empire Free Trade' campaign
        131
    joins Churchill's Coalition
        government 162–3
        Moscow trip (1941) 186
        resignation from (1942) 190
        in War Cabinet 175
    and restoration of gold standard 113
Begbie, Harold ('Gentleman with a
    Duster') 103
Belgium, German invasion of 69, 161
Bell, George, denounces area bombing
    194
Bell, Gertrude 68, 99
Beloff, Max 124
Ben-Moshe, Tuvia 59
Beresford, Lord Charles 67
Berlin, Isaiah, on Churchill 5, 238
Best, Geoffrey 73
Bevan, Aneurin 172
    attacks on Churchill 190, 219
Beveridge, William 43
    praises Churchill 220
Beveridge Report (1942) 213
Bevin, Ernest 213
    and Cold War 224
    denounces cooperation with
        Churchill 152

and Fulton speech (1946) 222
joins Churchill's Coalition
government 162
supports Churchill over Greece
209
Birkenhead, Earl of, *see* Smith, F E
(later Earl of Birkenhead)
Birrell, Augustine, on Churchill 47
'Black and Tans' 95–6
'Black Friday' (1910) 53
Bladon, Churchill buried at 245
Blandford, George, Marquess of, *see*
Marlborough 8th Duke of
Blenheim, battle of 8
Blenheim Palace 8
Bletchley Park 176
Blood, Sir Bindon 16
Blum, Leon 144
Blunt, W S 20, 83
Bolsheviks, and Russian Revolution
93–4
Bonar Law, Andrew 110
and Churchill:
exclusion from Coalition (1916)
84–5
a 'real danger' (1914) 74
and 'Ulster pogrom' myth 68–9
and Ulster 65
Bonham-Carter, Violet 233
Boothby, Lord 243
Bracken, Brendan 117, 151, 161
on Churchill 173
and Churchill's need of military
success 192
Churchill's Parliamentary Private
Secretary 156, 163
Bradbury, Sir John 114
Breslau 71
Briand, Aristide 229
Bridgeman, Sir Francis 59
Bridges, Sir Edward 183
British Broadcasting Corporation
(BBC), and General Strike
119
British Empire:
decline of 229–30
growth of 17
British European movement 228
British Expeditionary Force 164
British Gazette 118–19
British Housewives' League 219
Brockie, Sergeant-Major 23
Brodrick, St John 30–1
Brook, Norman 232, 238
Brooke, General Sir Alan 175–6, 192,
248
and Anglo-American relations 202
on Churchill 181, 183
publication of diaries 241–3
and Soviet ingratitude 186
Browne, Montague 239
Bryant, Arthur, and Alanbrooke diaries
241, 242
Budget League 44
Burnham, Charles 24
Butler, R A 133, 232
becomes Chancellor of the
Exchequer 232
and the 'Industrial Charter' 218–19
Buzzard, Dr Thomas 13

Cadogan, Sir Alexander, on Neville
Chamberlain 1
Caird, David 118
Cairo Conference (1921) 99, 101
Campbell Bannerman, Sir Henry 29, 36
Camrose, Lord 155, 220
Canada:
Churchill addresses Parliament
(1941) 187
lecture tour by Churchill (1900–01)
26
Carden, Admiral 76–7
Carlton Club meeting (1922) 107
Carr, E H, and British intervention in
Greece (1944) 209
Carrington, Charles 104
Carson, Sir Edward 67–8

Casablanca conference (1943) 199
Cassel, Sir Ernest 32
Cecil, Hugh 221
    as Churchill's best man 47
    and the Hughligans 31
Cecil, Lord Robert 127
Chamberlain, Austen 33, 103
    proposes Anglo-French alliance 123
Chamberlain, Hilda 226
Chamberlain, Joseph, tariff reform
    campaign 33
Chamberlain, Neville 213
    appeasement of Italy 147
    becomes Prime Minister 147
    British guarantee to Poland 153
    as candidate for Conservative
        leadership 122
    on Churchill 122–3, 135
    and Churchill's 'derating' scheme
        122
    on Churchill's letter-writing 226
    and Churchill's return to office
        155–6
    in Churchill's War Cabinet 162
    contributory pension scheme 115
    and Czechoslovakia 148–50
    discusses leadership succession 161
    and Munich agreement (1938) 150
    and Norway debate 160
    retirement of 173
    and return of 'treaty ports' to Ireland
        97
    as war minister 156
Chanak crisis (1922) 107
Channon, Chips 151, 210
Chant, Ormiston 12–13
Chaplin, Charlie 129
Charmley, John 252
Chartwell 116–17, 139, 220
Chartwell Trust 220
Chatfield, Lord 156, 160
chemical warfare, and Churchill:
    considers use of 195
    support for 102

Chequers 185
Cherwell, Lord, see Lindemann, F E
Churchill, Clementine 244
    and Alanbrooke diaries 242–3
    marriage 47
    relationship with Winston 48
    urges Churchill to resign
        Conservative leadership (1944)
        214
    warns Churchill of consequences of
        behaviour 173
    wartime work 172
Churchill, Diana 48, 139
    suicide of 244
Churchill, Gwendoline 82
Churchill, Jack 57, 82
    birth 10
    death of 221
    and North American tour (1929) 128
Churchill, Jennie 7
    Churchill's love of 11
    death of 108
    marriage 9
    plans 'Anglo-Saxon' magazine 27
Churchill, John, see Marlborough 1st
    Duke of
Churchill, John (nephew) 128
Churchill, Marigold 108
Churchill, Mary 108, 221
Churchill, Randolph, Lord 7–8
    Churchill's idealization of 3, 13
    cruel letter to Churchill 12
    decline and death 13
    and free trade 33
    marries Jennie Jerome 9
    political career 10
    and Tory Democracy 21
    and Ulster 65
Churchill, Randolph (son) 48, 155
    and Liverpool Wavertree by-election
        (1935) 139
    and North American tour (1929) 128
    and official biography of Churchill
        251

relationship with Churchill 172, 244
suggests meeting with Hitler 140
wartime activities 172
Churchill, Sarah 48, 139
and alcoholism 244
wartime work 172
Churchill, Winston:
1874 birth 7, 9
1874–93 childhood and education
10–12
1893–99 military career:
commissioned as cavalry officer
14
Egypt 17–19
in India 14, 16
resigns commission (1899) 19
at Sandhurst 12–13
self-education of 14–15
South Africa 24
1897–1900 as war correspondent:
north-west frontier 16
South Africa 20, 22–4
Sudan campaign 18–19
1899 fights Oldham by-election
21–2
1900 elected MP for Oldham 25
1901 maiden speech 30
1901 opposes army reforms 30–1
1902 idea of Middle Party 31–2
1903 opposes tariff reform campaign
33, 34
1904 crosses floor of Commons to
join Liberals 29, 34
1904–12 and women's suffrage
49–50
1905–08 Under-Secretary of State
for the Colonies 36–41
1908–10 President of the Board of
Trade 41–3
and budget crisis (1909) 44–5
and naval estimates crisis (1909)
43–4
1910–11 enthusiasm for Coalition
government 56

1910–11 Home Secretary 50–5
and 'Black Friday' 53
and industrial unrest 54
and penal policy 51–2
Sidney Street siege (1911) 54
and Tonypandy riots 53–4
1911–15 First Lord of the Admiralty
59–65
activism of 70
Anglo-French naval agreement 62
Conservatives force removal of 79
criticism of 73, 74
and defence of Antwerp (1914)
71–3
and development of the tank 75
and Gallipoli 76–81
German naval successes 71
naval expansion programme 62–3
orders fleet to battle stations 69
and reforms 59–62
and Room 40 70–1
and Ulster crisis 65–9
1914 asks for field command 74,
75
1915 Chancellor of the Duchy of
Lancaster 79
1915 resigns from government 80
1915–16 serves on Western Front
83–4
1916 exclusion from Lloyd George's
Coalition 84–5
1917–18 Minister of Munitions
87–91
1919–21 Secretary of State for War
and Air 92–6
advocates 'fusion' of Coalition
partners (1920) 106
and demobilization 92
and Ireland 95–6
and Russia 93–5
1921–22 Secretary of State for the
Colonies 96–103
and Chanak crisis 106–7
and Ireland 96–7

and Middle East 99–103
and use of air power 101–2
1922 loses seat 107
1924 on first Labour government 110
1924–29 Chancellor of the Exchequer 112–23
  and *British Gazette* 118–19
  derating scheme 122
  financial orthodoxy 115, 121
  first budget (April 1925) 115–16
  and General Strike 118–21
  indictment of Treasury and Bank of England 113–14
  and miners' dispute 119–20
  and miners' wage subsidy (1925) 114, 117–18
  and national insurance 115–16
  public expenditure 116
  restoration of gold standard 113–15
  and 'Ten Year Rule' 116
1930 Romanes lecture 131–2
1931–35 and India, defence of British rule 132–7
  and the Diehards 133–4
  resigns from shadow Cabinet 133
1932–39 and Nazi Germany threat 139–46
  advocates Air Defence Committee 141–2
  advocates collective security 144, 149
  campaigns for rearmament 141–2
  on Chamberlain's dilemma 148
  Churchill's isolation 151–2
  critical of Anglo-German naval agreement (1935) 141
  and Czechoslovakia 149
  denounces Chamberlain's policy 150–1
  and German rearmament 143
  and Munich agreement (1938) 150–1
opposes disarmament 140–1
prediction of war 144
rapprochement with Soviet Union 144–5
repelled by Nazi regime 140
and Spanish Civil War 145–6
warns against appeasement 148
1936 and Abdication crisis 146–7
1939–40 First Lord of the Admiralty 156–61
  early naval successes 158
  emergence as inspiring figure 157–8
  House of Commons speech 157
  and Norway 159–60
1940 Military Coordination Committee chairman 160
1940–45 Prime Minister 161–215
  Battle of Britain 165, 168
  becomes Conservative leader 173–4
  and Beveridge Report (1942) 213–14
  consolidates position 173–4
  and Cripps 189–90
  and de Gaulle 165, 202–3
  discontent with 188–91
  and division of Balkans 207
  and domestic politics 212–14
  establishes War Cabinet 162
  exuberance of 171–2
  and fall of France 164–5
  first speech to House of Commons (1940) 163–4
  forms Coalition 161–3
  general election (1945) 214–15
  and health 204
  and the Holocaust 198
  impact on Whitehall 172–3
  and India 191–2
  and intervention in Greece (1944) 207–9
  'kitchen cabinet' 163
  and leadership 165–6

and Middle East 192
and military conduct of war
174–7, 181–3
and Minister of Defence 174
and nuclear weapons 211–12
and 'Octagon' conference (1944)
204–5
and Operation Torch 192, 193
and Overlord 202, 204
and Palestine 198–9
pleads for advance on Berlin
(1945) 211
and Poland 205–7
and Potsdam conference (1945)
215
and Roosevelt 177, 180–1, 187,
199, 200, 201–2, 204–5, 211
ruthlessness of 165, 194–5
self-confidence 161
and Soviet Union 177, 185–7,
205–7
and Stalin 193, 207
and strategic bombing campaign
193–7, 227
and Teheran conference (1943)
201–2, 206
and TRIDENT meetings (1943)
200
and Ultra transcripts 176, 227
and United States 177–81, 187,
200–1
votes of confidence (1942) 188,
(1944) 214
wartime popularity 167–72
wartime travels 203–4
working methods 183–5
and Yalta conference (1945)
209–11
1945–51 Leader of the Opposition
216–31
attacks Labour over Europe 228
attacks socialism 218, 219–20
as elder statesman 217
and European unity 228–9

Fulton speech (1946) 221–3, 250
and Indian independence 229–30
and Korean War 217, 231
manifesto preparation 230
pays little attention to party
politics 217–18
uncomfortable with new policies
219
urges showdown with Soviet Union
224
Zurich speech (1946) 228
1951–55 Prime Minister 231–6
advocates discussions with Soviet
Union (1953–4) 235–6
and Anglo-American relations
234–5
composition of government 231–2
domestic policy 233
and European unity 234
health 232–3
invites Liberals to join
government 231
and nuclear danger 236
and Operation 'Robot' 233
'overlords' experiment 232
resignation (1955) 236
and Suez Canal 234, 235
1955 declines dukedom 236
1956 on Suez Crisis 239
1965 death of 244
1965 state funeral 2, 245
and alcohol 184–5
ambition of 22–3, 32, 247
ancestry 7–8
and Anglo-American relations 27
1951–5 administration 234–5
becomes consistently pro-
American 129
brief anti-Americanism 127
calls for military alliance (1946)
222–3
and 'English-speaking peoples'
concept 124–5
and First World War 125

granted Honorary Citizenship
240–1
hopes for post-war 200–1
opposes American naval parity
126–7
and Second World War 177–81,
187, 199, 200, 201–2, 204,
211
welcomes American naval
expansion 129
appearance 32
and Chartwell 116–17, 139
and Churchill College (Cambridge)
239–40
dress sense 172
extravagance of 138–9
finances:
lecture tours 25–6, 130
and Wall Street crash 130
writing 137–8, 220
image of 2–3
and Lloyd George 41
marriage 47
approach to 47, 48–9
importance of 220–1
Nobel Prize for Literature (1953)
237
North American tour (1900) 25–6
North American tour (1929) 128–9
and painting 82–3
political beliefs 35–6, 249
and Coalition government 31–2,
36
'Liberal in all but name' 15
move to the Right 64
reverence for constitution 246–7
and state intervention 40–1
relationship with parents 11, 13
reputation of 3–6
and 1951–5 administration 237
at Admiralty (1939–40) 157–9
and Alanbrooke diaries 241–3
amongst Conservatives 122–3
amongst Tory Diehards 134

and anti-Churchillians 243
and Antwerp affair 74
as Cabinet minister 247–8
Churchill on 243–4
and the Churchillian myth 5,
250–1
criticism from the Left 104–6
and Gallipoli 3–4, 79
and General Strike 120–1
the greatest occupant of Downing
Street 254
and iconoclastic views of 252–3
and inter-war years 134–5, 151–5,
248–9
as national hero 3, 4–5
and official biography 251–2
partial rehabilitation (1916) 85–6
and political style 247
post-war protection of 238–9
and Russian policy (1918–19) 95
suspicion of 45–7
and switching parties 29–30, 35
television dramatisations 253
and Tonypandy riots 53–4, 248
and 'Ulster pogrom' myth 68–9
in United States 179–80, 224,
240–1, 253
unstable and unreliable 103
and war memoirs 225–8, 249–50
and wartime leadership 165–6,
182–3, 249, 250
wartime popularity 167–72
and speeches:
preparation 32, 45
style 37
and wartime inspiration 168–9,
179
on Victorian era 28
and war 57–8
benefits of 89–90
and First World War strategy
86–7, 90
on idolization of military leaders
78

self-confidence of 248
views on 19–21, 69
on 'wars of peoples' 31
writings:
The Aftermath 108
The Eastern Front 108
The Gathering Storm 227
Great Contemporaries 138
A History of the English-Speaking Peoples 138, 240
Ian Hamilton's March 24
London to Ladysmith via Pretoria 24
Lord Randolph Churchill 34–5
Marlborough: His Life and Times 138
My African Journey 39
My Early Life 133
The People's Rights 45
The River War 18–19
Savrola 11, 16
The Second World War 225–8, 249–50
Step by Step 138
The Story of the Malakand Field Force 16
The World Crisis 108–10
Churchill, Winston Spencer (grandson) 172
Churchill Centre 253
Churchill College (Cambridge) 239–40
Clemenceau, Georges 90, 91
Clynes, J R, on Churchill 58
Cockran, Bourke 14
Cold War, and Churchill:
advocates discussions with Soviet Union 235–6
emphasis on individual freedom 219–20
Fulton Speech (1946) 221–3, 250
urges showdown with Soviet Union 224
Cole, G D H 120
Collins, Michael 96–7

Colville, John 173, 231
becomes Churchill convert 163
Colvin, Ian, on Churchill 112–13
Combined Chiefs of Staff, establishment of (1941) 187
Committee of Imperial Defence:
Air Defence Research Committee 142
Churchill invited to meeting of 59
communism, Churchill's loathing of 93–4
Congress party (India) 191
Connor, William 157
Conservative Party:
acceptance of state intervention 218–19
and Carlton Club meeting (1922) 107
and Churchill:
attacks by 42
attacks on 67–8
becomes leader 173–4
detested by 45–6
forces removal from Admiralty 79
insists on exclusion from Coalition (1916) 84–5
ostracism of 151
protests against his return to office 87
reconciliation with (1927) 121
suggestions that he should resign (1945) 217
wartime critics of 166–7
identity of 35
joins Asquith's Coalition 79
landslide victory (1924) 111
and League of Nations 143
revival of Protectionism 130–1, 132
and Ulster 65, 66, 67
Cooper, Duff 151
Cork, Admiral 160
Coronel, Battle of (1914) 71
Council of Europe 229
Cox, Sir Percy 99

Crawford, Earl of 68
  and Abdication crisis (1936) 147
  on Churchill 158–9
Creswell, Michael 141
Crete, German invasion of 181
Cripps, Sir Stafford:
  appointed ambassador at Moscow
    177
  enters War Cabinet 189–90
  as potential rival to Churchill 189
  wartime mission to India 191
Crowe, Sir Eyre 123
Cuba, Churchill's reporting from 14
Cunningham, Sir Andrew 175
Curragh Mutiny 67
Czechoslovakia 148–50
  German occupation of 153
  and Munich agreement (1938)
    150

D-Day landing (1944), success of
    204
Daily Express 168
Daily Graphic, Churchill's reports
    from Cuba 14
Daily Herald 157
  attacks on Churchill 104
Daily Mail 167
Daily Mirror 157
  hires Churchill as columnist 155
  'Whose finger?' 231
Daily Telegraph 220
  campaigns for Churchill's return to
    office 154–5
Daladier, Edouard 150
Dalton, Hugh 151
Damaskinos, Archbishop 208
Dardanelles Commission 86
  see also Gallipoli
Dardanelles Committee 79, 80
Daudi Chwa II 39
Davidson, J C C 118–19, 134
Davies, Clement 231
de Forest, Tuttie 32

de Gaulle, General Charles 177
  Churchill gives official recognition
    165
  differences with Churchill 202–3
  Roosevelt's hostility to 203
de Hirsch, Baron 32
de Robeck, Admiral 77
De Valera, Eamon 97, 237
Deakin, William 225
demobilization, Churchill and post-
    First World War 92
Denikin, General 94
Denmark, German invasion of 160
depression, and Churchill 244
devolution, Churchill's proposals for
    66
d'Eyncourt, Tennyson 75
Digby, Pamela 172
Dill, Sir John 175, 182
'direct action', post-First World War
    93
Disraeli, Benjamin 10
Dogger Bank, naval battles at 71
Dresden, Allied bombing of 195–6
Dulles, John Foster 235
Dundee:
  Churchill defeated (1922) 107
  Churchill returned for (1918) 92
  Churchill wins by-election (1908)
    42
Dunglass, Alec 210
Dunkirk 164
Dyson, Will 135

EAM (National Liberation Front) 208
Eden, Anthony 231
  becomes Foreign Secretary 174
  and Greece 181
  keeps distance from Churchill 148
  resignation (1938) 147
  and Suez Canal 234
  and Suez Crisis (1956) 239
Edinburgh, Churchill speaks in favour
    of a 'summit' 231

Edward VII:
　on Churchill 33
　death of 55
　succeeds to the throne 28
Edward VIII, and Abdication crisis
　(1936) 146
Egypt 17
Eisenhower, Dwight D 200, 211, 235,
　236
El Alamein, Montgomery's victory at
　(1942) 193
ELAS (People's National Army of
　Liberation) 208
elections, by-elections:
　Dundee (1908) 42
　Liverpool Wavertree (1935) 139
　North-West Manchester (1908) 42
　Oldham (1899) 21–2
　Westminster (Abbey) 110–11
elections, general:
　1900 ('khaki' election) 25
　1906 36
　1910 (December) 55
　1910 (January) 50, 55
　1918 ('Coupon') 92
　1922 107
　1923 110
　1924 111
　1929 127–8
　1935 143
　1945 214–15
　1950 230–1
　1951 231
Elford Adams, H L 104
Elgin, Lord 36, 38
Elizabeth II:
　and Churchill's state funeral 245
　succession of 232
Emmott, Alfred 25
Empire Free Trade 131
Empire Theatre, Churchill defends
　prostitutes 12–13
English-speaking peoples, Churchill's
　concept of 124–5

Ensor, R C K, and death of Victoria 27
'Ephesian', see Roberts, Carl Bechhofer
　('Ephesian')
Epping, Churchill elected MP for
　(1924) 111
Esher, Lord 44
eugenics, and Churchill 52
European Iron and Steel Community
　228
European unity, and Churchill 228–9,
　234
Everest, Elizabeth 10, 11
Ewart, Spencer 45–6

Falkland Islands, Battle of (1914) 71
Feiling, Keith 238
Feisal, Emir 99
　and Arab revolt 98
Fighter Command, see Royal Air Force
films, Churchill's late-night shows 185
Finland, Russian invasion of 159
Finney, Albert 253
First World War 69–91
Fisher, Admiral of the Fleet, Lord 60,
　76
　and Gallipoli 78, 80–1
Fisher, H A L 131–2
Fleet Air Arm 62
Fleming, Ann 245
Foch, Marshal 91
'Focus' (secret cross-party
　organization) 144
France:
　Anglo-French naval agreement
　　(1912) 62
　and Churchill:
　　love of 90–1
　　opposes Anglo-French alliance
　　　123
　　Oran 165
　　proposes union with 164–5
　fall of (1940) 164–5
　Vichy regime 165, 203
Franco, General 145

Fraser, Robert, warns against Churchill 151

Fraser, Sir Malcolm 118

free trade 115
  Churchill's retreat from 131–2
  Churchill's support of 33, 34

French, Sir John 83

fuel crisis (1946–7) 219

Fuller, J F C 238–9, 243

Fulton speech (1946) 221–3, 250
  and Anglo-American military
    alliance 222–3
  reaction to 222

Fyfe, Hamilton 157

Gallipoli 3, 76–81
  and Churchill's reputation 3–4, 79,
    248
  and Dardanelles Commission 86

Gallup opinion polls:
  support for Chamberlain (1939)
    158
  support for Churchill (1939) 154

Gamelin, General 164

Gandhi, Mahatma 93
  arrest of 191
  Churchill on 133
  released from jail 132–3

Gardiner, A G 46
  suspicion of Churchill 64

Garnett, Theresa 50

Garvin, J L:
  appreciation of Churchill 86
  supports Churchill 155

General Strike (1926) 118–21

Geneva:
  disarmament conference in (1927)
    126–7
  International Disarmament
    Conference (1932–4) 140–1

George II, King of Greece 208

George VI 204
  on Churchill 154
  death of 232

Germains, Victor Wallace, on Churchill 4

Germany:
  Anglo-German naval agreement
    (1935) 141
  and Anglo-German naval rivalry 44,
    62
  and Austria 148
  Churchill urges magnanimity
    towards 94
  and Czechoslovakia 148–50, 153
  invasion of Belgium (1914) 69
  invasion of Belgium (1940) 161
  invasion of Crete 181
  invasion of Denmark 160
  invasion of Greece 181
  invasion of Norway 160
  invasion of Poland 155
  invasion of Soviet Union 185–6
  'pastoralization' plan 205
  remilitarization of Rhineland
    143

Gilbert, Martin:
  on Alanbrooke diaries 242
  on Churchill and Gallipoli 81
  and official biography of Churchill
    251–2

Giraud, General 203

Gneisenau 188

Godesberg, agreement rejected by
    Cabinet 149–50

Goebbels, Joseph, denounces Churchill
    151

Goeben 71

gold standard, Churchill's restoration
    of 113–15

Gordon, General 18

Gort, Lord 164

Government Code and Cypher School
    71

Graf Spee 158

Great Slump (1929–32) 129–30

Great Terror (Soviet Union 1934–9)
    145

Greece:
    Churchill's intervention in (1944)
        207–9
    fall of (1941) 181
Greenwood, Arthur, in Churchill's War
    Cabinet 162
Grey, Edward, on Churchill 47
Guest, Amy 48–9
Guest, Frederick 27
    and marriage problems 48–9
Gwynne, H A 118, 119

Hague conference (1948) 228
Hague Peace Conference (1899),
    Churchill's attack on 19
Haig, Douglas 88
    and Churchill 91
    and tank development 75
Halabja 102
Haldane, Captain Aylmer 23
Halifax, Lord:
    appointed ambassador at Washington
        174
    on Churchill's 'kitchen cabinet'
        163
    in Churchill's War Cabinet 162
    and Italian offer of 'mediation' 164
    and succession to Chamberlain
        161
    see also Irwin, Lord
Hall, Amy 27
Hamilton, Sir Ian 24
    and Gallipoli 77
Hanfstaengl, Ernst 'Putzi' 140
Hankey, Maurice 75, 156
Harcourt, Sir William 30
Hardie, Keir 53, 54
Hardy, Robert 253
Harington, Sir Charles 107
Harriman, Averell 180
    mission to Moscow (1941) 186
Harris, Sir Arthur 193, 195–6, 197
Harrisson, Tom 168, 171
Harrow School, Churchill at 11–12

Harvard, Churchill's speech on
    Anglo-American relations
    (1943) 201
Harwood, Admiral 158
Hayek, F A 214–15
health:
    and Churchill in wartime 204
    stroke (1953) 232–3
Hearst, William Randolph 128–9
Henlein, Konrad 149
Hess, Rudolph 185
Hetherington, Major 75
Hiroshima 212
Hitler, Adolf:
    becomes Chancellor 140
    Churchill almost meets 140
Hoare-Laval plan (1935) 143
Hoare, Samuel 135, 137, 153, 162
Hobhouse, L T 40
Hobson, J A 40
Hogg, Quintin 230
Hollis, Colonel Leslie 174
Holocaust 198
Home Guard 165
Home Rule crisis (1912–14), and
    Churchill's role 65–9
Hope-Not, Operation 245
Hopkins, Harry 180, 184, 192
Hopwood, Sir Francis 37–8
Horne, Robert 103
horse-racing, Churchill's late
    enthusiasm for 221
House of Commons, Churchill's
    respect for 246–7
House of Lords:
    and budget crisis (1909) 44–5
    and Parliament Bill (1911) 55
Howard, John 23
Hozier, Clementine, see Churchill,
    Clementine
Hozier, Nellie 83
Hozier, William 108
Hughligans 31
Husky, Operation 200

Hussein, Saddam 102
Hussein, Sherif of Mecca 98
Hyam, Ronald, on Churchill at Colonial
    Office 38

Ibn Saud, King 185
immigration, Churchill on 233
imperialism, growth of 17
India:
    Churchill's defence of British rule
        132–7
        and the Diehards 133–4
        resigns from shadow Cabinet 133
    civil disobedience campaign 93
    and independence 229–30
    and Irwin Declaration 132, 136
    and Second World War 191–2
India Defence League 137
Industrial Intelligence Centre 141
Inonu, Ismet 200
Inskip, Sir Thomas 143–4
intelligence services:
    and Churchill 55, 70–1, 95
    and Ultra transcripts 176
International Disarmament Conference
    (Geneva 1932–4) 140–1
Iran 231
Iraq 97
    rebellion suppressed (1920) 98
    and role of Royal Air Force 101–2
Ireland:
    Anglo-Irish Treaty (1921) 96
    and 'Black and Tans' 95–6
    and Irish Free State 96–7
    Sinn Fein proclaim independent
        republic 93
    and Ulster crisis 65–9
Ironside, General 175
Irving, David 252
Irwin, Lord (later Lord Halifax) 122
    and Irwin Declaration on India 132,
        136
    see also Halifax, Lord
Islam, Churchill on 15

Ismay, Hastings 174, 231
    on Churchill as wartime leader
        182
    memoirs of 242
Italy:
    attack on Abyssinia 143
    declares war on Britain 176

Jacob, Colonel Ian 174
    on Churchill as strategist 181–2
    and Teheran conference 202
Japan, and Pearl Harbor attack 187
Jellicoe, Sir John 60
Jenkins, Roy, estimation of Churchill
    254
Jerome, Clara 7
Jerome, Jennie, see Churchill, Jennie
Jerome, Leonard 7
Jewish Brigade 198
Jewish National Home, Churchill on
    100–1
Jews:
    and Balfour Declaration (1917)
        98
    and Jewish National Home 100–1
    in Palestine 99
Joynson-Hicks, William 119

Katyn Forest massacre 206
Kemal, Mustapha 107
Kennedy, John F 241
Kenya, Churchill visits 39
Keynes, John Maynard:
    on Churchill in wartime 173
    The Economic Consequences of Mr
        Churchill 114
    elected to 'Other Club' 114
    on Morgenthau 179
    and restoration of gold standard 113,
        114
'khaki' election (1900) 25
Kimball, Warren 184
King, W L Mackenzie 120, 144, 154,
    212, 218, 224, 225

Kitchener, Lord:
  in Egypt 17
  and Gallipoli 77, 80
  and Sudan expeditionary force 18
  urges Dardanelles naval
    demonstration 76
Knollys, Lord 44
Kolchak, Admiral 94
Korda, Alexander 185
Korean War 217, 231

Labour Party:
  and Churchill:
    and General Strike 120–1
    his attacks on (1920) 95
    his relations with 54
    hostility towards 104
    joins his wartime Coalition 162
  electoral pact with Liberals (1906)
    39–40
  forms minority government (1924)
    110
  forms minority government (1929)
    127–8
  and League of Nations 143
  post-war government (1945–51) 218
  progress during First World War
    91–2
  refusal to serve under Chamberlain
    161
Lambert, Andrew 63
Lansbury, George 104
Last, Nella 167
Lavery, Hazel 82
Lavery, Sir John 82
Lawrence, T E 97, 98, 99, 144
League of Nations 143
lecture tours (Churchill):
  North America 25–6
  United Kingdom 25
  United States 130
Leicester West, Churchill defeated
  (1923) 110
Leigh, Vivien 185

Lend-Lease 178–9
Lenin, V I 93
Liberal Party:
  as Churchill's political home 248
  division of 91
  electoral pact with Labour Party
    (1906) 39–40
  identity of 35
  impact of tariff reform campaign
    33–4
  landslide victory (1906) 36
  and New Liberalism 40
  supports Labour minority
    government (1924) 110
  supports Labour minority
    government (1929) 127–8
  suspicion of Churchill 46–7, 63–4
Liddell Hart, Basil 161
Lindemann, F E ('the Prof') (later Lord
  Cherwell) 117, 141
  and bombing campaign 193
  head of Prime Minister's Statistical
    Section 163
  joins Churchill at Admiralty 156
  joins Churchill's Cabinet (1951) 231
  and Operation 'Robot' 233
  and 'pastoralization' of Germany 205
Lippmann, Walter 223
Lloyd, George 147
Lloyd George, David:
  advocates 'fusion' of Coalition
    partners 106
  and budget crisis (1909) 44
  and Churchill 41
    'a great danger' (1914) 74
    appoints as Minister of Munition
      87
    exclusion from Coalition (1916)
      84–5
    and Gallipoli 79
    passes over as Chancellor 103
    promises to restore to office 87
    views of 103–4, 135
  Coalition electoral victory (1918) 92

favours trade negotiations with
Bolsheviks 94–5
insists on Palestine mandate 97
and naval estimates crisis (1909)
43–4
and naval expansion programme 63
proposes Coalition government
(1910) 55–6
reputation of 1–2, 216
and Ulster 65
Local Defence Volunteers 165
Lothian, Lord 174, 178
Loucheur, Louis 88
Louis, Roger 234
Low, David 105–6, 167–8, 217
Lublin Committee 206
Lugard, Lord 39
Lusitania, sinking of 70

MacCallum Scott, Alexander 48, 85–6
MacDonald, Ramsay:
forms first Labour government (1924)
110
and India 132
and National government 133
Mack, Angela 174–5
McKenna, Reginald 44
and restoration of gold standard 114
Mackesy, General 160
Maclean, Fitzroy 205
McMahon Act (USA 1946) 212
Macmillan, Harold 151, 232, 233, 236,
239
Macready, General Neville, and
Tonypandy riots 53
Madge, Charles 168
Mahdi 18, 19
Maisky, Ivan 145, 155
Manchester Guardian 209
Marder, Arthur 79
Margate, Churchill's conference speech
(1953) 233
Margesson, David 156, 161
Marlborough 1st Duke of 8

Marlborough 7th Duke of 8, 9
Marlborough 8th Duke of (earlier,
George, Marquess of Blandford)
9, 10
Marlborough 9th Duke of ('Sunny'):
marries Consuelo Vanderbilt 27
in South African war 24
Marlborough, Duchess of (Consuelo
Vanderbilt) 27
marriage:
Churchill's approach to 47, 48–9
importance to Churchill 220–1
Marshall, General George C 192
Mass-Observation 167
and 1945 general election 215
and popular views of Churchill
168–71
Massingham, W H:
on Churchill at the Admiralty 63–4
impressed by Churchill 31
Masterman, Charles 40–1
Masterman, Lucy 46
Maudling, Reginald 219
Mawdsley, James 21
Maxwell-Fyfe, Sir David 217
Menpes, Mortimer, on Churchill 24–5
Menzies, Sir Stewart 176
Mesopotamia, *see* Iraq
Middle East:
Arab revolt (1916) 97–8
British operations in (1940) 176
and Churchill's settlement (1921–2)
99–103
Cairo Conference (1921) 99, 101
and Jewish National Home 100–1
and San Remo Conference (1920) 98
Mihailovic, Draza 205
Mikolajczyk, Stanislas 205, 206
militarism, *see* war, Churchill on
Milner, Lord 37
mine owners, attempt wage cuts 114
miners, wage subsidy (1925) 114,
117–18
Monckton, Walter 232, 233

Montagu, Edwin 103
Montgomery, General (later Field
    Marshal) Bernard 192
    and El Alamein 193
Moran, Lord 163
Morel, E D 107
Morgan, Brigadier J H 134
Morgenthau, Henry 179
    and 'pastoralization' of Germany
    205
Morning Post:
    and Churchill:
        attacks over Gallipoli 77–8
        criticises at Admiralty 73
        reports from South Africa 22
        reports from Sudan 18
    and General Strike 118
    and Ulster crisis 67
Morton, Desmond 89, 141, 163
Mosley, Sir Oswald 246
Mowat, C L 150
Mowat, Sir Francis 31, 33
Moyne, Lord 199
Munich agreement (1938) 150
Munich, Churchill visits 139–40
Mussadiq, Dr 231
Mussolini, Benito:
    Churchill praises 140
    and Munich conference (1938) 150

Nagasaki 212
Napoleon, Churchill compares
    himself with 58
Narvik 159–60
Nation, The 40
National government (1931) 133
National Insurance Act (1911) 43
national insurance, Churchill's
    extension of 115–16
National Review, attacks Churchill
    36, 37
National Trust 220
nationalization 218, 219
naval estimates crisis (1909) 43–4

Naval Review, established by Churchill
    60
Nehru, Jawaharlal 237
New Liberalism 40
New Statesman 120
New York Times 157–8
    on Churchill 224
    on Fulton speech 223
    and *History of the English-Speaking
        Peoples* 240
Newall, Sir Cyril 175
Nichols, Beverley 241
Nicolson, Harold 148, 156, 188, 211
Niemeyer, Otto 113, 114
Nobel Prize for Literature, awarded to
    Churchill 237
Norman, Montagu 113
    and restoration of gold standard 115
North Atlantic Treaty Organization
    (NATO), establishment of
    (1949) 224
North-West Manchester:
    Churchill elected MP for (1906) 36
    Churchill invited to stand as Liberal
        candidate 34
    Churchill loses by-election (1908)
        42
Norway:
    Churchill's intervention in 159–60
    German invasion of 160
Nover, Barnet 154–5
nuclear weapons:
    British programme 236
    Churchill and use of 212
    development programme 211–12

'Octagon' conference (1944) 204–5
Official Secrets Act, Churchill's
    passing of 55
Oldham:
    Churchill elected MP for (1900) 25
    Churchill fights by-election 21–2
Oliver, Vic 139
Olivier, Laurence 185

Omdurman, battle of (1898) 18
  treatment of wounded Dervishes
    20–1
Onassis, Aristotle 244
Opie, Iona and Peter 171
opinion polls, Gallup:
  support for Chamberlain (1939) 158
  support for Churchill (1939) 154
Oran, bombardment of French fleet
    (1940) 165
Orwell, George 207, 220
'Other Club' 173, 244
  founded by Churchill and F E Smith
    56
  Keynes elected to 114
Overlord, Operation 202, 204
'overlords' experiment 232
Overy, Richard 142
Owen, Frank, attacks on Churchill
    190
Oxford Union, 'King and Country'
    debate (1933) 134

painting, Churchill's enjoyment of
    82–3
Palestine:
  Arab population (1920) 99
  Arab riots (1920) 98
  and Balfour Declaration (1917) 98,
    100
  British mandate for 98
  Churchill's plan for partition of
    (1943) 198–9
  and Jewish National Home 100–1
  Jewish population (1920) 99
  Peel Commission on (1937) 100–1,
    137
Pall Mall Gazette, Churchill's African
    articles 39
Pankhurst, Emmeline 49
Papandreou, George 207
Parliament Bill (1911) 55
Pearl Harbor, Japanese attack on
    (1941) 187

Peel Commission on Palestine (1937)
    100–1, 137
penal policy, and Churchill 51–2
Petain, Marshal 165
Phillips, Sian 253
Picture Post 154
Pim, Captain 174, 203–4
Plowden, Pamela 47
Plymouth, Churchill visits after
    bombing raid (1941) 171
Poland:
  British guarantee to 153
  German invasion of 155
  Soviet suppression of 211
  wartime fate of 205–7
  and Yalta conference (1945) 210
Pond, Major James P 25
Ponting, Clive 252
Popper, Karl 220
Portal, Sir Charles 175, 193, 196
Potsdam conference (1945) 215
Pound, Admiral 159, 175
Prien, Gunther 158
Prince of Wales, HMS:
  Churchill-Roosevelt meeting on
    (1941) 180–1
  sunk by Japanese 188

Raico, Ralph 253
'Rainsborough, Thomas', see Owen,
    Frank
Ramsden, John 237, 250
rationing, post-war 218, 219
Rawlinson, General 91
Read, Herbert 109–10
Reade, Winwood 15
rearmament:
  and Baldwin 143
  Churchill's pre-war campaign
    141
Redgrave, Vanessa 253
Reith, John 119
religion, Churchill's views on 15–16
reparations 117, 126

Repulse, HMS, sunk by Japanese 188
Reston, James 157–8
Reves, Emery 138, 244
Reynaud, Paul 165
Reynolds, David 252–3
Reynolds News 157
Rhineland, Hitler's remilitarization of
    143
Richmond, Admiral 60, 68, 74
River Plate, Battle of the (1939) 158
Roberts, Andrew 166
Roberts, Carl Bechhofer ('Ephesian')
    121
Roman Catholicism, Churchill on 15
Romanes lecture, Churchill's proposal
    of Economic sub-Parliament
    (1930) 131
Rome, Allied capture of 204
Rommel, Erwin 181
Room 40 70–1
Roosevelt, Franklin D 83
    and Churchill 187, 199, 200
      first meeting (1941) 180–1
      'Octagon' conference (1944)
        204–5
      TRIDENT meetings (1943) 200
      wartime correspondence 177
    death of 211
    hostility towards de Gaulle 203
    and Lend-Lease 178–9
    and Stalin 201–2
    and Teheran conference 201–2
    and Yalta conference (1945) 209–10
Roosevelt, Theodore, on *Lord Randolph*
    Churchill 34–5
Rosebery, Lord 8, 31
    on Randolph Churchill 13
Roskill, Captain 182–3
Rowse, A L, and Churchill as saviour 4
Royal Air Force 62
    Fighter Command 165
    and Iraq 101–2
    and strategic bombing campaign
      193–4, 195

Royal Flying Corps 61
Royal Naval Air Service (RNAS) 61–2
Royal Naval Division, and defence of
    Antwerp 71–2
Royal Navy:
    and Anglo-German naval rivalry 44
    blockade of Germany 70
    and Churchill's reforms 59–62
    naval expansion programme 62–3
    Second World War 158–60
Royal Oak, HMS 158
Royal Scots Fusiliers 83
Russell, Wendy 244
Russia:
    allied intervention in (1918) 94
    civil war in 94
    and Russian Revolution 93
    see also Soviet Union
Russian Revolution, and Churchill's
    fears of 93–4

Sackville-West, Vita 148
Salisbury, Lord 232
Salisbury, Marquess of 8, 25
San Francisco Examiner 240
San Remo Conference (1920) 98
Sandhurst Royal Military Academy,
    Churchill at 12–13
Sandys, Duncan 139, 228
Sassoon, Siegfried 104, 105
    Churchill attempts to recruit 89
Scharnhorst 188
Schuman Plan 228, 234
Schwab, Charles M 128, 129
Scobie, General Ronald 207–8
Scott, C P 46–7
Scrymgeour, Edwin 107
Secret Service Bureau 55
Seely, John 67
Sèvres, Treaty of (1920) 106–7
Shelley, Norman 168
Shulman, Milton 241
Sicily, Allied invasion of 200
Sidney Street siege (1911) 54

INDEX

Simon Report on India (1930) 136
Simon, Sir John 136, 162
Simpson, Wallis 146
Sinclair, 'Archie' 83, 162, 196
Singapore:
  Churchill refuses to finance naval
    base (1924–5) 116
  surrender of (1942) 188
Sinn Fein 93
Sitwell, Osbert 105
Skidelsky, Robert 114
Smith, F E (later Earl of Birkenhead):
  Clementine's disapproval of 48
  death of 136
  and General Strike 119
  and India 135–6
  opposes American naval parity 127
  and the 'Other Club' 56
  and Ulster 66
Smith, Sir Hubert Llewellyn 42
Soames, Captain Christopher 221, 232
socialism, Churchill's attacks on 42,
    218, 219–20
Somervell, Robert 12
South African War:
  Churchill in 22–4
  Churchill's maiden speech on 30
Soviet Union:
  Anglo-Soviet Trade Treaty (1920) 95
  and Churchill:
    advocates discussions with
      (1953–4) 235–6
    Fulton Speech (1946) 221–3, 250
    pre-war rapprochement with
      144–5
    urges showdown with 224
  Cripps mission to (1940) 177
  German invasion of 185–6
  and Poland 205–7, 210, 211
  in Second World War 185–7
  successful atomic test (1949) 225
  wartime popularity in Britain 189
  see also Russia
Spaatz, Carl 196

Spanish Civil War 145–6
Special Operations Executive (SOE)
    177
Stalin, Joseph:
  and Churchill 207
    first meeting 193
  death of 235
  demands recognition of 1941
    frontiers 187
  and Poland 206, 210, 211
  and Potsdam conference (1945) 215
  pre-war terror 145
  and Spanish Civil War 146
  and Teheran conference (1944)
    201–2
  and Yalta conference (1945) 209–10
Star, The, Low's cartoons 105–6
Steed, Wickham, on Churchill 154
Stern Gang 199
Stevenson, Frances 79
Stokes, Richard, attacks area bombing
    194, 196
Strakosch, Sir Henry 139
strategic bombing campaign 193–7,
    227
  and United States Strategic Bombing
    Survey (1945) 243
Stuart, James 217
submarine warfare, First World War 70
Sudan 17–18
Sudetenland 148–9
Suez Canal 234, 235
Suez Crisis (1956), Churchill's opinion
    of 239
suffragettes 49–50
  and 'Black Friday' 53
Supreme Allied Headquarters Europe
    (SHAEF) 196
Supreme Allied War Council 94, 160
Sutherland, Graham, portrait of
    Churchill 237
Swinton, Lt Col Ernest 75
Sykes-Picot Agreement (1916) 98
Syria 98

Talbot, Captain 159
tank, Churchill's role in development of 75
tariff reform campaign 33
Taylor, A J P:
  on Alanbrooke diaries 242
  and Churchill as saviour 5
Teheran conference (1943):
  and Anglo-American tensions 201–2
  and Poland 206
Temple, William (Archbishop of Canterbury) 194
'Ten-Year Rule' 97, 116
Thompson, Dorothy 179
Tilden, Philip 116
Time, names Churchill man of the year (1950) 224
Tito, Josip Broz 200, 205
Tobruk, surrender of (1942) 192
Tonypandy riots (1910):
  and Churchill's reputation 248
  and Churchill's role 53–4
Torch, Operation 192, 193
Tory Democracy, and Churchill 21–2
Trade Boards Act (1909) 43
Trade Disputes and Trade Union Act (1927) 121
trade unions:
  Churchill's relations with 54, 152
  growth during First World War 92
Trades Union Congress, and General Strike 118
Transjordan 100
Trenchard, Air Marshal Hugh 101, 102
Tribune, wartime attacks on Churchill 190
TRIDENT meetings (1943) 200
Trondheim 160
Trotsky, Leon 93
Troup, Sir Edward 52, 248
Truman, Harry S 212, 221–2, 235
  and Cold War 224

Turkey:
  Churchill's wartime visit (1943) 200
  and Treaty of Sèvres (1920) 106–7
Twain, Mark 26

Uganda, Churchill visits 39
Ulster crisis 65–9
  and 'pogrom' myth 67–9
Ulster Unionists 66
Ulster Volunteers 66–7
Ultra transcripts 176, 227
United Europe, and Churchill's Zurich speech (1946) 228
United States:
  and British intervention in Greece (1944) 208
  and Churchill:
    Fulton speech (1946) 222–3
    lecture tours 25–6, 130
    reputation of 179–80, 224, 240–1, 253
  and destroyers-for-bases deal (1940) 178
  and First World War 70
  isolationism 125
  and Lend-Lease 178–9
  and naval expansion 126–7
  pro-British propaganda in 179
  and Second World War 177–81, 187, 199, 200, 211
  dominance of 202, 204
  and war debts 117, 125–6
United States Army Air Force (USAF), and bombing campaign 195
United States Strategic Bombing Survey (1945) 243

Vanderbilt, Consuelo 27
Versailles, Treaty of, and Sudetenland 148
Vichy regime 165, 203
Victoria, Queen, death of 27
Von Mises Institute 253

Wagnon, Hugh 180
Walden, Thomas 24
Wall Street Crash 129
war, Churchill on 19–21, 57–8, 69
  benefits of 89–90
  and First World War strategy 86–7,
    90
  and idolization of military leaders 78
  self-confidence in military affairs
    248
  and 'wars of peoples' 31
war debts 117
  and United States 125–6
Ward, Barrington 209
Warsaw uprising (1944) 206
Washington Naval Treaty (1922) 126
Washington Post 154–5, 180
  and Anglo-American relations 130
  editorial praising Churchill 86
Waugh, Evelyn 172, 245
Wavell, General 176, 182
  and Greece 181
  as Viceroy of India 191
Webb, Beatrice:
  on Churchill 32
  on Churchill and Lloyd George 47
Webb, Maurice 157
Weizmann, Chaim 100, 198
Welldon, J C 12
Welles, Sumner 178
Wells, H G:
  and Churchill in General Strike 121
  criticism of Churchill 209
  on The World Crisis 110

Westminster (Abbey), Churchill
    defeated in by-election (1924)
    110–11
Wigram, Ralph 141
Wilkie, Wendell 193
Williams, Edgar 76
Wilson, Sir Arthur 59
Wilson, Sir Charles (later Lord Moran)
    163
Wilson, Sir Henry 79, 95
  criticism of Churchill 103
Wilson, Sir Horace 162
Wingate, Orde 182
Women's Social and Political Union
    49–50
women's suffrage, Churchill's views on
    49–50
Wood, Ian S 69
Wood, Kingsley 161, 213
Woolton, Lord 162, 213, 232

Yalta conference (1945) 209–10
  House of Commons debate 210–11
Young, G M 238
Younger, George 87
Yugoslavia, Churchill's support of Tito
    205

Zionism, Churchill's support for 99,
    198–9
Zurich, University of, Churchill's
    speech at (1946) 228